ARKANA

POWER OF THE WITCH

Laurie Cabot has been practising witchcraft for more than forty years.
She founded the Witchcraft-as-a-science tradition in Salem, Massachusetts, where she conducts classes and lectures on the Craft. A
psychic counsellor with an international clientele, Cabot is also the
founder of the worldwide Witches' League for Public Awareness. She
and her daughters, Jody and Penny, are High Priestesses in the Council
of Isis.

Tom Cowan is a freelance writer and shamanic counsellor. He is a
student and teacher of the Old Religion and the folk magic of many
cultures. Cowan lectures extensively on dreams, shamanism and
mysticism. He is a published poet and holds a doctorate in history.

LAURIE CABOT WITH TOM COWAN

———————

POWER OF THE WITCH

ARKANA
PENGUIN BOOKS

ARKANA

Published by the Penguin Group
Penguin Books Ltd, 27 Wrights Lane, London W8 5TZ, England
Penguin Books USA Inc., 375 Hudson Street, New York, New York 10014, USA
Penguin Books Australia Ltd, Ringwood, Victoria, Australia
Penguin Books Canada Ltd, 10 Alcorn Avenue, Toronto, Ontario, Canada M4V 3B2
Penguin Books (NZ) Ltd, 182–190 Wairau Road, Auckland 10, New Zealand

Penguin Books Ltd, Registered Offices: Harmondsworth, Middlesex, England

First published in Great Britain by Michael Joseph 1990
Published in Penguin Books 1992
1 3 5 7 9 10 8 6 4 2

ACKNOWLEDGEMENTS

I'd like to make acknowledgements to the silent wisdom of the thousands of Witches who, under repression, could not have made their knowledge public. Their silent power and the power of the Goddess Isis have given me the courage and inspiration to express my own views and live completely as a Witch.

I am thankful to Lady Sybil Leek, HP, who bravely spoke out and opened the doorways, and to all the Witch Elders who have supported me in my life's goals.

I write this book to give love and honour to my daughters, Jody and Penny, and the lifelong support of Alice Keegan, my coven, the Black Doves of Isis and the Council of Isis Community.

Special thanks to Lady Zara, HP, Lord Azaradel, HP, Lord Theodore Mills, HP, Marlene McKinley, PhD, Tina Sciola, Ralph Turcott, Yoko Ono and John Lennon.

For a work of this scope, it was necessary to consult sources in many fields. We are especially indebted to the following works and highly recommend them to readers for further study:

Adler, Margot, *Drawing Down the Moon: Witches, Druids, Goddess-worshippers, and Other Pagans in America Today*, Beacon Press, Boston, 1979.

Alexander, Hartley Burr, *The World's Rim: Great Mysteries of the North American Indians*, University of Nebraska Press, Lincoln, 1953.

Bentov, Itzhak, *Stalking the Wild Pendulum*, E. P. Dutton, New York, 1977.

Bradley, Marion Zimmer, *The Mists of Avalon*, Ballantine Books, New York, 1982.

Campbell, Joseph, *The Way of the Animal Powers*, Harper and Row, San Francisco, 1983.

Capra, Fritjof, *The Tao of Physics*, Bantam Books, New York, 1975.

Cowan, Thomas, *How to Tap into Your Own Genius*, Simon and Schuster, New York, 1984.

Davis, Elizabeth Gould, *The First Sex*, Penguin Books, New York, 1971.

Evans, Arthur, *The God of Ecstasy: Sex Roles and the Madness of Dionysos*, St Martin's Press, New York, 1988.

Gittelson, Bernard and Laura Torbet, *Intangible Evidence*, Simon and Schuster, New York, 1987.

The Kybalion: Hermetic Philosophy by Three Initiates, The Yogi Publication Society, Chicago, 1912.

Martello, Leo Louis, *Witchcraft: The Old Religion*, Citadel Press, Secaucus, New Jersey, 1973.

Murray, Margaret A., *The God of the Witches*, Oxford University Press, London, 1970.

Peat, F. David, *Synchronicity: The Bridge between Matter and Mind*, Bantam Books, New York, 1987.

Sjöö, Monica and Barbara Mor, *The Great Cosmic Mother: Rediscovering the Religion of the Earth*, Harper and Row, San Francisco, 1987.

Starhawk, *Dreaming the Dark: Magic, Sex, and Politics*, Beacon Press, Boston, 1982.

Stone, Merlin, *When God Was a Woman*, Harcourt Brace Jovanovich, New York, 1976.

Tompkins, Peter and Christopher Bird, *The Secret Life of Plants*, Harper and Row, San Francisco, 1973.

Walker, Barbara, *The Woman's Encyclopedia of Myths and Secrets*, Harper and Row, San Francisco, 1983.

CONTENTS

INTRODUCTION

When you see me on the streets of Salem you know that I am a Witch. I dress like one. Some people shield their eyes when they pass me because they have been taught that you should not look a Witch in the eyes. They believe something awful might happen. Others come right up to me to look at the pentacle I wear around my neck or the rings on my fingers or to touch my black robe because they have heard that a Witch has healing power and something wonderful will happen to those who touch her.

There are other Witches besides me in Salem, just as there are Witches in every part of the world and always have been. Most Witches today do not wear traditional Witch clothing and jewellery for fairly obvious reasons – religious and political authorities, who still misunderstand our beliefs and practices, continue to harass us. A Witch friend of mine was recently fired from her job as a hair stylist because she wore her pentacle on a chain around her neck. Another friend was not allowed to put 'Wicca' on the admitting form at a local hospital when he was asked to state his religion; the clerk refused to type it and left the line blank. These Witches were open about who they were. Many, however, are not. You can't tell most Witches by the way they dress or by their jewellery, which is often hidden beneath their clothes.

1

You can spot them by their magic.

As a young girl growing up in California, I didn't know that I was a Witch. I didn't really know what the word *Witch* meant or what a Witch was. I didn't even realize that my talents were any different from other people's. Today I would say they were not different. I simply retained those talents and developed them while other children lost them.

The first 'media Witch' I ever saw was in Walt Disney's film *Snow White and the Seven Dwarfs*. Even though I was a small child, I sensed that it was not a true portrait of a Witch. I guess I accepted the fact that a wicked queen who had magical powers could turn herself into a hideous old hag, but I instinctively knew that there was more to it than that. I knew those powers could also be used for good. Wasn't the prince's kiss that woke Snow White from her sleep also magic? I resisted the notion that magic was the work of devils and evil-doers. I knew a magic kiss could undo evil.

Bible classes were confusing for me. We learned that we 'should not suffer a Witch to live,' but we also learned that it was wrong to kill. I was so worried about this command to kill Witches that I actually thought I had some moral duty to hunt down and kill them. I remember asking my mother if it was my personal responsibility to kill all the eccentric old ladies in the neighbourhood. She and my father told me that we should not harm anyone.

In time I began to wonder *why* the Bible said not to allow Witches to live. Were Witches the enemy? What were we supposed to fear from them? Was it their powers or what they did with those powers? I also wondered why Witches were always talked about as women. We read in the Bible that Moses performed magic to impress the Pharaoh and to feed and nurture the Israelites in the desert, and we learned that Jesus could do miracles. I became fascinated with the idea that there was some kind of spiritual power available to both men and women that could transform people's lives: heal the sick, provide food, raise the dead, walk on water, find wisdom and great truths in simple everyday objects like sheep, lilies, grape vines and fig trees.

Mary, the mother of Jesus, also fascinated me. I wondered how she could give birth to someone divine without being divine herself. I wondered if she were some kind of goddess, the source of life. Priests and nuns told us that she was not divine, but I never really believed that. She had too much power.

Our church had a glorious statue of Mary standing on a crescent moon, with a serpent coiled around her feet and the earth beneath. I thought a woman who could stand on earth, moon, and snake was not just an ordinary mortal. Later, as I learned more about Goddess legends from around the world, I discovered that the serpent was not always considered to be the symbol of evil as presented in the Old Testament story about the Garden of Eden. In other cultures the serpent is the symbol of earth wisdom and rebirth because it can live in the earth, in trees, in water, and it can shed its skin and renew its life over and over again. As I studied further I learned that energy moves in coils like a serpent, and that DNA molecules are also spirals, and that the electromagnetic energy running along the earth's ley lines moves in a similar manner. Coils, spirals, waves. It was science. But it was as serpentine and mysterious as the hidden life of snakes.

Throughout my childhood I suspected that there was more information and knowledge than people were giving me, and by some ability that I did not at the time understand I could sometimes pick up on that withheld information. For example, when I was four I overheard my father's friends discussing engineering and architecture. I sidled up to where they were sitting and wormed my way into the conversation with innocent questions. At first they humoured me with childlike answers, but soon, I was asking rather penetrating questions. They were amazed at how much I knew about a subject that was new to me. They were astounded. Much later I realized how I was able to hold my own with the adults. I was drawing in information from those around me and possibly from a higher source.

Once at a family gathering, when I was five, I heard my uncle talking about a valuable vintage car that he and his brothers and sisters owned jointly. He stood tall, a drink in his hand, and told them that the car had been stolen from the storage garage. As I listened to his long story I could also 'hear' him saying something else quite different, as if he were whispering secretly to himself – that he had *sold* the car and intended to keep the money! Being young, I could not distinguish between mental voices and spoken words, and so, being also naïve, I asked, 'But Uncle, I heard you say that you sold the car?'

The room fell silent. My delicate mother grew nervous and softly scolded me. 'Laurie, you shouldn't say such things!' I could tell both from my uncle's own nervousness and what was running through his clever mind that I had caught him in a lie. But who would listen to a five-year-old?

I think that what kept my Witch soul alive was that I knew I had a 'golden centre' where my spirit dwelled. Somewhere deep inside of me was a place that no one could touch. At night I often had a personal vision of a Blue Woman from the Sky who protected me. I didn't know if she was the Virgin Mary or the Blue Fairy from Walt Disney's *Pinocchio*. She was a little like both of them, but I was too young to make such fine distinctions. All I knew was that each night in bed I felt her soft hand, larger than life, scoop under me and I would fall asleep in her protective palm. Today I would say that the Blue Fairy was the Goddess appearing to me in the form that I could feel comfortable with at the time.

Fairies were part of my childhood. I knew where they

lived out in the garden and I would leave food for them, especially at the full moon, for I had heard stories that they come out to dance when the moon is round and bright. On cold nights I would make little flannel blankets to keep them warm. My mother grew upset with me over this and forbade me to go out at night to see them. She said I had seen too many Disney films! Life wasn't like that, she warned. But Olive, my Mexican nanny, knew better. She would help me sneak into the garden after my parents had gone to bed and place my doll dishes filled with food under the flowers. In the morning the food was always gone.

Ironically, one of my first experiences with altered states of consciousness took place at a Catholic Mass. To my six-year-old senses the church and its Roman liturgy were an enchanted adventure. The flickering of the candles and the scent of incense, the tall arched ceiling with its colourful paintings of saints and angels, the lulling rhythm of the organ and the hypnotic Latin chant carried me off into a deep, trancelike state. I felt euphoric as I mimed my prayers. I began to look forward to going to church with my father just to experience these spontaneous altered states.

As I think back over my childhood today I can recognize many incidents in which I discovered and used these un-orthodox techniques of power and knowledge. Most people can do the same. Why then do they forget them or repress them? The answer is rather simple: As children we listened to parents, teachers, and other adults disapprove of magic. In our desire to please them and be like them, we accepted their worldview that magical powers were wrong, dangerous or simply nonexistent. As the years went by those talents were 'conditioned' out of us. Some fortunate children, however, escape this conditioning. They are born into families where psychic abilities are understood, accepted and even en-couraged. When they have 'strange' experiences their parents reassure them that nothing is wrong with them. These children learn that the world, as the Yaqui sorcerer told anthropologist Carlos Castenada, 'is stupendous, awesome, mysterious, unfathomable' and that they 'must assume responsibility for being here, in this marvellous world . . . in this marvellous time'. These children learn to expect the unexpected and not limit their knowledge to what can pass through the five senses.

I wish someone had told me about precognition the year that old Mr Bancroft died. One day Kenny, the boy next door, came running over to tell me that the man who lived in the old yellow Victorian house that I had always felt drawn towards when I passed it on the way to school each day, had died of a heart attack. I immediately told my mother what Kenny had said, and she replied, 'What? Mr Bancroft hasn't died.' She looked at me in a funny way. But she was right. Mr Bancroft was quite alive. I felt confused and said nothing more about it.

A week later Mr Bancroft died of a heart attack. I waited after school for Kenny and asked him how he knew a week ago that Mr Bancroft would die of heart attack. He, too, looked at me in a puzzled way. 'I don't know what you're talking about,' he said. 'I never told you that.' Years later I realized that either Kenny had had a precognitive experience and told me about it and then had repressed it, or I had had a precognitive experience, or we both had. But no one was there to explain these things to us. Sure, it might have been a coincidence, but as I had never seen Mr Bancroft or known of anyone who had ever had a heart attack, an extra-sensory explanation is much less unlikely than such a strange coincidence.

Many other incidents similar to this one occurred as I grew older. When I got to high school I decided to find out just what was going on. I asked teachers what these experiences could possibly mean and studied the books they gave me. In time I came to understand what all these strange occurrences meant. They meant I was a Witch.

The magical experiences in childhood and adolescence that both confused and excited me fell into four categories: receiving knowledge not available to other people through the normal channels of information; healing others with herbs, spells, and touch; going into altered states of consciousness; and communicating with spirits. As I studied and read I learned that these were the traditional powers attributed to Witches, shamans, native medicine peoples and many kinds of natural healers. The wise women and men of all ancient cultures possessed them. Some authorities even suggested that all so-called primitive peoples possessed them to some degree. When I talked this over with friends and teachers, most were shocked that I took these notions so seriously. They couldn't understand how an intelligent person could believe what to them seemed like make-believe. They called it hocus-pocus. They called it the supernatural. But no matter what they said, I knew what was natural for me. I never shared their shock. Deep inside me these things made sense. Deep inside I was thrilled.

The ancient power of magic is both spiritual and scientific. In recent years I have met many 'New Age' people who ignore the need to ground themselves scientifically. It takes more than wishful thinking to be a competent, practising Witch. I have come to call many of these people 'white-lighters' because all they want to do is worship and be spiritual. I have nothing against worship and spiritual works. But many people forget that magical workings impose upon us the responsibility of knowing *how* our magic works. We must know both the physical and metaphysical principles that underlie all magic and spiritual work so that we can use our powers correctly and for the good of all.

When it comes right down to it, Witches are still human. We are not disembodied beings composed solely of white light; we don't live in a blissful state of astral happiness. We

7

laugh, we bleed, we cry. We must know how to live *in* the world, not just 'between the worlds'. I hope that the wisdom and knowledge that you learn from this book will ground you in both worlds and awaken your responsibility for both worlds. It is only by being responsible human beings that we can be responsible Witches. And only responsible Witches will survive.

. I .

THE ANCIENT POWER OF MAGIC

Certain things are everlasting. Magic is one of them. It comes from the Persian and Greek roots *magus* and *magos* which mean wise. The English word magi, meaning wise men, comes from them. Witches are among the wise ones who participate in the work of creation in order to nourish the people and protect the earth. Magic belongs to no one culture, society or tribe – it is part of the universal wisdom. Magic-makers in every century and in every culture have played similar roles and shared similar characteristics. Whether they were called Witches, shamans, priests, priestesses, sages, medicine people or mystics, they knew how to heal the sick, summon the herds, grow crops, assist at births, track the influence of stars and planets and build temples and sacred mounds. They knew the secrets of the earth, the powers of the moon, the longings of the human heart. They invented language, writing, metallurgy, law, agriculture and the arts. Their rituals and ceremonies, their spells and incantations, their prayers and sacrifices were expressions of their oneness with the source of all life, the Great Mother of all living things.

First and foremost the magic-makers were healers who could diagnose illness and prescribe the correct medicine and ritual to heal their patients. Always performed in a social context that included the family and relatives, the ancient healers' magic worked because it was holistic, drawing on the patient's own healing power and working with the elements and spirits of the patient's environment. It dealt with both the physical and spiritual causes of disease – the invasion of harmful spirits or substances and the debilitating effects of soul loss. Ancient healers could withdraw the harmful objects from the body and retrieve lost souls.

Ancient magic workers were also spiritual leaders and counsellors who officiated at important rites of passage. They performed marriages, sanctified births, anointed the newborn, initiated young people into adulthood and led the souls of the dying into the next world. Because they stood 'between the worlds' of spirit and matter, they could serve as bridges and mediators between the human and the divine. People came to them with their visions and dreams. Sometimes they alone could help an individual discover his or her guardian spirits and sacred names.

As compelling seers, prophets and visionaries, they answered questions about the past and the future. They interpreted omens. They advised on auspicious times to plant, get married, travel, go on vision quests. Some of them had the power to raise storms, bring rain and calm seas.

They were the Animal Masters, who understood our kinship with all creatures. They knew the minds and hearts of the beasts and were at home with wild things. They could communicate with animals and plants and prowl in sacred places. They knew the arcane language with which creation speaks to itself. They knew how to listen.

And the wise ones were master storytellers who knew the ancient myths – for even ancient peoples had ancient myths that contained their collective folk memory. As custodians of legend and custom, they could recite poems and sing songs for hours or days at a time, mesmerizing their listeners with the magic of their voices. They were the original bards.

When we think about the gifts and talents that these ancient magic-workers possessed, something inside us glimmers. We resonate to them because we know that we, too, possess these gifts and talents. On some level of consciousness we know that these skills are not supernatural but natural, and that *we have used them* – in memory, in imagination, in another life, in our dreams. We understand the deep truths that the Witch, the shaman and the mystic embody, truths so old the world will never get rid of them. Although many modern people will not admit it, the Witch's worldview makes sense today. We still sense a connectedness with nature that has not been totally lost. We instinctively know that all creation contains a magnificent vitality, that everything is alive, that all creatures contain spirit. In our heart of hearts we agree with the philosopher Thales, who told the ancient Greeks, 'All things are filled with gods.'

Every culture has had its magicians and visionaries. We find them in the histories of Sumer, Crete, India, Egypt, Greece, Africa, the Americas, Polynesia, Tibet, Siberia and the Middle East. In Western Europe they appeared as the Druids, the priests and priestesses of the Celtic race whose origins are still shrouded in the mists of history. The migrating Celts spread Druidic wisdom and magic from China to Spain. In mining and metalworking, sculpture and art, poetry and literature, law and social customs the Celtic peoples left an indelible stamp on European culture. From their scientific and spiritual customs the modern Witch derives much of her Craft. With a remarkable ability to blend both the practical and the metaphysical – the Celts developed the traction plough, rectangular field systems and crop rotation, as well as theories about the immortality of the soul and reincarnation – the Druidic leaders of the Celts stand as shining models for the modern Witch.

A Witch's knowledge is old. Her worldview is ancient. People who pride themselves on being modern often dismiss

Witchcraft as fantasy, superstition or make-believe. Biased accounts of ancient people, written by historians who were convinced of their own culture's superiority, have made our ancestors' civilizations look barbaric, ignorant and savage. But the truth about the ancient ways can't be suppressed. Witchcraft thrived in the so-called primitive cultures of the past; it thrived in the highly developed cultures of the past. It thrives today.

MAGICAL CHILDHOODS

What is true in the macrocosm is true in the microcosm. Many modern Witches trace their first encounters with magic back to very early times in their childhoods, when their innocence and ability to wonder paralleled that of our earliest ancestors. In fact, even when recognized later in life, magic fills us with a sense of awe as it breaks forth in our lives. Adults feel a kind of childlike wonder and surprise during their first magical experiences.

Just as the child loses its sense of oneness with the universe as it develops ego boundaries and learns how to protect its separate and distinct body from the rest of the world, human societies lost that sense of unity as they evolved away from nature. As men and women created societies more and more removed from the natural world, they found themselves working against nature, subduing it, exploiting it. In time they thought of nature as neither intelligent nor divine. Eventually they came to view it as the enemy.

But Witches have never forgotten the basic truth about creation: the world is *not* our enemy; neither is it inert, dumb matter. The earth and all living things share the same life force; the earth and all living things are composed of Divine Intelligence. All life is a web of interconnected beings, and we are woven into it as sisters and brothers of the All.

If you think back into your early childhood, you will probably remember an incident when you knew something others didn't know, an occasion when knowledge came spontaneously and intuitively. Perhaps you read someone's thoughts, knew what was inside a present before you unwrapped it, made an improbable wish and it came true. You may have felt a strong kinship with nature, a bond with animals and plants, a certain power coming to you from the stars. You may have seen spirits or little people or heard them in the night. Ancient tales of Gods and Goddesses may have resonated with something deep in your soul, and you knew the old myths were as true as the scriptures you may have read in church or temple. They may have seemed even more true.

A WITCH'S MAGIC

To me the word *Witch* is a delicious word, filled with the most ancient memories that go back to our earliest ancestors, who lived close to natural cycles and understood and appreciated the power and energy that we share with the cosmos. The word *Witch* can stir these memories and feelings even in the most sceptical mind.

The word itself has evolved through many centuries and cultures. There are different opinions about its origins. In old Anglo-Saxon, *wicca* and *wicce* (masculine and feminine respectively) refer to a seer or one who can divine information by means of magic. From these root words we derive the word *Wicca*, a term many in the Craft use today to refer to our beliefs and practices. *Wych* in Saxon and *wicce* in Old English mean to 'turn, bend, shape'. An even earlier Indo-European root word, *wic*, or *weik*, also means to 'bend or shape'. As Witches we *bend* the energies of nature and humanity to promote healing, growth and life. We *turn* the

Wheel of the Year as the seasons go by. We *shape* our lives and environments so they promote the good things of the earth. The word *Witch* has also been traced back to the old Germanic root *wit* – to know. And this, too, gives some insight into what a Witch is – a person of knowledge, a person versed in both scientific and spiritual truths.

In the origins of many languages the concept of 'Witch' was part of a constellation of words for 'wise' or 'wise ones'. In English we see this most clearly in the word *magic*, which derives from the Greek *magos* and the Old Persian word *magus*. Both these words mean 'seer' or 'wizard'. In Old English the word *wizard* meant 'one who is wise'. In many languages *Witch* is the hidden word, concealed in the common, everyday terms for wisdom. In French the word for midwife (a term that in rural areas often meant 'Witch', just as 'country nurse' did in English-speaking countries) is *sage-femme*, 'wise woman'.

Wisdom enriches the soul, not just the mind. It is different from mere intelligence, information, and cleverness, which dwell only in the mind. Wisdom goes deeper than that. When the brain, with its multitudinous facts and pieces of information, ceases to exist, the soul will endure. The ageless wisdom of the soul will survive.

The Greek word for soul is *psyche*. We often think of psychics as being gifted and rare individuals because they can tap into this universal wisdom, but the gift is not rare. We all have it; we are each en-souled individuals. Everyone has psychic powers or soul powers, and each of us can relearn – or remember – how to use them.

Although both men and women share the power of magic, the word *Witch* has commonly been associated with women rather than men, but men in the Craft are also called Witches. During the Burning Times 80 per cent of the people who were executed for practising Witchcraft were women. Even today most practitioners of the Craft are women, although the number of men is on the rise. There is a good reason for thinking of Witchcraft as a woman's Craft. A Witch's power deals with life, and women are biologically more engaged in producing life and nourishing it than are men. It is not a coincidence that as more men assist in childbirth and take on the responsibilities of caring for newborn infants, more men are becoming interested in the Craft. The spirit of the times is leading both men and women to reconnect with the mysteries of life that are found in the natural rhythms of woman, earth and moon – for the mysteries of life are the mysteries of magic.

Magic is knowledge and power that come from the ability to shift consciousness at will into a non-ordinary, visionary state of awareness. Traditionally certain tools and methods have been used to cause this shift: dance, song, music, colours, scents, drumming, fasting, vigils, meditation, breathing exercises, certain natural foods and drinks, and forms of hypnosis. Dramatic, mystical environments, such as sacred groves, valleys, mountains, churches or temples, will also shift consciousness. In almost every culture some form of visionary trance is used for the sacred rituals that open the doorways to the Higher Intelligence or for working magic.

From Neolithic times the practice of Witchcraft has always centred on symbolic rituals that stimulate the imagination and shift awareness. Hunting rituals, vision quests and healing ceremonies were always performed in the rich context of the symbols and metaphors unique to each culture. Today a Witch's meditations and spells continue this practice. A Witch's work is mind work and uses powerful metaphors, allegories and images that unlock the powers of the mind. The Huichol Indians of Mexico tell us that the mind has a secret doorway that they call the *nierika*. For most people it remains closed until the time of death. But the Witch knows how to open and pass through that doorway even in life and bring back through it the visions of non-ordinary realities that give purpose and meaning to life.

The images and symbols of Witchcraft have a mysterious and magical quality because they tap into something deeper and more mysterious than ourselves. They trigger the ageless truths that dwell in the unconscious which, as the great psychologist and student of world religions Carl Jung suggested, merge with the instinctive responses of the animal kingdom and may even encompass all of creation. The deepest knowledge, just on the other side of the *nierika*, is always knowledge of the universe. It is always present, even though, like a candle flame in the blinding sunlight, it seems invisible and unknowable. But magic takes us to those deep realms of power and knowledge. Magic leads us into the soft moonlight, where a candle flame glows steady and bright. It can take us through the *nierika* and bring us back again.

Deep inner knowledge from the unconscious cannot always be expressed in words; it often requires poetry, song and ritual. Somewhere in the centre of your soul is a sense of identity that you can never convey to another human being by words alone. You know there is more to you than you can see or express, just as you know there is more to the universe than you now understand. At best you can only give hints and glimpses of your deepest self by the things you like, what you fear, how you play, the way you smile. Guarded in the centre of your being is the secret of who you are and how you personally connect to the rest of the universe.

A Witch's knowledge of herself, of nature, of the divine power behind the cosmos can be best expressed through myth, symbol, ritual, drama and ceremony. Jung tells us that the structure of the mind results from the interplay of archetypal energies that can be known only in images and symbols and sensed in ritual and numinous events. And so we find that from the earliest times holy men and women of every culture have created practices rich in symbols and metaphors that the deep unconscious mind intuitively recognizes and understands: drums, gems, feathers, shells, wands, bowls, cups, cauldrons, sacred tools and clothing made from sacred plants, animals, and metals filled with power. These are the images that reveal the patterns of knowledge that lie beneath the physical universe. These are the images that lead us to the secret power hidden in the centre of things, including our own hearts. With these rites and images, we can – as Witches say – 'draw down the moon'.

· 2 ·

THE OLD RELIGION

From the earliest days of human life on this planet, men and women have wondered and worshipped in the face of life's many mysteries. Out of the need to wonder and worship came understanding, and from understanding came meaning. In modern times we often think that understanding and meaning replace mystery, but nothing could be further from the truth. When understanding and meaning are truly incorporated into our hearts and minds we discover that the mysteries never disappear. They grow richer and deeper. The need to wonder, worship and understand are all parts of the same human desire, and these three needs find a unity of expression in ancient spiritual practices. The same ancient mysteries lie at the heart of my own spiritual beliefs. It is what Witches call 'the Old Religion'.

All religion is about creation – not simply the tales and legends of how a creator or creators brought forth the universe, but how living men, women and children participate in the ongoing generation of the universe. Creation is never finished, it is an eternal process. In some native traditions people sing the sun up at dawn and chant it down at dusk. There is profound wisdom in this that cannot be repudiated by the contention that the sun could very well rise and set without human assistance. The turning of day into night and winter into spring *should* be human as well as divine activities. As followers of the Old Religion, Witches take an active part in what we call turning the Wheel of the Year and participating in the course of the seasons. We are co-creators of the universe.

OUR MOTHER, THE EARTH

Religion is about creation, and for that reason religion should be about the earth. To many people this comes as a surprise because modern religious thinking emphasizes salvation over creation and focuses on heaven and hell rather than earth. But pagans believed that biological processes are spiritual processes and that there is divine meaning in every natural event.

As participants in the ongoing drama of creation our ancestors believed that the great mysteries of life were the mysteries of transformation: how things turn into other things, how things grow, die and are reborn. Perhaps nowhere in their experience did they see these events more personally and intimately than in the transformations of woman. The ability to conceive a new human life, give birth, produce milk and to bleed with the phases of the moon was awe-inspiring. The centrality of woman in the life of the community could not be denied. She alone had the power to produce and nurture life. Without her new life would die. Woman reflected the cyclic changes that paralleled the seasonal changes of the earth and the monthly phases of the moon. It was not superstition, nor spiritual fantasy, that made early observers notice that both woman and nature shared the great role of motherhood. It was biological fact.

The earliest works of art that depict human figures are of mothers. Dating back 35,000 to 10,000 BC and discovered all across Europe and in Africa, these 'Venus figurines', as they are called by archaeologists, show the fullness of motherhood and the ripeness of feminine nature. Carved in bone, ivory and stone or shaped out of clay, these small miniatures, with large bellies, full breasts and powerful thighs, were not simply the erotic art of their day. As the highly respected authority on world mythologies Joseph Campbell emphasizes in *The Way of the Animal Powers*, 'This definitely is *not* a work of naturalistic art, but a conceived abstraction, delivering a symbolic statement.' From their positions in holy places and grave sites they represented something sacred. The female organs were clearly 'numinous centres,' as Monica Sjöö and Barbara Mor tell us in their comprehensive and inspiring study of the worldwide Goddess traditions, *The Great Cosmic Mother: Rediscovering the Religion of the Earth*. At a time when the male role in conception was not understood, or only vaguely understood, the mother's body was viewed as the only source of life, just as the earth was the only source of biological life.

There are no similar depictions of men dating back this far. Indeed, the role of the male in conception is a rather recent discovery, dating back only about five thousand years. The father's role in conception was probably not widely understood until about 300 BC. The great pioneer anthropologist Bronislaw Malinowski discovered twentieth-century Stone Age cultures in Polynesia that only dimly understood the male contribution. It is not surprising that the father's role should have gone unnoticed for so long. Since a woman does not become pregnant with every act of intercourse, nor does she know she is pregnant until days or weeks have passed, the connection between conception and sexual activity with males is not immediately obvious. To our ancestors it appeared that the male 'opened' the vagina but that the actual placement of the young life in the womb was the work of divine power, perhaps the light of the moon, maybe a spirit visitor. Or from the worldwide distribution of myths about parthenogenesis, perhaps the woman had the power to produce life solely on her own. At any rate, the concept of fatherhood and permanent mating developed rather late in human history. As anthropologist Lewis Henry Morgan put it, 'It was not until *recorded* civilization commenced that it [the patriarchal family] became established.'

Even earlier than the Cro-Magnon societies that carved the Venus figures, we find Neanderthal grave sites, dating back many millennia, with their dead buried in a curled-up foetal position, their bones painted with red ochre. Symbolically the deceased have re-entered the womb of the earth. They are once again red with the blood of the mother. They have literally and symbolically returned to her, thus completing what our Ice Age ancestors knew to be the complete cycle of life – from womb to womb, from a single mother to the Great Mother.

From a wealth of archaeological, historical and anthropological evidence – Goddess statues, burial customs, cave paintings of woman giving birth, the newborn still connected to her by the umbilical cord – I believe it is clear that our ancestors understood the intimate connection between female power and earth power. Woman was the source of life. Woman's recurrent cycles paralleled the recurrent cycles of nature. The great 'myth of the eternal return' (to use the wonderful phrase from Mircea Eliade, the renowned scholar of world religions) was the myth played over and over again in the life cycle of every woman, in each pregnancy that produced a new human life, and in the mysterious bleeding that occurred each moon and ceased when the womb retained its blood and grew fuller and fuller like the waxing moon. By so closely identifying woman with the earth, and the earth with divine power, our ancestors found it reasonable to assume that the divine power behind creation was female. Monica Sjöö and Barbara Mor have said it very succinctly: '*God was female for at least the first 200,000 years of human life on earth.*' For Witches, God is still female.

The Old Religion, with its strong matrifocal perspective, was a religion of ecstasy. Archaeological evidence of primal religious experiences – cave drawings, pictures in tombs and on pottery – show human figures with large awestruck eyes, human beings dancing with wild animals, flying with birds, sharing the watery realms with fish and snakes. Religious practices and shamanistic rituals that have survived into our own time among indigenous peoples also indicate ecstatic religious experiences – dancing, drumming, chanting, re-enacting primal creation myths and inducing trance. From all the scattered evidence reaching through the centuries, it appears that ecstatic religious experiences were the norm for pre-Christian cultures. And so they should have been in religions that centred on woman's experience. The Great Goddess and her priestesses were living examples of the integration of body, mind and spirit. For them there was no dichotomy between mind and body, between spirit and matter.

Followers of the Old Religion believe the universe was created in ecstasy out of the body and mind of the Great Mother of all living things. The oldest creation myths from around the world recount the many ways that human beings have perceived this original birth of earth, sky, plants, animals and the first human couple. From north-west India we learn about Kujum-Chantu, the Divine Mother, who created the physical landscapes of the earth out of the various parts of her own body. A Pelasgian creation tale from the eastern Mediterranean explains how Euronyme, the Goddess of All Things, danced the earth into existence. From Venezuela comes the story of Puana, the Snake who created Kuma, the first woman, from whom sprang all living things and all the customs of the Yaruros people. A Huron story tells of the Woman Who Fell from the Sky, a divine woman, who with the help of Turtle, began human life on earth. The Fon people in Dahomey, Africa, revere Nan Buluku, the Great Mother, who created the world. From ancient China comes the creation story of how the universe was in the shape of a hen's egg containing a mysterious *something* not yet born. From this feminine environment sprang Phan Ku, the first being who created the earth. A Tahitian myth also relates how the first spark of life began inside a great egg, where Ta-aroa waited for ages to be born before beginning the great work of creation with his companion, Tu. Among the many Greek myths of creation is that of Gaia, the Earth, who appeared out of the Chaos or Void and who brought forth Heaven and the Sea, and then created the mighty Titans. In Babylonia we hear the story of the divine mothers, Apsu and Tiamat, who created the gods. A Sumerian myth explains how the Sea Goddess Nammu, called 'the mother, the ancestress', gave birth to the gods. The ancient Mayans told many tales of the Maker and Former, who had many names, among them both Grandfather and Grandmother.

In Hebrew legends the all-powerful Yahweh was originally the Goddess Iahu-'Anat, a name that, as Elizabeth Gould Davis tells us in *The First Sex*, was 'stolen from that of the Sumerian goddess'. The name Yahweh has also been related to the Canaanite moon deity, Yareah, who was possibly androgynous or bisexual. Even in Genesis we find indications that mother deities were present at the creation. In one of the two creation accounts, Elohim, the word translated as a singular 'God', is actually a plural noun, and according to some biblical scholars would be better translated as 'creative nature spirits'. That Elohim was plural and partially feminine is clear from the words of Genesis that say 'Let *us* make man in *our* image and likeness. Male and female He [!] created them.' If the 'image and likeness' of the creator is both male and female, we can assume that at least some of those 'creative spirits' had feminine natures.

THE TRIPLE MOON GODDESS

In many parts of the world the original Goddess is referred to as the Great Moon Goddess, a triune deity. She is the great female trinity of Maiden, Mother and Crone. And in many written accounts, as well as in the artwork that has survived, we see this triple nature – sometimes depicted as three faces – reflected in the three phases of the moon. Here, too, the earliest human worshippers understood that one and the same mystery or power operated in both woman and the moon. As Joseph Campbell put it, 'The initial observation which gave birth in the mind of man to a mythology of one mystery informing earthly and celestial things was ... the celestial order of the waxing moon and the earthly order of the womb.' So not only was the Goddess reflected in the three phases of the moon, but the biological cycles of every woman found expression there too. Every woman could identify with the Great Goddess by identifying her own bodily transformation with the moon's monthly waxing and waning.

A Witch's spells and rituals are always performed in conjunction with the phases of the moon, and female Witches align their magical work with their own menstrual cycles. By observing the three lunar phases and meditating on the Goddess's traditions associated with them, we discover the special powers and mysteries of the moon and the unique wisdom it teaches us about the Divine Mother of the universe.

The Maiden
The crescent moon, virginal and delicate, grows stronger and brighter each night, appearing higher and higher in the sky as it comes to greater fullness. Ancient men and women have interpreted this phase of the moon to represent the young girl growing stronger with each passing day. She is the pure,

24

independent athlete and huntress, who in Mediterranean Goddess lore was called Diana and Artemis. As she matures into a powerful woman warrior, or Amazon, she learns to defend herself and the children that she will someday give birth to.

In some cultures this free and independent Goddess is the Lady of the Wild Things and presides over the hunting rituals. In her hand she holds the hunting horn, taken from the cows and bulls that are her special animals. The horn is shaped like the crescent moon. One of her earliest representations is the 21,000-year-old figure discovered in France that archaeologists have named the Venus of Laussel. It depicts a woman stained with red ochre holding the hunting horn in triumph. The art historian Siegfried Giedion calls her 'the most vigorously sculptured representation of the human body in the whole of primeval art'. Joseph Campbell points out that as a mythic personage – i.e. an image of someone that transcends the merely human – she was so well known that 'the reference of the elevated horn would have been ... readily understood'. What Stone Age people readily understood was that the woman with the horn could assure success on the hunt because as a woman she knew the intimate mysteries and movements of the wild herds. Ironically, the language our contemporary historians have traditionally used to speak of Ice Age hunters speaks of violence, slaughter and men. However, as historian William Irwin Thompson notes, 'every statue and painting we discover cries out to us that this Ice Age humanity was a culture of art, the love of animals, and woman'.

The Mother
The full moon, when the night sky is flooded with light, is represented as a mother Goddess, her womb swollen with new life. Witches and magic-workers everywhere have always found this to be a time of great power. It is a time that draws

us to sacred places, like the hidden springs and caves that Neolithic women might have used as their original birthing places. In his fascinating study *The Great Mother*, Erich Neumann suggests, 'The earliest sacred precinct of the primordial age was probably that in which the women gave birth.' Here women could withdraw into the Great Mother and, in privacy and with fresh running waters nearby, give birth in safety and in a sacred manner. And so down to this day temples, churches, sacred groves and sanctuaries have a womblike stillness and quality that suggest protection and safety from the world of men, warfare, and disruption. As we enter these places, often lit as by the light of the full moon, we feel born into a more sacred life, and we feel closer to the source of all life.

In the mother aspect of the full moon, the Goddess of the Hunt also becomes the Queen of the Harvest, the Great Corn Mother, who bestows her bounty upon the earth. The Romans called her Ceres, from whose name the word *cereal* is derived. She is the same as the Greek Demeter, a name composed of Δ, the feminine letter delta, and *meter*, or 'mother'. In Asia she was called 'the Doorway of the Mysterious Feminine . . . the root from which Heaven and Earth sprang'. In America she was the Corn Maiden, who brought maize to nourish the people. In all her manifestations she is the source of crops and vegetation that become our food. When she departs in the winter months – as Demeter seeking her daughter Kore in the Underworld – the land lies barren. When she returns in the spring all turns green again.

In many Middle Eastern, Mediterranean and ancient European traditions the Mother Goddess gives birth to a son, a young hunter who in time becomes her lover and mate. Although this may sound contradictory and incestuous to modern ears, we must keep in mind that as 'mythical types,' all women are potential mothers, and all men are grown sons.

According to many ancient legends, the young God must

die. Here we find ancient myth and social customs aligning. Because women were vital to the survival of the tribe, for only they could give birth and nourish the newborn, the dangerous job of stalking and killing the wild beasts became the males' responsibility. By 7000 BC the Son of the Divine Mother was fairly well established in European legends as a Hunter God, often depicted wearing horns. There were strategic and sacramental reasons for this. As ritual the horned head-dress honoured the spirit of the animal and identified the young hunter with the animal he hoped to kill. In ecstatic religious rites a person *becomes* the God or Goddess who is being honoured by dressing, speaking and acting like the deity. So, by wearing the horns and antlers, the hunter became the hunted in body, mind and spirit. He looked like the prey; he thought like the prey; he embodied the spirit of his prey. The identification with the hunted was thought to ensure a successful hunt.

Strategically, the hunter wore the very horns and hide of the beast for safety and success. By concealing his human shape and scent he could approach the herd without scaring it away. American Indians donned buffalo robes, complete with head and horns, to approach a buffalo in this same way up into the nineteenth century. Stalking and killing a large horned animal was dangerous. Many hunters were gored or trampled to death. Around tribal fires the successful hunter was honoured and given the horns or antlers of the slain beast to wear as a sign of victory and an expression of gratitude on the part of the tribe, for he had put his life in danger. In time this hunter-son of the Great Goddess was honoured as a Horned God, and his willingness to sacrifice his life for the good of the community was celebrated in song and ritual.

The hunter often met his death in the winter months, the season of the hunt when hides were thick with fur and meat was easily preserved in the cold, frosty air. This drama of a winter death was also seen in nature as the winter sun grew faint and weak, and everything appeared dead or sleeping, and when the long winter nights encouraged our Stone Age ancestors to retreat into the warm, womblike darkness of their lodges. It was the season of ice and death. Joseph Campbell tells us in *The Way of the Animal Powers* that 'the annual disappearances and reappearances of the birds and beasts must also have contributed to this sense of a general time-factored mystery', a mystery that all things have their times to die and be reborn. A religion based on the cycles of nature would make this a sacred truth. Those who followed that religion could celebrate even the season of death because they knew that it was to be followed by a season of rebirth. If the Son must die, he would be reborn, just as the sun would return in the spring. The Earth and Woman see to it. These were the mysteries of the Great Mother Goddess, the Great Womb of the Earth.

In Britain and north-western Europe, in Ohio and Mississippi, and in many other parts of the globe, Neolithic farming cultures constructed great earth mounds. According to Sjöö and Mor, 'the beehive shape of so many Neolithic earth mounds was quite intentional and symbolic. Beekeeping was a metaphor for settled agriculture, and for the peaceful abundance of the earth in those times. And the honeybee was like the full moon, making illumination in the night.' Shaped like the full breasts of the Goddess of Milk and like the beehive ruled by the great Queen Bee, earth mounds were the results of human efforts to swell up the earth to resemble the hills and mountains that were honoured as the sacred breasts and belly of the Goddess. The beehive imagery recalls the tales of 'lands flowing with milk and honey' – the milk of mothers, the golden honey from the Queen. From Africa and Thrace come legends of women warriors who fed on honey and mare's milk. In whatever form we find it, all nourishment comes from the Goddess of Earth and Moon, and all mothers are strong because of her power within their bodies.

When I cast a magic circle beneath the full moon, I draw its power down into the chalice of clear spring water I hold in my hands. As I gaze into the cup I see my own face in the moon's silver reflection. Then, at the correct moment, I plunge my ritual dagger into the chalice, splitting the water, shattering the moon's image into many smaller parts, like shards of crystal. Slowly, deliciously, I drink the power and energy of the moon. I feel it go down my throat, tingling throughout my entire body. The Goddess is then within me. I have swallowed the moon.

When Witches place their feet or hands into a pond, a lake, or any pool of water beneath the full moon, they draw up the moon's reflected power through their fingers and toes. We pull her power into our bodies whenever we swim in moonlight. Ancient rituals called for brewing potions in a cauldron beneath a full moon so the Goddess's own light could be stirred into the brew. Even indoors in the cold New England winters, meeting in my living-room before the fire, my coven brings the moon's full shape into our presence by standing in a circle. Or a single candle reflected in the chalice helps us envision the moon, for every reflected light shares the moon's own nature, casting a magic glow in which things unseen can be seen.

The Crone

At some point in every woman's life the menstrual cycle ends. She ceases to bleed with the moon. She retains her blood for ever, or so it must have seemed to our ancestors. She holds her power, and so she is power-full. She is an elder. She is the wise old crone. Like the waning moon, her body shrinks, her energies wane and she eventually disappears into the dark night of death, just as the moon disappears for three dark nights. At death her body is replaced into the earth, and at some point she will be reborn, fresh and virginal as the new moon on its first visible night, hanging like a jewel in the western sky at sunset.

The Greek Goddess Hecate, Goddess of Night, Death, and Crossroads, embodied this Crone. Her rule during the moon's absence made the night exceptionally dark. The frightened paid her homage during these three nights, seeking her favour and protection. Wherever three roads crossed Hecate could be found, for here life and death were thought to pass each other. Even today Witches will leave cakes at crossroads or in the woods at the dark of the moon to honour her.

At death Hecate was said to meet the departed souls and lead them to the Underworld. In Egypt the Dark Moon Goddess was called Heqit, Heket or Hekat, and she was also the Goddess of midwives, for the power that leads souls into death is the same power that pulls them into life. And so Hecate became known as the Queen of the Witches in the Middle Ages, for the wise old country nurses, versed in the ways of the Goddess, were the midwives. From years of experience they acquired the practical skills for assisting at births and the spiritual insights that could explain the mystery of birth.

And so from birth, to puberty, to motherhood, to old age and death, the eternal return of life is intimately bound up in every woman, no matter what phase of her own life she is currently in. The eternal return of life is seen and felt in every season of the earth. And there is no phase or point on this great wheel that is not sacred, and there is no phase or point on the wheel that is overlooked in a Witch's yearly celebrations.

In these ways our ancestors wondered and worshipped. In these ways they understood their place in the great mysteries of creation and found meaning for their lives. And in these ways Witches today continue the old customs and make life holy.

GODDESS CULTURES

The deepest values and beliefs of a people shape not only their spiritual practices but the way they organize their lives. Out of the shared perceptions of what is real arise the social structures that reflect a people's notion of truth. It is not surprising, therefore, that we find Neolithic societies organized around women.

In the early years of the twentieth century the archaeologist Arthur Evans discovered the ruins of a lost culture at the town of Knossos on the island of Crete. The paintings and artefacts that he found depict a joyous, playful, sensuous, peace-loving culture where women held positions of honour and power and where men were subservient and presumably held second-class status. At first scholars thought this Minoan culture on Crete to be a kind of fluke. But other towns in the eastern Mediterranean have been uncovered that reflect a similar matrifocal organization to that on Crete. In Anatolia (present-day Turkey) the towns of Catal Hüyük, Mersin, Hacilar and Alalakh were also matrifocal Goddess cultures. At the other end of the Mediterranean, Marseilles and Syracuse were Goddess-worshipping centres, and perhaps the most famous of all was at Ephesus, a Greek city on the west coast of Anatolia.

What were these women-centred, Goddess-worshipping cultures like? Many scholars have noted their strong resemblances to the larger number of European myths and legends about a Golden Age, suggesting that the myths arose as latter-day accounts of what had once been reality. The absence of military fortifications and weaponry indicate that they were peace-loving cultures. There seems to have been no large-scale, organized warfare, only the minor, personal skirmishes and conflicts that arise in any human society. Weapons were small, personal instruments, which suggest they were used primarily for defence.

Goddess centres also lacked a bureaucratic political structure; people lived in clanlike extended families run by mothers. There was no slavery. Women functioned as priestesses, artists, agriculturists and small-game hunters. Food was abundant and supplied by gathering, foraging, hunting and later small-scale farming. In short, these Neolithic Goddess cultures seem to have sown the seeds for Western thinkers' fascination with Utopia, not as a future possibility, however, but as a dream about a reality we have lost.

It is not surprising that ancient life centred on mothers. Bloodlines, kinship and property rights naturally descended through mothers because the mother-child relationship was always paramount. A child always knew its mother. Even after fatherhood was understood, mothers and children did not always know who the father was.

Matrifocal societies may indeed have had the characteristics of a Golden Age simply because the primary bonding was between children and mothers. As psychiatrist Erich Fromm has pointed out, children must *win* their father's love, usually by obedience and conformity. A mother's love is unconditional, which breeds goodwill. Cultures based on mother love and reinforced by religious rites centring on the Mother Goddess would have been peaceful, easy-going, life-nurturing societies built on trust. The sacredness of all life would have been stressed, and violent, destructive behaviour discouraged. Humanistic values arising from the natural playfulness of mother and child, rather than obedience to an authoritarian figure, would have cemented social relations.

The Goddess centres discovered around the Mediterranean are representative of the matrifocal cultures in other parts of the world. Their discovery has led some scholars to suggest that Neolithic civilization, especially in temperate climates, was matrifocal everywhere and that women were the originators of human culture. Because of woman's centrality in human life and society, she would have been the developer of the arts and skills necessary for civilization to advance. Women's labour provided the bulk of the food supplies, if the hunting-gathering societies that still exist in our own day are any indication. Here women provide 60 per cent of the food, and social myths and customs indicate that the gathering and preparation of food were always female responsibilities. As part of the food preparation women would have developed processing, preserving and storage techniques.

To provide clothing women learned weaving skills and the art of tanning and dyeing hides. Among the first attempts at art may have been the designs that women painted on leather or wove into textiles. Women were probably the primary fire keepers, a sacred and vital function in primeval societies. In eighty-four tribal societies that have survived into the twentieth century, women are still the primary builders and keepers of fires, and many of these cultures have legends about woman being the original discoverer of fire. Ovens were traditionally built to resemble womblike mounds and were referred to as a kind of belly or womb. Woman's role in the ritual maintenance of fire continued down through the centuries, as seen in the vestal virgins of Rome and the Irish nuns of St Brigid at Kildare, who tended sacred fires until the time of Henry VIII. As fire keepers women would have been in charge of pottery, ceramics and metallurgy.

As the primary gatherers of herbs, grains, nuts, berries and roots, women would in all likelihood have been the original herbalists and pharmacologists. With their knowledge of medicinal herbs and remedies, women were the first official healers and health-care providers. (The World Health Organization relates that 95 per cent of all health care even today is provided by women.) Cataloguing and explaining to their daughters the various parts of plants and showing how to prepare them, pointing out which were poisonous, and cataloguing herbs and cross-referencing them with specific ailments may have entailed the refinement of communication that led to the development of language as we know it. Anthropologists who suggest this theory point out that hunting large game, the male's primary function, would not have required such meticulous detailing and cataloguing of information. Hence vocabulary and sentence structure would not have been as extensive or complex. Hunting is best taught and executed by silent observation and imitation.

Women's experience also shaped our ancestors' concept of time. The earliest calendars were lunar calendars based on the twenty-eight-day cycle of the moon and the thirteen moons in a year. Chinese women developed lunar calendars three thousand years ago, and lunar calendars have been discovered at Neolithic sites across Europe. They were also used by tribal people in the Americas up into modern times. Since menstrual cycles follow lunar cycles – and still do today when women live away from artificial lights – Neolithic women would not have escaped noticing the strong connection between the two. They probably even identified the two as being parallel aspects of the same phenomenon – an indication that the Goddess who manifested in the moon each month also manifested in their own bodies. The Gaelic words for menstruation and calendar still reflect this close identification. They are *miosach* and *miosachan* respectively. As Stone Age women etched or notched moon-time on to wood or stone to track menstrual cycles, calculate pregnancies and predict births, they developed the earliest forms of mathematics and astronomy, two fields which scholars believe originated in conjunction with one another.

If women and women's mysteries inspired astrology and calendrical sciences, then women's influence was most likely the inspiration for the stone circles and megalithic structures that were built all over the globe. Many of these were laid out to mark the passage of time by means of celestial events such as the appearance of certain constellations in the sky at appointed times of the year or the rising of the sun at the summer and winter solstices. In other words, Stonehenge and Avebury in England, and their counterparts in other areas of the world, were huge astronomical observatories. One of the most recently discovered examples is an Irish tomb outside Dublin built in alignment with the rising sun at the winter solstice so that the first rays at dawn on 21 December enter a small slit in the roof of the tomb and throw pools of light which illuminate designs carved on the floor in the inner chamber. This old Celtic tomb, erected over five thousand years ago, is older than Stonehenge and the pyramids.

In many of these stone circles, or 'medicine wheels' as they are called in Native America, sacred rituals were performed in conjunction with solar, lunar and stellar sightings. Even today astonishingly accurate observations can be made using these structures, even though the stones themselves look crude and clumsy. The mathematical precision with which they were laid out and constructed clearly indicates that these old tribespeople were sophisticated engineers and geometricians. It also indicates that they felt a powerful need to construct, by means of their own physical labour, earth structures that would be in harmony with celestial events. They intuitively understood that harmony and balance need to be affirmed by human endeavour, that it was their responsibility to express and live according to the patterns of harmony they saw around them. The same should apply to us living today – for of all the earth's creatures, human beings have the power to ignore, even destroy, the balance of nature. Today the haunting stones and medicine wheels appear like sentinels guarding sacred places as well as sacred concepts. They seem to say to us, 'Be careful. Enter this sacred space only if you vow to uphold the harmonies and beauties of creation.'

It is well known that in small groups of women living or working together, menstrual cycles harmonize and align with each other. Scholars believe this was the norm in tribal life. Thus all or most of the women would share their menstrual times together, and the monthly period would have been recognized as a time when woman experienced the divine power inherent in the earth and moon most intensely. In many indigenous cultures women still spend these days in meditation and sacred rituals.

When human life and social activity coincide with the natural cycles of the earth and moon, ovulation and menstruation occur regularly in conjunction with lunar phases. The former coincide with the full moon, the latter with the new moon. Modern life has not totally destroyed this conjunction. More births occur around the full moon than during any other time of the month, which makes sense considering that the human gestation period lasts the equivalent of nine lunar months.

As one sifts through the scattered bits of information gathered from cultures around the world and dating back thousands of years to pre-recorded history, a pattern begins to emerge. The most intimate female experiences – ovulation, menstruation, gestation, birth, the production of milk – and the clocking of these experiences formed and shaped our ancestors' conceptions of time. And the way a people measure time determines the timing and nature of their important social activities and rituals which become the foundation for civilization. For these reasons, it is suggested by many scholars that women were the real culture bearers and founders of civilization in these prehistoric times.

Witches practise many of the same arts and skills that lie at the base of human culture and were once considered sacred to the Goddess. As we cook, sew, brew potions, prepare herbs, build fires, collect healing stones, set up altars, read the omens in the movements of earth and sky, perform healing rituals for the sick, we recite the prayers and chants that we hope are similar to those chanted by our Neolithic grandmothers. We continue to use the old names for the Goddess. In Crete, the place where Goddess culture flowered for the last time in all its purity, were worshipped the famous Greek Goddesses – all aspects of the one Goddess – whose names touch something deep and sacred in our unconscious, names that we invoke in many of our rituals: Aphrodite, Athene, Demeter, Persephone, Artemis, Hecate. Witches continue to honour the Great Goddess depicted in Cretan art as the Lady of the Beasts, the Lady in tune with the wild things of nature, the Lady who can pick up serpents and channel energy from the sky and the earth, the Lady who knows the secrets of herbs and plants.

The sacred-bull rituals of Crete continue to inspire Witches' understanding of the Horned God. The sacred marriage between the Goddess and her Son, representing the sacredness of life in the eternal union of male and female, finds symbolic representation in our coven circles. Although modern Witches no longer practise sexual rites in mixed covens of men and women, the ancient sexual acts of Goddess worshippers depicted in art and legend continue to provide us with imagery and poetry that call to mind the powerful energies, at once human and divine, that produce new life.

THE CELTS

My own Craft traditions, as well as my family heritage, go back to the Celtic races of north-western Europe, where Goddess spirituality and matrifocal societies survived the longest on the European continent. By the time Celtic societies are recorded in history, hostile patriarchal states had arisen around them, the most powerful being the Roman Empire. Like earlier Goddess peoples, the Celts were pressured into adopting organized warfare, proving the truth of the old adage that if you have to fight a bear, you will grow claws. But many of the matriarchal customs and folkways persisted, especially those related to the rôle and status of women and those influencing spiritual beliefs and practices. Among the Celtic tribes the Old Religion survived, and in its survival and transformation we discover the origins of the European Witchcraft traditions.

The Roman historian Tacitus noted that: 'all the [Celtic] tribes have a common worship of the Mother of the Gods and the belief that she intervenes in human affairs and visits the nations in her care ... It is a season of rejoicing, and festivity reigns wherever she deigns to go. They do not go to battle or wear arms; every weapon is under lock; peace and quiet are known at these times [until the Goddess returns to her sanctuary] which is on an island in the ocean amidst a grove of sacred oaks.' The Druid priests and priestesses of the Celts held the oak tree in special honour because it was sacred to the Goddess Dana. The Celts who settled in Britain were called the Tuatha de Danann, or 'people of the Goddess Dana', a northern European variation of Diana, who was worshipped in groves of sacred oaks.

In Celtic societies hereditary monarchies were matrilineal. Temporary male chieftains were elected. Women served as lawyers, judges, sages, physicians and poets. Boys and girls studied together in the academies; the teachers were usually women. Women held the balance of power in tribal councils and often led armies into battle. In fact the proper training of male warriors included instruction by the famous women warriors of the day whose heroic reputations were won by their valour and bravery in battle. The great Irish hero Cu Chulainn, for example, studied for a year and a day with the warrior–goddess Skatha. Women taught the magical and sacred arts as well as the military. According to some traditions, Merlin learned his skills from the Goddess in the guise of the Lady of the Lake, or Viviane (She Who Lives). As Morgan le Fay, she was turned into an evil sorceress by Christian writers who hoped to discredit the Celtic belief in Merlin.

From Roman observers we derive an interesting picture of the importance women played. The Roman historian Ammianus Marcellinus wrote that: 'a whole troop of foreigners would not be able to withstand a single Gaul [Celt] if he called his wife to his assistance, who is usually very strong, and with blue eyes'. Julius Caesar noted that 'the matrons decide when troops should attack and when withdraw'. Women's dominance in society and military matters allowed Roman generals to use the Celtic male egos as military strategy. According to Tacitus, on one occasion the Romans gave the Celtic armies their choice of submitting to Rome or remaining independent under the rule of Celtic women. 'The lower classes murmured that if [they] must choose between masters, [they would rather choose the Romans] than the women of Gaul.'

Celtic women were not weak or soft. Reports indicate that physically many were about the same height and build as men. The further back we go into the past, the more men and women seem to have been equal in size. The bones of both men and women discovered at various prehistoric sites are about the same in terms of size and weight. Over the centuries, however, men have evolved to be physically larger and stronger than women. Scholars suggest that this was due to a combination of physical activity that required greater muscularity on the part of males and the possibility that women selected the larger males as mates, especially after they became dependent upon husbands for survival, thereby producing larger male offspring.

It is interesting how historians can shape our images of these Celtic women by their choice of words. Boadicea, one of the last women warriors of Britain, who routed Roman armies and captured key British cities, is described in a Latin account by Dio Cassius. As translated by male historian G. R. Dudley, she was 'huge of frame', 'terrifying of aspect', wore a 'tunic of many colours' and a 'great twisted golden necklace'. She 'grasped a long spear' and was regarded by her troops with 'fear'. Agnes Strickland's translation presents a more flattering description. Boadicea was 'tall of person', wore 'a loose gown of changeable colours', and had a 'chain of gold' around her neck. She 'bore a spear' and was 'regarded with reverential silence' by her troops.

The Brehon Laws, passed down in Irish Celtic society from prehistoric times, provide detailed insight into the status of women. Celtic women could inherit estates and the titles that went with them; a woman could make legal contracts independent of her husband; women could appear in court and bring suits against men; a woman could choose her husband (most neighbouring peoples allowed only the male to select a wife); women did not legally become part of the husband's family; husbands and wives enjoyed equal status in marriage; marriages lasted for a year, at which time they could be renewed if mutually agreed upon; divorce required mutual consent; daughters inherited equally with sons. A divorced woman retained her property, plus the dowry, which in the Brehon legal system was required of both the husband and wife (it usually consisted of oxen, horses, shield, lance and swords). The wife could also demand from one-third to one-half of her husband's wealth. Sex was not viewed in rigid moralistic terms: a woman was not 'guilty' of adultery if she had sexual relations outside of marriage; male homosexuality was common and accepted, especially among warriors. The Christian church challenged these laws and many other Celtic customs regarding women, in particular the right to divorce, inherit property, bear arms and be physicians.

The chief priests and priestesses of the Celts were the Druids. The word *druid* is related to the Greek *dryad*, a 'nature spirit' or 'tree nymph'. The term was also applied to priestesses of Artemis, the Moon Goddess, called the Mother of All Creatures. One of her popular manifestations was as the great Bear Mother. (Artemis's Saxon name was Ursel, the Bear, later assimilated into Christian mythology as St Ursula.) The Celtic Druids and the Greek dryads were two phases of a long spiritual tradition among European peoples. Originally the priesthood was all female; later males were admitted. Druidical knowledge was taught orally and consequently there are no written accounts of their exact teachings, but contemporary scholarship suggests that there is a virtually unbroken line of magical practices from the early dryad mysteries of the Greeks down through the later Druids, finally showing up in the incantations and spells of those who would come to be called 'wise women', or 'Witches'.

The ancient nature spirits, called 'dryads' in Greece and 'druids' in Scotland, were shapeshifters who lived in trees and forests. They often took the shape of birds and snakes and could read thoughts and prophesy things to come. In these magical skills we get a glimmer of the Witch's power. She, too, is a shapeshifter: as a bird her consciousness can soar across the skies; as a snake she can slip into the earth to mine its sacred knowledge and wisdom. She, too, can see into the thoughts and feelings of others, as well as peer into the future.

The Druidesses in Britain were divided into three classes. The highest class lived as celibates in convents. These sisterhoods tended the Goddess's sacred fires, and they were assimilated into the Christian era as nuns. The other two classes married and lived either at the temples or with their husbands and families. They were servants and assistants at rites sacred to the Goddess. With the coming of Christianity, they were called 'Witches'.

THE REVOLT OF THE SKY GODS

As we read mythologies and sacred literature written around 2500 to 1500 BC, we notice a shift in sensibilities. The strong Goddesses who dominated thought and feeling for several hundred thousand years are slowly replaced by powerful male Sky Gods. The Son/Hunter/Lover, who as child and consort to the Great Mother always held a subordinate position, now becomes the primary deity. New names appear: Marduk, Indra, Apollo, Zeus, Thor, Jupiter, Jehovah – Sky Gods reigning with the power of the sun, challenging the older Goddesses of earth and moon: Ceres, Cybele, Athene, Diana, Artemis, Tiamat, Anat, Isis, Ishtar, Astarte, Minerva, Dana.

The solar Gods became the heroes and the earth and moon Goddesses became the villains, and many of the old tales were rewritten and revised to reflect this shift in consciousness. In many of them the Goddess – or the feminine power – is identified with a serpent or dragon, both of which represent the primal powers of the earth and the watery regions subject to the pull and tug of the moon. In the new patriarchal religions these serpents and dragons are always presented as evil. Marduk slays Tiamat, Indra kills Danu and her son Vrta, Apollo slays Gaia's Python, Perseus decapitates Medusa with her serpentine hair. These stories persist even into Christian times, where we find St George slaying the dragon in England and St Patrick driving the snakes from Ireland.

Sacred mythology began to reflect a dualism that was probably unknown in Neolithic times or that was certainly relegated to a minor role in the scheme of things. Sun and Sky opposed to Earth and Moon, Light opposed to Dark, Life opposed to Death, Male opposed to Female. Earlier, all things were part of the Great Mother, including the power to destroy, the mystery of death and the darkness of night. Polarities were not viewed in moral terms. It was not a question of good versus evil. Each had positive and negative aspects, all necessary ingredients in the Great Wheel of Created Life. Death, for example, although it always elicits a certain fear of the unknown, was a vital part of creation. It was not 'the wages of sin' or a curse for disobedience. Native Americans retained this healthy notion of death as part of the Great Circle of Life even into our own times, as expressed in the saying that 'Today is a good day to die'. This attitude totally baffled patriarchal missionaries and the United States Cavalry.

Along with the slaying of the animal power sacred to the Goddess, the revisions also claimed that the original creation had been the work of a solitary Father God rather than a divine Mother. Whereas earlier creation stories told of virgin births and births brought about by androgynous or bisexual beings, the new myths spoke primarily of the creation from a masculine source. We even find Goddesses springing from the heads of male Gods!

Among the many revisions was the old Assyrian story of Adam and Eve, rewritten so that Eve is born of Adam's rib rather than the reverse, as it appeared in the older version. In an old Mesopotamian legend Eve creates a male, Adam, and makes him her mate, following the usual Goddess/Son myth. In the Genesis version God makes Adam out of clay with his 'hands', and then Eve from Adam's rib. It seems that the biblical writers wanted to distance God as much as possible from the act of birthing, which makes the point very strongly that creation is not a feminine activity and has nothing to do with wombs, blood and giving birth.

In some of the books of the Judeo-Christian scriptures that were arbitrarily rejected from the official canon, Adam admits that Eve is his superior: 'She taught me the work of knowledge.' In a Gnostic text Eve is the Mother of All the Living and actually creates Jehovah. It reads, 'He was even ignorant of his own Mother . . . It was because he was foolish and ignorant of his Mother that he said, "I am God; there is none beside me." ' In some versions Eve chastises and punishes God for His cruel treatment of human beings. Barbara Walker, author of *The Woman's Encyclopedia of*

POWER OF THE WITCH

Myths and Secrets, says, 'One of Christianity's best-kept secrets was that the Mother of All Living was the Creatress who chastised God.' Witches find it interesting that the name Jehovah is formed by the four Hebrew letters *Yod-He-Vau-He*. The first, *Yod*, means 'I', the next three, *He-Vau-He*, mean both 'life' and 'woman'. The Latin version of these three letters is *E-V-E*. In other words, the name of Jehovah is feminine and it means 'I am woman; I am life.' Today a popular chant among Witches is based on these ancient letters: 'Io! Evohe!'

As mythologies drifted further and further away from the original religious view of the Great Goddess, the dualism that has come to dominate so much of Western thinking grew stronger and stronger. Life was seen primarily as a struggle between the forces of good and the forces of evil, rather than a dynamic dance of all things working together for the good life. Life on earth became less important than the life to come. Everything associated with this life – earth, the body, sex, woman – became suspect if not outright evil. The folk saying that 'cleanliness is next to godliness' sums it up quite well: earthiness is to be rejected as a religious concept; it is dirty and impure. Woman is to be rejected as a spiritual leader who reflects the image of the divine Feminine. She is dirty and impure.

A curious thing happened to the male gods as they consolidated their hold over the human imagination. Although a few retained their shapeshifting power, most gradually lost their animal identities. We find only a few gods retaining the heads of animals and birds, such as Anubis, the jackal-headed God of Egypt, and the eagle-headed genie carved in a ninth-century palace in Mesopotamia. In the Jewish, Christian and Muslim traditions, the male God also lost any hint of androgyny. In time God became completely human and completely male. As we will see in the chapter on Witchcraft as a science, this inability to shapeshift and transform oneself runs contrary to the nature of reality. The ability to transform energy into matter, and vice versa, is the way the universe operates. On the spiritual level it means that a God *as God* can become other beings, even created beings, because God is one with creation. But the new versions of the old myths were intent on separating and distancing the creator from creation. And they succeeded.

The solitary God became standard in Jewish, Christian and Muslim cultures. At one time historians of religion who interpreted the past in the light of their own patriarchal values argued that the evolution from polytheism to monotheism was a mark of advanced civilization. They said it was a sign of human development to stop believing in many gods and goddesses in favour of a single, male god. However, they were wrong on two counts. Firstly, as anthropologist Paul Radin showed early in this century, a belief in many gods does not preclude a belief in a Supreme Being. In fact most cultures that honour more than one god retain a strong and abiding belief in a Great Spirit or All-Father or All-Mother, or some divine power or force that lies behind everything, including the lesser gods. In other words the history of religious thought does not progress from some naïve belief in many gods to a 'better' belief in just one all-powerful, male deity.

Secondly, it is highly questionable that the arrival of monotheistic thinking – in its rigid, inflexible form – was a mark of advancing civilization. With the arrival of Father Gods came the degradation of the earth, woman, the body, sex and most natural tasks in which earlier people found joy and happiness, what has come to be called 'work': collecting and processing food, building shelters, crafting tools and useful objects, etc. Furthermore, cultures that develop around the notion of an authoritarian Father God inevitably oppress those who do not fit the image of the all-powerful, adult, human male: children, women, homosexuals and the nonhuman communities of animal, plant and mineral life with which we live and share our planet. In rigid patriarchal thinking these have no value in themselves except as they serve the male-dominated institutions. They are valuable only as far as they can be exploited for patriarchal purposes.

What were the original patriarchal purposes? In what web of events did patriarchy originate?

Goddess cultures thrived in warm, temperate climates where animal and plant life was abundant. Everyone had relatively equal access to the resources of life, and there was no need to create institutions of power or to submit to them for survival. Early European history recounts that these Goddess cultures were invaded by lighter-skinned, fairer-haired peoples from colder, harsher climates to the north. These Aryan invaders worshipped male Sky Gods or Thunder Gods, who usually resided on mountaintops, aloof from the inhospitable earth, as the invaders perceived it. Historians have described several waves of these Aryan invasions in India, the Middle East, Egypt, Greece and Crete. Most occurred between 2500 and 1500 BC, the same era when the sacred myths were being revised.

Why did they come? In less hospitable climates there was a greater incentive to acquire and stockpile food and resources. Survival depended on it. Groups that lacked the necessities of life raided other more fortunate settlements and took what they needed by force. In time this gave rise to a warrior class, and warfare became an essential institution for survival and growth in a way that it was not in the warmer cultures to the south.

Interestingly, the patriarchal raids from the north coincided with important developments in metallurgy. Although exact dates aren't known, historians surmise that around 2500 BC the patriarchal Hittites developed the technology to smelt iron. From the Stone Age to the Bronze Age, weapons were simple and crude – axes, clubs, slings, projectiles –

personal objects available to everyone. No one had a monopoly on the means of warfare. Matriarchal cultures were relatively peaceful; when violence occurred it consisted of sporadic, personal skirmishes. But with the ability to manufacture stronger, heavier weapons the nature of warfare changed. Training was necessary to learn how to use the newer weapons. Strength and skills – and the time to develop them – became paramount. Raiding parties became all-male clubs since the male, who is free from childbearing and child-rearing, had the time to become the 'professional' warrior and could afford to be away from the camp for long periods of time. Historians surmise that the new developments in metallurgy transformed it into a male industry geared up for war. The earlier tin, gold and silver industries, run primarily by women, had produced jewellery, ornaments and domestic objects.

Patriarchal invasions occurred over many centuries. Not every one was successful, and there were reversals, but in some places the two cultures co-existed rather well and blended their religious beliefs. Matriarchal cultures did not disappear overnight, but slowly they were eroded by the very nature of the new warfare. Organized warfare was for spoils. And among the spoils of war were women and children. Male warriors could rape women, steal children and enslave prisoners. In time the status of women fell to that of children and slaves, and social customs changed to reflect this. Patriarchal families became the norm. A woman became subservient to her husband, who legally owned her, all her property and her children. Men emerged socially, economically and politically dominant, and eventually patriarchal institutions, laws, values and social customs reflected the myth of male superiority.

Patriarchal societies organized around warfare were based on violent, militaristic values, and the all-male, warrior ethic – and way of life – was legitimized by the pronouncements of a single, jealous, warlike Father God. Authoritarianism, discipline, competition, notions of 'might makes right', 'to the victor belong the spoils', and severe punishment for deviant behaviour became mainstays in the male ethos. Since the Bronze Age these values have characterized Western politics, religion, economics, education and family life.

Ironically, since the patriarchal revolution of the Bronze Age coincided with *written* history, it appears that this is the way things have always been. But patriarchy is a rather recent development over the last four thousand years. It is still a new experiment when compared with the hundreds of thousands of years that human beings have lived in matriarchal societies. And a mere drop in the ocean compared to the 3.5 billion years that other forms of life have existed on the planet.

· 3 ·

WHAT THEY SAY ABOUT WITCHES

Sitting next to me on a television chat show was a minister who conjured up my worst fears – that the lies that produced the Burning Times were still alive and well across the nation. In spite of my best efforts to convince him that the Witches' code is 'And it harm none, do what you will', he persisted in making blanket statements about all Witches being evil. I tried to tell him that I have never used the Craft for evil or to harm anyone, but he refused to believe me. To him all Witches were bad. I was a Witch, therefore I was bad.

This minister, a religious zealot who seemed obsessed with the biblical injunction that one 'should not suffer a Witch to live', continued to make false statements about me and Witchcraft in general and to arouse the audience against me. It was hard to take seriously his commitment to his own code of ethics, which commands him not to 'bear false witness against his neighbour'. I was his neighbour on the programme and he was making false statements about me. Finally, in desperation, and to lighten a rather tense exchange with a bit of humour, I turned to him and said, 'You should be glad I'm *not* a bad Witch or you'd be in a lot of trouble right now.' It baffled me how he could continue to antagonize me if he really believed that I had the power and will to inflict harm on him. He replied very glibly, 'My Jesus will protect me.' So that was it, a showdown to see who had more power, 'his Jesus' or me.

What the minister never realized is that because I am a Witch, I can parry attacks without attacking back. I can protect myself and neutralize the harm that he would do without inflicting harm on him. In fact the Witches' law states that if a Witch does harm, it returns to her threefold. I think the difference between the minister and me is that he *would* do me harm given the chance. He was, in fact, inciting the audience to mistrust and fear me.

This closed-mindedness reaches every corner of our society. I do not deny that Witches are human and consequently capable of harm, just as Christians, Muslims and Jews are capable of harm. Anyone's talents or skills can be perverted and used for the wrong purposes, but most Witches do not misuse their powers. Furthermore, Witches have the power to neutralize their enemies in ways that will not do the enemy harm. If the patriarchal religions of Christianity, Islam and Judaism taught their peoples how to counteract evil without doing harm in return, without taking up the sword and brandishing nuclear weapons, for example, there would be a lot less violence and bloodshed in the world today and Western history might not have been the depressing story of war and persecution that it is.

But, unfortunately, the man who attacked me on the show follows a long line of Witch-hunters, inquisitors, judges, torturers and executioners who were responsible for the systematic torture and execution of six to nine million people in Western Europe from the twelfth to the seventeenth centuries. (We will never know, of course, exactly how many people died. Some estimates range as high as thirteen million.) The church's goal was to destroy the beliefs and spiritual practices of many communities of people who still practised the Old Religion. This was certainly not a high-water-mark for religious leaders who supposedly practise the teachings of a man whose message was to live peacefully with others, to turn the other cheek, to put down the sword.

For all the rights and freedoms that American society offers most of its citizens, there is still a long way to go in securing religious liberty for groups that are not part of the mainstream religions. It was only fifteen years ago that President Carter signed the freedom of religion act for Native Americans, and even today they are still struggling to get their religious practices accepted in schools, prisons and hospitals. Witchcraft is even further behind.

Society exploits us at Halloween and ignores us at Yuletide – as if the winter solstice was sacred only for Christians and Jews. A few years ago the Salem Chamber of Commerce decided that the town should celebrate the December festivities under the slogan 'Holiday Happenings', an umbrella term that included both Jewish Chanukah and our Celtic Yuletide. All three groups worked together stringing lights around town, since all three religions were celebrating the ancient earth mystery of the birth of a new sun on the winter solstice, the longest night of the year. Recently, however, the mayor's council went back to promoting the holiday season as Christmas only, thus excluding Jews and Witches from public recognition. Each year I watch with great interest the local squabbles that erupt in different towns around the country over putting up manger scenes in public places. Why can't our nation admit that it is a pluralistic society and provide space and money so that people of all faiths can celebrate their sacred days publicly without fear of reprisal from narrow-minded hate groups?

In many cases people are well-meaning but uneducated – they just don't know the facts. In other cases, however, people are guilty of outright bigotry, which I define as *wilful* ignorance: they choose not to listen to the facts or, listening

POWER OF THE WITCH

to them, they refuse to accept them. They blind themselves; they turn their hearts and minds to stone. They don't want to know the truth because it might upset their prejudices, which bolster their own misguided positions. They appear on nationwide television and radio talk shows to slander us. Our civil rights should safeguard us against such slander.

The truth about European Witchcraft has not been well told until very recent times. With the repeal of the anti-Witchcraft laws in the middle of this century, the resurgence of interest in the Craft, and the personal accounts and studies that have been published by courageous writers in the Craft, the truth is finally getting out. When the first books written by Craft members appeared in the 1950s, some Witches felt that the age-old tradition of secrecy and silence had been violated. It's true that Witches practised in secret and kept their activities and identities hidden. They were, after all, frightened. But I feel that so much has changed in our century, so much is now open and above ground in so many walks of life, that we would be letting a golden opportunity slip by were we not to speak openly and clearly about who we are and what we do. We must inform society about the truth of the Craft; we need to erase the grey area of myth and misconception that allows our detractors to say whatever they please about us. Although vows of secrecy were necessary in the past for individual Witches and covens to survive, they made it worse in the long run. No one spoke for us or about us except those who did not know us and those who hated us. We can't let that happen again. We must speak for and about ourselves. We have nothing to hide.

An argument that I hear even from Craft members is that we should not identify ourselves or reveal our so-called secrets because the Burning Times could happen again. My answer to that is: yes, I suppose anything could happen again, but I think it is much less likely to happen if the truth about us is known so that people will be less inclined to believe the lies upon which the Burning Times were built. Lies can be used to justify killing us only if real people are made to believe those lies and act upon them. My hope is that when real people hear the truth, they will recognize the lies for what they are. And the Burning Times will never happen again.

THE BURNING TIMES

How did the lies start? Where did the negative image of the Witch begin? And how did it become so ingrained in our culture that it's almost impossible for some people to hear the word *Witch* without thinking of evil?

The answers to these questions have roots that lie deep in the past, growing out of the patriarchal revolution that we looked at in the previous chapter. Patriarchy culminated in Europe in the fourth century when the church and the Roman Empire joined forces. Under Constantine, Christianity became the official religion of the empire. Bishops followed Roman armies into the territories and, under their protection, preached what they call the 'good news'. But as it fell on the ears of those who worshipped in the Old Ways of their ancestors, it was hardly good news.

The history of Christianity is the history of persecution. Christian forces have consistently harassed, persecuted, tortured and put to death people whose spirituality differed from their own – Pagans, Jews, Muslims. Even groups within the Christian community itself, such as the Waldensians and Albigensians, suffered under the strong arm of the church. Any group or individual whom the ecclesiastical authorities branded a heretic could be tried and executed.

As Christianity spread around the globe indigenous peoples who stood in its way or disagreed with its teachings were accused of devil worship. We find this argument justifying the persecution of native peoples in Europe as well as in the Americas, Africa, Polynesia, the Orient and within the Arctic Circle. Christian armies and clergy, blinded by a patriarchal and monotheistic worldview, have seldom understood the value of spiritual paths different from their own. They have repeatedly failed to see the sacred wisdom in other cultural traditions based on different perceptions of the divine power. In many instances they have not even bothered to look for it. They have shown no compassion, understanding or tolerance for native pantheons.

When Constantine made Christianity the official religion of the Roman Empire, the war against native religions commenced in earnest. Sacred shrines were sacked and looted, springs and wells polluted, priests and priestesses discredited or executed. The first Christian emperor himself embodied the fierce violence that in time would be directed against Witches. He boiled his wife alive, murdered both his son and his brother-in-law and whipped a nephew to death. During his rule the seeds were sown for the political-military-ecclesiastical establishment that would dominate medieval society. He gave bishops the authority to set aside judgements of the civil courts, and he instructed the courts to enforce all episcopal decrees.

Over the next thousand years patriarchal prejudices against women became institutionalized in the church-state structures of medieval Europe. In the century after Constantine, for example, St Augustine argued that women did not have souls. This abominable theory was eventually debated at the Council at Mâcon in the sixth century, and Celtic bishops from Britain argued successfully against it. Thus it did not become official church doctrine. Nevertheless, the idea continued to find supporters among individual churchmen for centuries to come.

Later, St Thomas Aquinas constructed a rationale for treating women like slaves. He wrote, 'Woman is in subjection because of the laws of nature, but a slave only by the laws of circumstance . . . Woman is subject to man because of the weakness of her mind as well as of her body.' This infamous argument was carried further by Gratian, a canon lawyer of the twelfth century: 'Man, but not woman, is made in the image of God. It is plain from this that women should be subject to their husbands, and should be as slaves.' So by the teachings of the church fathers, women fell from being a natural reflection of the Great Goddess and Mother of All Living Things to the lowly position of a slave, not made in the image of God, and possibly not having a soul.

The respected historians Will and Mary Durant have written that 'medieval Christendom was a moral setback' for Western civilization. Many non-Catholic historians have agreed with them. Otto Rank has pointed out perhaps the reason for this moral setback. The history of civilization, he says, was 'the gradual masculinization of human civilization'. Certainly, in its extreme and paranoid style, the male ethos, blinded by its own patriarchal values, has run rampant in its subjection of half the human race and in its desecration of the earth and its resources.

Christendom did not become the dominant faith overnight, and for centuries the Old Religion and Christianity co-existed. In AD 500 the Franks' Salic law made it legal to practise magic. A law promulgated in 643 made it illegal to burn a person for practising magic, and in 785 the church Synod of Paderborn set the penalty of death for burning a Witch. For a while it appears that not only did the church not fear Witchcraft, it didn't even take it seriously. The Canon Episcopi declared that Witchcraft was a delusion and it was a heresy to believe in it. But by the time of the Reformation attitudes had changed. Both John Calvin and John Knox claimed that to deny Witchcraft was to deny the authority of the Bible, and two centuries later John Wesley stated, 'The giving up of Witchcraft is in effect the giving up of the Bible.' Clearly, Witchcraft was here to stay – Christendom needed it to preserve the integrity of the Bible.

For a long time the Christians, too, practised magic. St Jerome, for example, preached that a sapphire amulet 'procures favour with princes, pacifies enemies and obtains freedom from captivity'. And he didn't mean that it could be used as money to buy these favours! Pope Urban V promoted a cake of wax called the Agnus Dei, or Lamb of God, which protected against harm from lightning, fire and water. (I'm not sure how it was used.) The church routinely sold charms to prevent disease and enhance sexual potency. From the seventh to the fifteenth centuries church literature discussed the widespread belief that a priest could cause death by saying the Mass for the Dead against a living person. Presumably, some priests performed this black magic. Until a late date both civil and church authorities used Witches to raise thunderstorms during battle if a good, rousing tempest would help their cause. The church fathers explained this by saying that God *allowed* the Witches' power to work. Even today remnants of Christian magic can be found around the world in the form of medals, holy water, relics, statues for automobile dashboards and any blessed object that is used for protection or special favours.

So for a number of years magic seems to have been favourably regarded, even by some people within the church. Witches continued to hold respected positions as healers, nurses, midwives, seers and wise ones versed in the folk customs and beliefs of the people. Throughout Europe there were strong pockets of Old Believers.

But gradually the Christians began to distinguish between sorcery and magic. In 1310, for example, the Council of Treves made conjuring, divination and love potions illegal. These were considered magic. And yet books on sorcery were published under the auspices of the church even with ecclesiastical approval. Von Nettesheim, one author of approved books on sorcery, actually learned his magic from Abbot John Trithemius. What was the difference? The difference was the sex of the practitioner. Men performed sorcery. Women did magic. Sorcery was acceptable, magic was not. In reality, of course, magic is magic. What the church was aiming for was not the elimination of magic or sorcery but the elimination of women practitioners.

Another development in church politics set the stage for the persecution of Witches. It is clear from written correspondence by priests who served in the Inquisition that when the Albigensian and Waldensian heresies had been stamped out in the thirteenth century, church inquisitors worried about their careers. In 1375 a French inquisitor complained that all the rich heretics had been put to death. 'It is a pity,' he wrote, 'that so salutary an institution as ours should be so uncertain of its future.' Witch-hunting was big business. Nobles, kings, judges, bishops, local priests, courts, townships, magistrates and bureaucratic clerks at all levels, not to mention the actual Witch-hunters, inquisitors, torturers and executioners, profited by the industry. Everyone received a share of the property and riches of the condemned heretics. Should such a 'salutary' institution go out of business? Pope John XXII thought not. He mandated that the Inquisition could prosecute anyone who performed magic. Soon inquisitors were finding magic-workers everywhere. The entire population of Navarre in France was suspected of being Witches!

The word *Witch* has meant different things to different people in different periods of history. One of its acquired meanings in the late Middle Ages was 'woman', especially any woman who criticized the patriarchal policies of the Christian church. In the fourteenth century, for example, women who belonged to the Reforming Franciscans were burned at the stake for Witchcraft and heresy. Church literature grew increasingly strident in its teaching that

57

women were a threat to the community because they knew magic. Over the years the campaign worked: in the popular mind women who knew the ways of the Craft were considered evil.

The single most influential piece of propaganda in this campaign was commissioned by Pope Innocent VIII in 1484 after he declared Witchcraft to be a heresy. He instructed the Dominican monks Heinrich Kraemer and Jacob Sprenger to publish a manual for Witch-hunters. Two years later the work appeared with the title *Malleus malificarum*, or 'The Witches' Hammer'. The manual was used for the next two hundred and fifty years in the church's attempt to destroy the Old Religion of Western Europe, demean women healers and spiritual leaders and create divisiveness in local communities in order to strengthen the political and economic factions that the church supported (and that in turn supported the church).

Demeaning Witches demeaned all women, for Kraemer and Sprenger's arguments against Witches grew out of their patriarchal fears about women in general. According to the *Malleus malificarum*, no woman has a right to her own thoughts: 'When a woman thinks alone, she thinks evil.' (This, incidentally, was an argument that was used at the turn of the present century to deny women the vote – they might think and vote independently of their husbands!) The two monks rehashed Aquinas's argument about women being physically and intellectually inferior to men. 'They are feebler both in mind and body ... Women are intellectually like children ... [They] have weaker memories, and it is a natural vice in them not to be disciplined but to follow their own impulses without a sense of what is due.' In short, Kraemer and Sprenger's propaganda about woman is summed up in their words that 'she is a liar by nature ... Woman is a wheedling and secret enemy.'

The Christian clergy were not alone in their condemnation

of women. The writers of the Talmud wrote, 'Women are naturally inclined to witchcraft' and 'The more women there are, the more witchcraft there will be.'

Could it be that these male writers intuited woman's innate power and correctly saw its relationship to divine power? Woman's power is of the Goddess. Whereas some people have found that notion comforting, patriarchal church leaders found it threatening. In their attempts to monopolize all visionary experience, all the healing arts and all magical practices that enhance human life, they turned the source of life, woman, into an enemy. And they waged war against that 'enemy' so effectively that some European towns were left with only one woman.

In Kraemer and Sprenger's manual Witches were depicted with all the same characteristics that the church had used to describe Jews in the centuries before: they were said to worship the devil; to steal the Eucharist and crucifixes from Catholic churches; to blaspheme and pervert Christian practices; to ride on goats. Kraemer and Sprenger even used the same descriptions for Witches that had been used for Jews: horns, tails, and claws – i.e. the stylized images that artists had devised to depict the Christian devil.

The motives that orchestrated and precipitated participation in the Witch-hunts were a tangled web of fears, suspicions and sadistic fantasies. It's not always easy to discern logic or reason. But we can start with one of the major problems that church leaders faced regarding their conquest of European communities: it was never complete.

Throughout Europe there were people who continued to worship the old Gods in the old ways. The church's frustration over this led it to destroy sacred trees and groves, pollute healing wells and springs and build their own churches and cathedrals on ancient power spots where people had communed with spirits and deities since Neolithic times. Even today many churches and Christian sites, such as

Lourdes, Fatima and Chartres, are built on sites that were sacred to the Goddess and the old Gods throughout history. They will probably continue to be places of power and inspiration long after the Christian churches disappear. In many churches and cathedrals in Europe I was happy to find images of imps and dwarfs, the little people of Celtic lore, that the pagan artisans chiselled into the stonework to honour our ancestors. The little people are still there. Their power is still present. I have felt it.

Where people continued to worship and live in the old ways sacred to the Goddess, church leaders whipped up fears and fantasies about their arch nemesis, Satan. They did this by twisting and distorting the time-honoured archetypal images of divinity, namely that of the Great Cosmic Mother and her other Self and consort, the Horned God.

As Christianity and the old nature religions clashed in Europe, missionaries used the image of the Divine Son, the Horned God, as a representation of the Christian Satan. In time any horned figure called up images of Satanic mischief. Ironically, wearing horns as a symbol of honour and respect was a widespread custom, originating, as we saw in the previous chapter, in Neolithic hunting cultures. The horned head-dress eventually became stylized as the royal crown. This was a logical development since a repeatedly successful hunter assumed an increasingly prominent and respected role in the tribe, which evolved into that of chieftain or king. William G. Gray, a scholar of Western spiritual traditions, has pointed out that the Stone Age tradition of the hunter who laid down his life for the tribe was extended to that of the king who laid down his life for the people. 'The hunter-son must die' became 'the king must die'.

But wearing horns was a widespread custom not confined to Neolithic hunting societies. The ancient Greek Gods Pan and Dionysus were depicted wearing horns, as was Diana, the huntress, and the Egyptian Isis. Alexander the Great and

Moses, neither actually Gods, were honoured among their followers with horns as a sign of their prowess and the divine favour that seemed to bless their exploits. Horns were a physical representation of the light of wisdom and divine knowledge that radiates from them (much like halos). Deuteronomy tells us that Moses' 'glory is like the firstling of his bullock, and his horns like the horns of unicorns'. Horns were also used on Greek, Roman and Italian war helmets up to the fourteenth century as a symbol of strength and valour. And as William G. Gray and Dr Leo Martello have each pointed out, Jesus, with his crown of thorns, has become another image of the great Western archetype of the king who laid down his life for his people.

Many customs and terms continue to reflect the importance that horns once held in local folklore. The word *scorn* comes from the Italian word that means 'without horns', for to be without horns was a sign of disgrace, shame or contempt. Holding up the index and little fingers in the form of horns was a gesture to ward off the evil eye. Today it means 'bull'. The lucky horseshoe is shaped like curved horns. And since it was the male animal that had horns, the horn easily became a phallic symbol. Leo Martello has called our attention to the fact that the contemporary adjective 'horny', which up until recently applied only to men, is also derived from these concepts.

Among the old European nature religions the male deities (the goat-footed, Greek nature God Pan, the Roman Faunus, the Celtic Cernunnos) represented the Son of the Great Cosmic Mother. Together Mother and Son embodied the powerful, lusty, life forces of the earth. The priestesses of the Old Religion honoured the Goddess and her Horned Consort by adorning their priests with horns and wearing the crescent, horn-shaped moon on their own foreheads. Against these old religious practices the church waged a bitter campaign. Among their weapons were the teachings that woman was

61

evil, Witchcraft was the work of the devil and the horned representations of the God and Goddess were images of Satan. Underlying these attacks were the fears of women, sex, nature and the human body. Official church doctrine, worked out over the centuries by an all-male, celibate clergy, preached that woman was the source of all evil (since Eve trafficked with the serpent), that the earth was cursed by God (as a punishment for that sin), and that sex and the body were dirty and vile. 'The world, the flesh, and the devil' is the way it was – and is still – summed up.

The church never accepted the ancient belief that the earth was sacred, alive with Gods and divine spirits. It could not understand or tolerate a spirituality that celebrated the human body, or the bodies of animals for that matter. As Christians beat their breasts, accused themselves of sins of the flesh and moaned about the drudgery of living in 'a valley of tears', Goddess worshippers sang, danced, feasted and discovered, as the Charge of the Goddess puts it, that 'all acts of love and pleasure are my rituals'. Protestants deplored the joyous activities of earthy rituals, like singing, dancing, chanting and merrymaking, even more than Catholics. Protestant theology attributed many of these directly to the devil. In the Old Religion, however, these were sacraments.

During the Burning Times a Christian conspiracy, consisting of both ecclesiastical and civil authorities, sought systematically to eliminate the old festivals. Church directives instructed local clergy to substitute Christian holy days for the pagan festivals. Christmas was established to conflict with the winter solstice, Easter with the spring equinox, the feast of St John the Baptist with the summer solstice, All Saints' Day with the Celtic New Year, Samhain. And so it went throughout the year whenever there was a local pagan festival.

The authorities also preached against the merrymaking

that took place on these holy days, especially rituals that involved sexual rites. In many pre-Christian cultures making love was a sacramental re-enactment of the creation. A church that mistrusted sex and women found it difficult to accept the idea that women's sexuality could be sacred. A spirituality that celebrated 'acts of pleasure' because they were sacred to the Goddess was a considerable threat to celibate priests and friars who found it difficult to tolerate lusty thoughts even in themselves.

Dominican scholar Matthew Fox has noted that the 'fall from paradise' myth created a theology 'that cannot deal with the holiness of sexuality'. As he writes in *Original Blessing*, his plea for a more mystical, earthy, feminist Christianity: 'It is no secret that the models of sanctity that the patriarchal period of Christianity has held up to us have rarely been laypersons.' The ideal in the Catholic Church has always been celibacy, and an active sexual life outside of marriage has always been discouraged. A woman was allowed to express her sexuality only as a sex partner for a husband. In other words, a woman's sexuality must be limited to a patriarchal marriage, where it can be controlled by a man. Even within marriage, sex was suspect. It was still 'the flesh', which traditional Christian theology tells us is weak. A celibate clergy and virginal nuns convey a pretty clear message (as does the message recently reaffirmed by the Vatican that women cannot be priests because they do not have male bodies!).

Some Christian thinkers have long suspected that sex was the original sin and that eating the fruit of the tree of knowledge was a metaphor, which mercifully avoided the need to actually say 'it' in a sacred book! It has been taught that Eve the temptress was a seductress, and that every woman is Eve. This argument was used during the Burning Times and up into our own era to create suspicion about women's motives.

Clearly, the church could not tolerate the old earth religions of pre-Christian cultures. But the interesting question is: why, after hundreds of years of 'co-existence' between Christian communities and pockets of Old Believers, did such a venomous and bloodthirsty attack upon Witches begin in the late fifteenth century and continue for over two hundred years? The lack of action by the early medieval church has been attributed to its lacking the political machinery to carry out any widespread campaign against Witches. In the early Middle Ages the church had not yet cemented its position in European societies. Its influence was thinly scattered. Toleration was thus a necessity. But by the late Middle Ages the picture had changed. The church had become a major political and economic force in Europe. The Inquisition was powerful. The Crusades had created military and economic arrangements between local bishops and wealthy nobles (some bishops *were* wealthy nobles). The machinery was in place for a widespread persecution of dissenters.

Whose interests did the Witch-hunts serve? asks Starhawk in her perceptive book on Witchcraft, *Dreaming the Dark*. Stated that way, our attention is drawn to other factions, apart from the Christian churches, that also had vested interests in eliminating Witches and anyone they chose to label a Witch. Who were these other interests that supported and engaged in the persecution?

For one, the growing commercial elements in late medieval societies were beginning to consider land as a commodity that could be bought, owned and sold. The traditional outlook, so sacred to the earth-centred cultures of our ancestors, had been that no one owned the land – not even the lords owned it in the sense that they could sell their land if they wanted. Land belonged to the community; even peasants had rights, such as collecting firewood in the forests and grazing their animals on the commons, and the right to *live* on the land. The lords of the realm were honour-bound to respect these rights. As a market economy developed, however, the so-called landowners began expropriating the land for themselves and driving out peasants who stood in the way. The capitalist notion of private property began to edge out the old communal attitudes that land was sacred and belonged to the people as a whole. Capitalist pioneers in America found the same communal attitudes among native peoples and had to wage war – physical and ideological – to eliminate indigenous societies here whose concepts of land and spirit stood in the way of what was called 'progress'.

The enclosure movement, which began in the high Middle Ages and continued down into the nineteenth century, severely disrupted peasant life. By 'enclosing' common lands to be run under their own jurisdiction, landowners deprived peasants of their age-old rights. The feudal concept of land as an organism shared by all elements of society was gradually eroded by a market economy. In the process entire villages were depopulated. Thousands of peasant families were driven further into the unsettled areas or lured into the towns and growing cities to work as wage earners for the new industries. Village pagan life was disrupted, neighbours began to fear neighbours, and, as often happens, scapegoats were needed to explain the unsettled times. How easy it was for the church and wealthy interests to exploit this situation by launching Witch-hunts in local areas against individuals who believed in the old ways and fought for a way of life based on the oneness of the land and the sacredness of the earth.

In addition to wealthy commercial interests and landowners eager to exploit the land, the medical profession also took an interest in the persecution of Witches and those healers who offered an alternative to the medical practices taught in the universities of the day. The effort to establish a professional medical community involved restricting medical knowledge to those who took formal courses of study. They, of course, could then set their own fees and exclude anyone they did not deem fit to practise. It is not surprising that they deemed women unfit to be healers. As the *Malleus malificarum* stated, 'If a woman dare to cure without having studied, she is a Witch and must die.' It was as simple as that.

Witches had, of course, studied, but not in the universities. They studied in nature, learned from older women in the community, experimented on their own, asked advice from the plants and herbs themselves. What really galled the medical profession and the church was that Witches were *good* at healing. In 1322 a woman was arrested for practising medicine and tried by the medical faculty at the University of Paris. Although the verdict stated that she was 'wiser in the art of surgery and medicine than the greatest master or doctor in Paris', it did little to win the male medical profession's respect for women healers.

Many Witch remedies were painless and more effective than the bleeding, leeching and purging that were standard medical practices until the twentieth century. And for many people a Witch's charms and spells were the only available medicine. Witches were also scapegoats for ignorant physicians. When a doctor couldn't cure someone he could always blame it on a Witch. Ironically, miraculous cures, when performed by a doctor, were attributed to God or the intervention of saints. Witches' miraculous cures were the work of the devil!

A Witch's healing skills were also subversive of religious orthodoxy. Eliminating pain was un-Christian. Because of Adam and Eve's fall, people were supposed to suffer, especially in childbirth, for the God of the Old Testament had cursed woman and told her that she would have to bear children in pain and in sorrow. Kraemer and Sprenger claimed that 'no one does more harm to the Catholic faith than midwives'. What they had in mind was both the painless

66

births that defied the patriarchal God's curse on woman and the fact that Witches did not baptize the newborn. Witches had painkillers, anti-inflammatory treatments, digestive aids, contraceptive drugs and many other herbal and natural treatments that today are the bases of many pharmaceutical products. Their knowledge of how to ease childbirth and hasten recovery made them the best midwives. No wonder the medical profession launched a campaign to eliminate midwifery as a legitimate calling!

It was a long campaign. It took until the twentieth century in America (and considerable money and propaganda from the American Medical Association) to eliminate midwifery from the available options for childbirth. Fortunately, in the last couple of decades, women are once again asking for midwives and natural forms of childbirth. Many doctors are still against midwives, but I have yet to hear any of them employ the old sixteenth-century argument that if a midwife can provide a comfortable, safe and easy birth, she must be in league with the devil.

Women were denied professional status as healers by an all-male, medical-religious establishment eager to discredit natural healing techniques as being superstitious, ineffective and even dangerous. We now know from anthropological studies of peoples in Africa, Polynesia and North and South America that one of the most effective ways to destroy a culture is to destroy confidence in its healers and spiritual leaders. When these two roles are undermined, people become demoralized, their way of life collapses and they are more easily assimilated into the value system of the invading forces, be they political or ecclesiastical. The rising professions, in league with church authorities, did precisely that all across Europe. They created the image of the Witch as a meddlesome, superstitious huckster of ineffectual and dangerous cures and remedies. And they said her Horned God was the Christian Satan.

To justify the millions of executions, the church created a systematic demonology around pre-Christian folk beliefs, practices and holidays. To these were added the fantasies about pacts with the devil, bizarre and sadistic sexual rites and obscene travesties of Catholic ceremonies. The worst Christian fears about salvation and eternal punishment were projected on to innocent people who were accused of being in league with the devil. The sexual nature of the hysteria over Witches seems a logical result of the sexual repression based on religious doctrine. In a sense the Witch-hunts were more about sex than about devil worship. Of course, when the 'accused' women were asked if they dreamed of the devil, many said they did. The devil was a major theme in medieval and Renaissance culture. The devil was talked about, feared, depicted and blamed for all that went wrong. It is normal for people to dream about the cultural images that make up so much of their lives. I am sure Witch-hunters also dreamed about the devil, and they probably also dreamed about Witches dreaming about the devil!

Armed with the *Malleus malificarum*, Witch-hunters entered villages and hamlets and began their search. The official guidebook suggested that children made the best informers because they were easily intimidated. A routine custom was to give teenage girls two hundred lashes on their bare backs to encourage them to accuse their mothers or grandmothers of Witchcraft. So-called evidence of Witchcraft was varied, illogical and unevenly applied. For example, if on being accused, a woman muttered, looked down to the ground or did not shed tears, she was a Witch. If she remained silent, she was a Witch. Dissimilar eyes and pale blue eyes were thought to indicate a Witch, as did the 'devil's mark' (often a smaller, third nipple, which about one out of three women has). A wart, mole or birthmark also qualified as a mark of the devil, as could freckles.

If the 'devil's mark' could not be found, an inquisitor

intent on establishing a given woman as a Witch could assume that the mark was cleverly concealed so that it would go undetected. A formal search of the woman's entire body was then conducted, usually in public before curious on-lookers who were often more interested in seeing the woman nude than in finding the mark of the devil. Searching a woman's body for signs of the devil led to such widespread cases of rape that bishops eventually wrote directives to discourage the 'zeal' with which inquisitors pursued their quarry.

The search might be conducted with a 'Witch pricker', an instrument resembling an ice pick. Professional Witch-hunters (who were paid only when they could convince the local authorities that they had captured a Witch) often used two prickers, a normal one and another with a retractable point that slid up into the handle. After drawing blood on various parts of the body with a regular pricker to establish its sharpness, the Witch-hunter could then secretly switch prick-ers and 'plunge' the blade of the retractable pricker up to the hilt into the body of the accused woman. Feeling no pain was evidence of a Witch.

The principle of 'corpus delecti' was not necessary to establish the 'crime' of Witchcraft. One did not need an actual victim or evidence of a bona fide crime. Hearsay, accusations and bogus testimony of others in the community was sufficient. In Salem Village a common sign of Witchcraft was 'mischief after anger'. In other words, if two women quarrelled and the children of one of them became sick or her cow died, she could assume that this 'mischief' was the work of the woman with whom she had quarrelled. The mischief was 'magic'; the woman was a 'Witch'. Inability to recite the Lord's Prayer in public before an investigating committee without stumbling over the words was also con-sidered a sign of Witchcraft.

According to Barbara Walker's *Woman's Encyclopedia of*

Myths and Secrets, a woman who lived alone was considered a Witch, especially if she resisted courtship. In England a woman was murdered by a group of soldiers who saw her surfing on a river. '. . . She fleeted on the board standing firm bolt upright,' they reported, and so they assumed she was practising magic. When she came onshore they shaved her head, beat her and shot her to death. One woman playfully ran down a hill in front of her empty bucket, calling it to follow her. Those who saw her little game thought it was sorcery. She was brought before the authorities for Witchcraft. A Scottish Witch was arrested for bathing neighbourhood children, a practice in hygiene that was frowned upon in that day.

There were rules about torture, as if that somehow made it more humane. For example, torture was never to last more than one hour. But inquisitors could stop a session just short of an hour and so begin again. There were three approved bouts: one to elicit a confession, a second to determine the motive and a third to incriminate accomplices and sympathizers. Sometimes torture went around the clock. Ankles were broken, breasts cut off, eyes gouged out, sulphur poured into hair on the head and other parts of the body and set on fire, limbs pulled out of sockets, sinews twisted from joints, shoulder blades dislocated, red-hot needles thrust beneath fingernails and toenails and thumbs crushed in thumbscrews. Victims were given scalding baths in water mixed with lime, hoisted on ropes and then dropped, suspended by their thumbs with weights attached to their ankles, hung head-down and revolved, singed with torches, raped with sharp instruments, pressed beneath heavy stones. Sometimes family members were forced to watch another tortured before their own ordeal. On the way to the stake victims might have their tongues cut out and their mouths scoured with a red-hot poker to prevent them from blaspheming or shouting obscenities during the execution. The inquisitor Nicholas Remy was astonished that, as he noted, so many Witches had 'a positive desire for death'. It is hard to believe that he could not understand why.

It takes about half an hour to die from smoke and blisters. Slow-burning charcoal can prolong the agony for an entire day.

When the execution was over a public dinner was usually held to celebrate 'an act pleasing to God'.

THE SALEM TRIALS

In my town no one was burned at the stake. Witches were hanged or crushed beneath heavy stones. The twenty people executed in Salem have always seemed a small number when compared with the millions who suffered in Europe, but proportionally those killed, those imprisoned, and those accused but not yet arrested were a sizeable percentage of the population for a sparsely populated area. It was a true hysteria. People from all walks of life had been accused: a minister who had graduated from Harvard and owned a large estate in England; the wealthiest shipowner in Salem; Captain John Alden, the son of John and Priscilla, the legendary lovers of Plymouth Colony; even the wife of the governor of the Bay Colony. No one was safe.

It all started in the Reverend Paris's kitchen, where Tituba, a slave woman from Barbados, entertained the Reverend's daughter and her girlfriends during the cold winter months of 1691. The girls asked Tituba, who knew methods of divination, about their future husbands, a normal concern of most young girls around puberty. In time the girls began to have fits, showed extreme moodiness, adopted odd postures and gestures and had visions. (A generation later in North-ampton, Massachusetts, the same type of behaviour among young people would lead the Reverend Jonathan Edwards to declare that a spiritual 'quickening' was occurring and thus would begin the first 'Great Awakening' in the history of American religious revivals. In Salem Village this same behaviour was interpreted by church leaders as the work of the devil.)

Hearings were held over the next few months at which the girls and others who became afflicted with the same behaviour (it had become a kind of teenage fad) accused adult members in the community of tormenting them. They had bizarre fantasies of otherwise respectable people engaged in lurid activities with the devil. As the winter turned into spring, natural misfortunes were blamed on the devil working through certain members of the village. According to the theories of the day, the devil could work only through someone with that person's cooperation. Someone who had made a pact with the devil. Someone who was a 'Witch'.

Accusations were made, people arrested, hearings were held, and by spring the jails were overflowing. Then it spread. 'Witches' were discovered in Beverly, Topsfield, Andover, Ipswich, Lynn and virtually every town in Essex County. In Andover there were actually more arrests than in Salem Village. Authorities in Boston sent representatives to conduct trials.

In June the first trials began, and Bridget Bishop was hanged after having been in jail since April. Events moved quickly. In July, Rebecca Nurse, Sarah Good, Elizabeth How, Sarah Wild and Susanna Martin were hanged. The August trials found John Willard, John and Elizabeth Proctor, George Jacobs, Martha Carrier and the Reverend George Burroughs guilty. All were executed, except Elizabeth Proctor, who was pregnant and given a stay of execution until her baby was born. The September trials sent Martha Cory, Alice Parker, Ann Pudeator, Mary Esty, Margaret Scott, Mary Parker, Wilmot Reed and Samual Wardwell to the gallows. Martha Cory's husband, Giles, was pressed to death beneath the weight of stones. And as the gruesome summer ended over a hundred people were still awaiting trial, and several hundred others had been accused.

Finally, cooler heads began to prevail. Increase Mather preached in Cambridge that the issue of acceptable evidence for 'Witchcraft' rested on very shaky ground, especially the notion of spectral evidence, or the devil's ability to take the shape of someone in the community. While not denying that the devil could assume the shape of a man or woman, 'proving' that he or she had made an initial pact with the devil was rather difficult. Could the devil not assume the shape of an innocent person as well? Some people were beginning to think so. In the end, Increase Mather argued that it would be better for one 'Witch' to escape execution than to put ten 'innocent' people to death. His arguments carried the day, and the Witch-hunt soon ended.

A question that often arises about the twenty people executed and the hundreds accused is: were they really Witches? Historical evidence is sketchy. I am sure that some or many of them, like their counterparts in Europe, still retained many of the Old Religion's practices – herbalism, special potions, divination, natural healing techniques. Some may have even celebrated the old nature holidays. We know that Massachusetts settlers at Merrymount erected a Maypole earlier in the century. But the question of whether or not they were Goddess worshippers has never been proven. Surely there were Witches among their ancestors, but they themselves may not have been Witches in the sense that they were our co-religionists. Most were probably devout Christians. Nevertheless, I think we must claim them as Witches. Certainly they died for our freedom. They refused to admit that they had committed any crime. (Interestingly, not one of those who confessed to Witchcraft was hanged. They repented and were admitted back into the community. We

73

could also ask whether those who confessed were Witches or did they confess to save their own lives? Much is lost in the pages of history.)

If the victims of the Witch-hunt in Salem and nearby towns were not Witches, then the Witch Museum not far from my house is not really about Witchcraft and visitors who tour it by the thousands each year are not really learning the truth about who we are or what we practise. Over the years Salem Witches have protested this to the board of the Museum and we finally arranged for them to alert tourists to this fact. What visitors learn about on their tours of the Museum is not the religion of the Goddess, but about what can happen to a Christian community that succumbs to an irrational fear of the devil and projects this evil image on to members of the community.

As the eighteenth century progressed people grew more sceptical about Witchcraft. The spirit of the times – the rationality of the Enlightenment – convinced people that magic was hocus-pocus and people who practised it were practising self-delusion. The new era was also more sceptical about religion in general and less zealous in persecuting unbelievers. The wrath that had fuelled the Witch-hunts subsided. In 1712 the last person was executed for Witchcraft in England, although the anti-Witchcraft laws stayed on the statute books until the twentieth century. In Scotland the last execution took place in 1727 and the laws were repealed in 1736. Of course, all over Europe and in America there were sporadic trials and executions from time to time. In Hungary in 1928, for example, the courts acquitted a family who had beaten an old woman to death on the suspicion that she was a Witch. With or without the laws and the civil or church authorities to back them up, people continue to harass Witches and often do them serious physical harm.

A photographer once asked me if I would pose for a picture beside the tombstone of Judge Hathorne, one of the magistrates who persecuted Witches in Salem and nearby towns in the seventeenth century. I agreed, and now whenever I look at that photo I say to Judge Hathorne and his cohorts, 'We survived. We're still here.'

WITCHES TODAY

Around the turn of our present century, renewed public interest in spiritualism and metaphysics, encouraged in part by the new fields of psychology and anthropology, stirred up interest in the Craft once again, but this time among more sympathetic people. The occult (broadly defined to include metaphysical issues) was quite respectable among major writers and artists such as W. B. Yeats, James Joyce, William James and Bernard Shaw. The works of Sigmund Freud and Carl Jung discussed the powers of the unconscious, and Jung's works argued a strong case that the collective themes, symbols and images that have been part of the human mind since the beginning of time continue to survive in modern consciousness. Field studies in anthropology discovered the counterparts to European Witches among shamans, medicine people, visionaries and native healers around the world, and Westerners learned that these people are not threats to a community but actually its lifeblood. Without them the indigenous cultures could not exist.

In 1921, Margaret Murray, a folklorist and anthropologist, published *The Witch Cult in Western Europe*, followed by *The God of the Witches* in 1933. In these two books she argued that Witchcraft was the ancient religion of Western Europe, a pre-Christian religion that honoured fertility deities, particularly a double-faced Horned God, called Janus or Dianus in Latin. She believed that the Craft was an organized religion, celebrating the two main feasts of 1 May and 31 October, and eight 'sabbats', or holidays, throughout the year. She described visionary, shamanic practices centring on covens of thirteen people. In general, the 'Witch cult', as she called it, was a joyous religion, celebrating the fertility cycles of the year with feasting, dancing and singing. It had nothing to do with devil worship.

Other scholars found errors in Murray's work, such as the fact that she failed to prove that the Craft was formally organized and that this organization extended across Europe. She also failed to establish that the coven of thirteen people and the traditional sabbats as we know them existed before the time of the Inquisition. But her work, as well as the criticism against it, raised important issues about who we are and uncovered exciting new ways to look at our history. Perhaps her greatest contribution to the 'new image' of the Witch in the twentieth century was to prove that pre-Christian practices did not die out with the so-called conversion of pagan peoples to the church and to show convincingly that the Horned God of our ancestors was not the Christian Satan.

In the middle of the century Gerald B. Gardner, an amateur anthropologist and folklorist, wrote and published the first books on the Craft by a practising Witch. In the 1930s he claimed to have discovered a coven in England that had followed the Old Ways rather continuously since very early times. He was initiated into the Craft by that group of Witches and founded his own coven on the Isle of Man. In 1949 he published (under a pen name) *High Magic's Aid*, a historical novel, and once the anti-Witchcraft laws in England were repealed in 1951, he published two important works under his own name: *Witchcraft Today* (1954) and *The Meaning of Witchcraft* (1959). These books represented the first notable break with the secrecy and silence that had surrounded the Craft. Gardner's description of the Craft became the standard approach for many Witches looking for a manual or guide for practising the Craft. Today there are many Gardnerian Witches and covens that continue to practise more or less faithfully along Gardnerian lines. For them Gardner appeared as a herald of the Old Ways. (However, Witches brought up in family traditions assert that what they learned from their parents and grandparents did not resemble Garner's version of the Craft.)

Basically, Gardner's version contributed much to modern Witchcraft: fertility-oriented rituals to honour the Horned God of the Forests and the Triple Goddess with chanting, dancing and meditation, celebrated on the eight sabbats and at the new and full moons. The ritual of drawing down the moon, reciting the Charge of the Goddess, invoking the Horned God and Goddess, performing healing ceremonies and other works of positive magic are central to the Gardnerian tradition. Covens are led by a high priest and high priestess, who train and initiate others in the Gardnerian way, passing on their Books of Shadows to initiates who study them to learn the laws and liturgies of the Craft.

Not all Gardnerian Witches follow Gardner's prescriptions rigorously. A cardinal tenet of Gardner's that has been discarded by most modern witches is the tradition of practising 'sky-clad', or in the nude. There is no widespread historical evidence for this custom before Gardner, who was a naturist even before discovering the Craft. In fact the oldest traditions seem to indicate that Witches preferred long black robes, especially during the Burning Times when they would be less conspicuous in the forest, where they went at night to do their rituals. Certainly the preference among most Witches today both in Britain and the United States is to wear robes, a practice that has always been an important part of magical ritual and contributes as much to a Witch's power as practising sky-clad.

Other traditions that have contributed to the modern image of the Witch are the Dianic practices that stem primarily from Margaret Murray's works and Sir James Frazer's very influential *The Golden Bough*. In Dianic covens great emphasis is placed on the Goddess and on the role of priestesses. Covens and organizations are matrifocal and concentrate on women's issues. The current women's movement has inspired much of the political activism that some covens engage in. Recent studies in women's spirituality have also influenced coven practices and coven lore, just as the Dianic tradition itself has contributed important material to women's spiritual issues among mainstream theologians. This cross-fertilization has been very exciting for Witches and religious scholars alike.

Many Dianic covens are extremely creative in developing new rituals and taking the Craft 'out of the broom closets' and into the streets. Some sponsor public rituals on the sabbats and on occasions when Witches' presence can demonstrate on behalf of social and political issues. Although radical feminism, including lesbianism, has found a place in Dianic covens, not all covens are focused solely on women's issues. The great environmental and social crises that face our society today inspire Witches to use their power and magic to work change within society.

One of the most recent works on Witches and other neo-pagans in America is Margot Adler's excellent work, *Drawing Down the Moon*. After interviewing individual Witches and covens around the USA and joining them in rituals and celebrations, she compiled her findings in a clear, well-written account. Her book is an excellent study of the beliefs, customs and life-styles of neo-pagan groups. The marvellous variety she presents attests to the vigour of pagan communities as well as the dedication of individual Witches.

In modern times these more accurate pictures of Witchcraft are slowly reaching the general public, but there is still a great re-education campaign that must be undertaken if we are ever to correct the inaccurate image of the Witch as an evil-doer in league with the devil. Contemporary culture continues to reinforce the old images that come from the Burning Times.

THE WITCHES' LEAGUE FOR PUBLIC AWARENESS

When Warner Brothers announced that it would make a film version of John Updike's novel *The Witches of Eastwick*, Salem Witches decided to protest against the inaccurate image it would present of Witches. This was the catalyst that led to the founding of the Witches' League for Public Awareness. I summoned Witches in the Salem and Boston areas and we met, fifty to seventy-five strong, with our babies and children, on the steps of the Massachusetts Film Bureau in Boston to protest against its decision to allow the filming of the movie in the Commonwealth. The media, of course, turned out, and within days our protest was seen all across the country. We probably helped to publicize the film by stirring up controversy over it, but we also did ourselves good by speaking out and not standing idly by while Hollywood created yet another film depicting the Witch as an evil-doer.

Witches all across the States responded favourably to our taking a public stand, as they realized that Updike's so-called Witches – not real Witches but bored housewives with psychic abilities – would be perceived by the general public as being representative of the truth and would fuel the myth that Witches do evil by conjuring up the devil and having sex with him. It would be *Rosemary's Baby* all over again. Letters poured in, and we discovered that the Witches' League had grass-roots support from individual Witches and entire covens from Maine to California.

Our goal was to have a disclaimer run at the beginning of the film or with the credits stating that although the word

Witches appeared in the title of the movie, it was being used in the popular and inaccurate sense of a person who does harm to others and trafficks with the devil. Or the disclaimer could simply say that the film should not be construed to imply that a person who practises Witchcraft is engaged in devil worship. (There was a precedent for this. The film *The Godfather* disclaimed that the film implied that all Italian-Americans were engaged in organized crime.) The Witches' League also sent 'awareness packets' to the three actresses pointing out the disservice their protrayals would cause to thousands of women around the world by perpetuating a gross misconception about us. We also offered to advise on the script or story line. We received no reply from the actresses, their agents or Warner Brothers.

But the reply from Witches throughout the States was stupendous. We began writing to them, networking, setting up guidelines for handling similar threats to our integrity and exploring possibilities for educational work in local communities. Two years later we now have fifteen councils that cover the entire United States and parts of Ireland, England and Canada. Each council head oversees volunteer activities such as letter-writing campaigns, monitoring television programmes, news reports and newspaper accounts of Witchcraft, and reporting back to our central office in Salem. In addition to being a watchdog on misinformation about the Craft, we review books and articles on the Craft and recommend the better ones to libraries and schools. We also keep tabs on congressional bills that deal with civil rights and religious liberties. We do not, however, take on personal cases involving infringement of civil rights in jobs or housing or violence. In those cases we suggest that a Witch contact the American Civil Liberties Union or the Witches' Anti-defamation League, founded by Dr Leo Martello.

One of the Witches' League's major commitments is to counteract the misunderstanding that has come to surround one of our festive, joyous celebrations, Samhain, or Halloween as it has come to be called. Each year the feast is used to regurgitate all the inaccurate and degrading myths about the Craft. And now there are movements in some communities to abolish it, such as the New Hampshire town where a murderer dressed up like the ghoul in *Friday the Thirteenth* and killed someone. All across the country parents worry about their children on this special night, afraid they will do harm to others or destroy property and afraid that others will do harm to them. Is there any better proof that mental projections become real? The lurid fantasies and misconceptions of a society now prowl the streets and neighbourhoods doing evil.

In Salem we send letters to local wholesalers and shopkeepers in October reminding them that Halloween is the Witches' feast of Samhain, a high holy day and the old Celtic New Year. We encourage them not to decorate their stores and windows with images of repulsive-looking Witches with pointed hats, riding broomsticks and cackling through broken teeth. (Witches go to dentists just like everyone else.) We also discourage images of ghouls, ghosts, Dracula, vampires, Frankenstein and people with their bodies ripped apart. We point out that there are plenty of colourful Halloween images that are not offensive and that do not play upon society's fears and pollute the minds of children and adults. Most Salem businesses comply. The ones that do not receive a personal visit by one of our delegates, who tries to educate them as to how their decorations demean Witches and the feast of Samhain while encouraging their children to do mischief. In most cases it is simply ignorance, and people are willing to listen and learn, and often take down the offensive images of green-skinned hags.

An area that I believe requires constant monitoring is children's television. So many children's stories and films present the Witch as a cranky old crone who hates little children. Witches have been part of Western mythology for centuries, going back to the folktales collected by the Brothers Grimm and retold in various forms from generation to generation. But until the last century or so the tales were literally *told*, not seen. Children *heard* about Witches. It was up to their young imaginations to determine what they looked like. If a child knew a local Witch in the neighbourhood, first-hand experience would convince the child that not all Witches were evil like the ones in the fairy tales. Today children see Witches only in the form determined by artists and media directors. Little is left to their imaginations. What's more, since most Witches do not live openly and publicly as Witches, children have no reference with which to compare the media Witch. Are we sexy and voluptuous like Elvira? Are we pointy-nosed and grovelling like the Wicked Witch of the West in *The Wizard of Oz*? Do we rage and writhe like the evil stepmother in Walt Disney's *Snow White and the Seven Dwarfs*?

Recently I was having dinner in a Mexican restaurant in the nearby town of Danvers (the original site of Salem Village, by the way) and a polite young waiter came up to my table. 'You're Laurie Cabot, aren't you?' he said rather shyly. I said I was and asked him his name. 'Randy,' he replied. 'I met you when I was a child.' I told him he had a better memory than I did and asked him how we met. He said his mother was walking with him and she ran into me on the street and we stopped and talked for a few moments. I asked the young waiter how long ago that was, and he replied, 'Twenty years ago.' Then he added, 'I always thought it would be nice to meet you again,' and excused himself politely to return to his tables.

And so we did meet again. It made me realize that an entire generation has grown up in the Salem area who know me. I'm sure some of them have heard the old lies and slanders from their parents. But then there is Randy, who knows that he lives in a community with a Witch – actually a lot of Witches – and no harm has come. Randy must have seen me over the years on television or in the newspapers. I've taught the Science of Witchcraft at Salem College and lectured all over Salem and the United States. I am interviewed every year at Halloween by local and national television and radio stations. I sponsored the Salem Witches' Ball at Halloween for many years. I am on the board of the Salem Chamber of Commerce. I ran for mayor. On days when the lies and slanders about Witchcraft seem to be too much to bear, I think about Randy and others like him, and I know that having lived publicly as a Witch has been worth it.

And yet I continue to wonder how many people were influenced by the nightmarish scene from Disney's *Snow White* where the evil queen turns herself into a hideous hag by drinking a potion. How can I say loud enough, how can my voice reach far enough, to assure people, and especially children, that that is *not* the way one becomes a Witch?

THE DIFFERENCES BETWEEN WITCHCRAFT AND SATANISM

Recently Geraldo Rivera produced a programme on Satanism for prime-time network television in the USA. I held my breath all the way through. How relieved I was to see that he managed to get through the entire hour without mentioning Witchcraft. But then just as I was about to take up my pen and write him a note of congratulation, the programme ended with a list of things for parents to watch out for if they worry about their children getting involved with Satanic cults. And there it was – Witchcraft!

There is much confusion about who is dangerous and who is not. The police departments around the country have special guidelines for what they call 'occult' crimes. These are crimes that appear to be committed by individuals or groups who are mixed up in various cruel and sadistic practices, often involving ritual torture and death, usually of animals but sometimes human beings. It's important for police departments and the FBI to apprehend these criminals and prevent future atrocities. But they, like so many others in our society, confuse the evidence.

Witches have worked with FBI agents to help investigate bizarre crimes. I have received phone calls from police departments from all over the USA to advise them in their search for psychotic offenders who use the trappings of religion in their crimes. Any crackpot can vandalize churches and synagogues and use sacred objects in a crime. The real Satanists mock Witchcraft symbols like the pentacle just as they do the crucifix. Any sadist can commit murder, rape, mutilate a victim, and then claim to be a Witch or a Satanist.

It really isn't that difficult to distinguish the Craft from Satanism. Witches wear the pentacle with the point up. Satanists reverse it with the point down, just as they reverse the crucifix. Witches never use a crucifix for any purpose, upside down or right side up. We never use the numbers 666. We do not sacrifice animals for any purpose. We do nothing Christian backwards. Specifically, we do not say the Lord's Prayer backwards. We do not celebrate Black Masses or any other colour of Mass. We use no Christian artefacts, and therefore we never need to break into Christian churches to steal them. Witches do not *use* children in our rituals. When our own children participate in Craft ceremonies, they do so on the same terms as adults. We do no physical harm to anyone, nor do we project harm on to others. Furthermore, we do not recruit or proselytize.

Getting the record straight is difficult. The Witches' League for Public Awareness sends thousands of pamphlets and letters explaining the Craft to businesses, schools, religious groups and law-enforcement agencies around the world. One of our latest projects is to convince the publishers of the major dictionaries and encyclopedias to rewrite their definitions of Witches and Witchcraft to reflect the truth about us and leave out the business about 'ugly, old hags' and 'pacts with the devil'. We would like them to say that Witchcraft is an art and science that all peoples and cultures have practised in one way or another. We would like our roots in the pre-Christian European nature religions to be taken seriously and discussed with respect. We would like definitions to stop equating us with evil.

We are also trying to advise the producers of the daily soap operas, which are viewed by millions of people each day, to stop referring to wicked and conniving women as 'Witches'. The scriptwriters use the word in the Kraemer and Sprenger sense of 'evil woman'. Such script-writing is totally unnecessary and demeans Witches and women. It is also hard to explain to our children why characters on television use a word that refers to their mothers for such backbiting and bitchy women.

I know that slowly and surely people are getting the message. On my way home after the television show recording I stopped in a petrol station in Cleveland to fill up the tank. I heard someone call out my name and wondered who it could be, since I don't know very many people in that area. It was a mother and father with their little children who had stopped for petrol and had recognized me from the show. They said they were happy to have seen me and were glad that I had 'stood up' to that minister. As I drove on I wondered about that family. Were they Witches?

·4·

THE CRAFT OF THE WISE

As I read through my Book of Shadows I am always reminded of how rich and varied the Craft is and always has been. My eye scans the pages; certain words, informed with memory and individual magic, loom up and nearly leap off the page: coven, wand, solstice, crystals, love, vervain, poppets, cats, chants – and the magical names of coveners I have known over the years. The early entries date back more than twenty years; the more recent ones record rituals we did last year, potions I brewed a month ago, a dream I awoke from just last night. In my personal journal and commonplace book I record and catalogue my life as a Witch. When I leave this book – actually many volumes now – to my daughters Jody and Penny, they will have a full account of how I lived: my rituals, spells, recipes, meditations, practices, the important events in my life. In these pages they will learn how I upheld and practised the Craft.

It is not common for a Witch to show her Book of Shadows to others, except to close members of the Craft. There was a time when just possessing a book of magic could bring persecution and death. Here is an entry in a Book of Shadows written by a Witch in the twelfth century:

Keep a book in your own hand of write. Let brothers and

sisters copy what they will but never let this book out of
your hand, and never keep the writings of another, for
if it be found in their hand of write they will be taken
and tortured ... Learn as much as you may by heart
and when danger is past rewrite your book.

Fortunately, we live in more enlightened times where we
don't have to keep our journals secret and commit our most
important rituals and spells to memory for fear of being
persecuted. Nevertheless, a Witch's Book of Shadows is a
private record and is usually not given to others to read, but
I will share with you some of the basic practices that have
meant so much to me, the practices that we have come to call
the Craft of the Wise or Witchcraft. It will give you an
insight into the kinds of things that make up the Craft: the
people, the training, the covens, the rituals and spells, and
the tools of magic that bring blessings to the earth.

PENTACLES: THE SIGN OF THE CRAFT

On many pages I have drawn small pentacles, as I do when I
sign my name on letters and documents. I believe the
pentacle to be one of the oldest geometric symbols known to
humans. It consists of a five-pointed star inside a circle. It is
the key symbol in the Craft. It is the Witch's mandala, a
geometric diagram of all existence, that encompasses both
creatrix and creation.

The pentacle has a rich history in the magical and spiritual
customs of many cultures. In Greece it was the symbol of
Demeter's daughter Kore, the Goddess of vegetation and the
fruits of the field, because the apple contains a star composed
of five seeds in its core. Today gypsies call the five-seeded
pentacle in the apple 'the Star of Knowledge'. Pythagorean
mystics honoured the pentacle, which they called 'Pentalpha',

because it consisted of five interwoven alphas: the Greek letter, α which stood for birth and beginnings. In Egypt a five-pointed star represented the great underground womb of Mother Earth. The Celtic tribes also saw it as a sign of the Goddess of the Underworld, Morgan. In Babylon the pentacle was an amulet of protection and healing. In Judaic-Christian traditions the pentacle was the first of the Seven Seals, which represented the secret name of God; and King Solomon wore a pentacle on his ring as a sign of his power to work magic. Among the old European tribespeople the pentacle represented the Horned God, a shapeshifter who had five manifestations: a human, a bull, a ram, a goat and a stag. The Celtic hero Gawain had a pentacle inscribed on his shield.

The star is always drawn with one continuous stroke, with one point upright, and to me it represents the continuous outline of the human body: the head at the top, the two arms, the legs, the mystic centre where all points cross. It is a symbol of the human body that goes back millennia, and it resonates with something old and sacred in our souls. Even people who know little about Witchcraft feel this when they look at Leonardo da Vinci's famous representation of the Microcosmic Man that shows the muscular male body, arms and legs outstretched, standing as a five-pointed figure in the perfect circle. It looks as if he could lift off the page and soar. Instinctively, we know that this proud, self-confident, almost defiant stance is at the heart of what it means to be human. Perhaps it is the strength of the triangle, one of the strongest geometric figures, that resonates with our sense of purpose.

The five points also represent the five senses, through which earthly knowledge enters the mind. The centre can stand for the sixth sense, the deep unconscious, or the ethereal connection of each human being with the All or the Higher Self.

The circle around the pentagram represents the totality of

all intelligence. It is the sign for the God and Goddess, the fullness of cosmic intelligence. The circle pulls in light and directs it toward the centre along its many radii. Each time I see a pentacle I am reminded of the encircling power of the All that surrounds and protects us, assuring us that each human being is at the centre of divine life. Our Divine Mother encloses each of us in her womb. No matter where we are, what we do, in her we live and move and have our being. Other religious groups and even political bodies have instinctively understood the power and meaning of this sacred emblem. While travelling through Europe I was startled but overjoyed to find the pentacle pieced into mosaics and stained-glass windows in Catholic cathedrals. The states of Oklahoma and Texas use the pentacle as a part of their state seals.

To use a scientific metaphor (although as we will see in the next chapter, 'metaphor' may be an understatement), the pentacle is a circuit charged with energy. The star reflects and refracts light, and light carries information (something else we will look at more closely in the next chapter). When made of silver it draws in light just as the moon does, retaining all the rays except those reflected as silver. When made of gold it draws in and carries the strength of the sun. Metallurgists tell us that molecules of silver are crescent-shaped, like the moon, and molecules of gold have spires or rays, like the rays of the sun. By wearing a pentacle on our bodies we are constantly drawing down and in the moon power or sun power found in light. The circle is the never-ending, perfect intelligence that fills the universe and runs down the arms of the star, inward to the human body, uniting All That Is and the individual in perfect wisdom. Such is the ideal. Of course, not every Witch fully realizes the ideal in her life or his life. We must co-operate with the power of the pentacle, allowing its power to shape our consciousness. We must return to it often, meditating on its mystic meanings and seeking within it the universal wisdom.

As a sacred symbol we put the pentacle everywhere, much like Christians use a cross and Jews a Star of David. Each Witch wears a pentacle somewhere on his or her body, frequently on a chain around the neck, or as a bracelet, sometimes as a logo on a shirt or jacket. Witches who are 'out' in their lives display it quite openly; others, out of fear of discrimination or persecution, wear it beneath shirts or blouses or woven secretly into the hem of their clothes. In whichever ways are appropriate each Witch needs to live in the presence of a pentacle and draw in the energy that is unique to it and to her.

The power of the pentacle affects each of us differently but it always operates in the same way, bringing wisdom and protection to whoever wears it. Some Witches have been lured by its ancient structure since they were little children. Even before they knew what it stood for they were drawn into its deep meaning and purpose. They resonated with it, and it led them to the Craft. Others begin to understand the symbol only after being introduced to Witchcraft. But for each of us learning the secrets of the pentacle is a lifelong process. Because the pentacle represents perfect wisdom it is as much a path as it is the source and goal of our lives.

BECOMING A WITCH

In the earliest pages of my Book of Shadows are the names of three important women – all Witches – who introduced me to the Craft and the pentacle. I was sixteen years old when I met them, a young girl scouring the Boston Public Library for books that would explain why I felt so different from my friends and school acquaintances. I knew I was different, but I didn't yet know that I was a Witch. I hunted for books that would teach me about metaphysical matters and explain the mysteries of nature and, if such books existed, how spirit and matter co-operate in sustaining the physical world.

A very kind and knowledgeable librarian seemed to understand what I was looking for. She seemed to intuit my inarticulate yearnings. She sensed that my search was for more than just book knowledge, that I was searching for my very self. I trusted her. In time I discovered that she was one of the wise, and that, in some undefined way which I could not then put into words, she was like me. She directed me to books on nature, history, science and religion, which collectively transported me back to a time before Christianity. I read Robert Graves's *The White Goddess*, Sir James Frazer's *The Golden Bough, Isis Unveiled* by Madame Blavatsky, and many articles on sleep, dreams, parapsychology and mythology.

I read about eras when people accepted personal visions and experiences like the ones I was having as completely good and natural. I learned about societies where the search for truth was a shamanic, not a priestly experience; that is, where individuals seeking spiritual wisdom embarked, like troubadours and knights perilous, on lonely, often dangerous journeys; where quests for spiritual power required physical and psychological crises; where the hero was tested time and again by nature, human challenges and his or her own deepest fears and longings. It was a search for the wisdom of the cosmos, not the doctrines of an ecclesiastical hierarchy. In short, it was not a search for churches. It was a search for castles, hidden in the centre of magical kingdoms.

In the course of my reading and study I learned that the powers and longings that seemed so strong in me, and so different from everyone around me, were once valued and respected. My librarian friend guided my reading so that I learned the Old Ways of the Craft from its earliest beginnings. Over the months we developed a strong relationship based on mutual interests, and as I learned that the word *Witch* applied to me, I realized it applied also to her.

The librarian and two of her friends initiated me into the Craft. Each of them was a remarkable woman in her own right. One was a musician, the other a professor at a local college. The initiation ritual they used over forty years ago is still the one I use today. As I read it over again in my Book of Shadows I see that it has changed very little. And so it is with much in the Craft. Although there is always room for innovation – and Witches are notoriously imaginative in creating new rituals – the Old Ways stay with us and ground us, reminding us that our practice originates deep in human history. I feel privileged that the three Witches who taught me the Craft were themselves grounded in ancient ways; each was a keeper of sacred knowledge and a teacher and storyteller who could pass that knowledge on to the next generation. And each encouraged me to try and understand the scientific basis for the Craft.

That small, quiet coven of four was my first introduction to the Craft as a craft, as something one *does*. The triple nature of the Goddess was perfectly manifested in us for one of the coveners was quite elderly, the other two were mothers and I was the young girl.

I fell I was very fortunate to be led to these three wonderful women when I needed them, but then that's the way the Goddess works. Most people in the Craft relate similar experiences. When the time was ready for them and they had reached a level of spiritual or intellectual development necessary for joining the Craft, they met the right persons or groups or read the right books that served as their introduction.

Most people find the Craft (or it finds them) at the time in their lives when they need it. Others feel a calling to it for many years. They feel led. Some power or force larger than themselves enters their lives and opens windows for them. A voice calls; they feel challenged to discover states of consciousness that go higher and deeper than the social and cultural norms with which they have grown up. In my Book of Shadows are the names of many men and women I have been privileged to introduce to the Craft over the years. Now that I am an elder in the Craft I can look back on those who came to me for instruction, and I am constantly reminded how wise the Goddess can be in selecting the individuals she wants to serve her in the Craft. Even now their individual names rekindle in me the same hopeful enthusiasm they once felt – that we all once felt – when the windows were flung open, shutters thrown back, and we saw for the first time the beauty and glory of the world through the eyes of a Witch. Or perhaps I should say that it was the first time we knew we were looking at the world with the eyes of a Witch.

There are many ways to 'become' a Witch – to discover your own Witch eyes, your own Witch soul. In early times knowledge was passed from mother to daughter, from grandmother to granddaughter. Learning the ways of the Craft was as commonplace as learning how to cook soup, birth a child, build a fire. Family traditions made up a great part of Witchcraft, and it is through them that most of our knowledge was preserved and passed down through the ages. Today there are very few Witches of my age who learned the Craft from their mothers and grandmothers because Witchcraft was illegal in most places until the middle of the twentieth century. But we have moved into a new era. Since the Wiccan revival that followed the repeal of the anti-Witchcraft laws, more men and women in the Craft are teaching their children the ways of power. My own daughters, Jody and Penny, and my 'adopted' daughter Alice Keegan, are the second generation in a new line of Witches.

Most Witches practising today did not learn the Craft in their families. They read books, they took courses, they studied it on their own. There is nothing wrong in taking courses or workshops offered by someone in your community, provided she or he is a reputable, initiated Witch, well versed in the Craft.

Many people are introduced to the Craft through friends or acquaintances. You learn that a co-worker, a neighbour or some friend of a friend is a Witch, and as you get to know her or him, you grow more interested in what makes the person tick. Eventually, you are led to the Craft and at some point you realize that what they do and what they believe have always made sense to you. You know that somewhere in your secret heart you should be doing that too. And at some point you say, 'I am ready.'

COVENS

Most people who are serious about studying the Craft find a person or coven who will accept newcomers as apprentices. Traditionally, there are three to thirteen people in a coven, but many groups are fairly flexible in terms of size and the mix of men and women. The number thirteen most likely originated for each of the thirteen moons that occur every year. A lunar month is a few days short of a calendar month, so there are thirteen moons, not twelve, in every calendar year. Although it has been pointed out many times that Jesus's 'coven' consisted of thirteen (twelve apostles and himself), this fact has little to do with a Witch's coven. The association with Jesus was probably just another attempt by the Inquisition during the Burning Times to draw unfavourable analogies between Christianity and paganism by creating the myth that Witches pervert Christian customs. Covens have nothing to do with Christianity. Rather, they are living vestiges of the old lunar calendars that measured time and events around the twenty-eight-day menstrual cycle.

Furthermore, thirteen is just a good number of people in terms of simple group dynamics. Thirteen people stimulate creativity and provide a sufficient number of members for sharing tasks and responsibilities. A group of thirteen does not become unwieldy. It is small enough for everyone to get a chance to participate, speak out, be heard and, most of all, be known as an individual. Because the coven of thirteen is so rooted in Craft traditions, it has become a widespread belief among Witches that thirteen people have more power than any other number of people.

There is also a beautiful geometric aspect to a circle of thirteen people. Twelve is the number of spheres it takes to surround a thirteenth sphere, so that each of the twelve touches the surface of the thirteenth – a sphere enclosed by spheres! Being the three-dimensional form of a circle, the sphere is the perfect shape, all points equidistant from the centre, no beginning, no end and only one smooth surface. In a sense that is the ideal coven: all members equal in the circle, tasks and responsibilities revolving among all coveners, the group continually replacing itself with new members as older members leave or pass on, and a unified family spirit based on mutual respect, harmony and balance.

Both men and women can belong to the same coven, although some covens prefer all one or the other. When both sexes are present the ritual of drawing down the God and Goddess is more perfectly realized and the unique male and female energies, both physical and spiritual, are allowed full expression. That perfect yin and yang combination that empowers everything in the universe comes into full play. (We will look at this principle of gender in both physical and metaphysical terms in the next chapter.)

Some women's covens, especially feminist groups, favour sacred space composed solely of female energy. In today's world, where most families are composed solely of mothers and their children, women need psychological support and a safe forum for discussing women's issues. An all-women's coven provides the kind of sanctuary and sisterhood where a woman can speak openly and honestly about herself, release frustrations and heal the wounds she receives from a patriarchal society. In a circle of loving women we can draw strength and energy to return to our lives and work.

In ancient times both men and women held special rituals that were excluded from the other sex to discover and experience their own mysteries. At these special times each learned what it meant to be male or female and how that experience fitted into the great plan for the cosmos. Today we have lost much of the sacred quality of these mysteries. Young girls are often told very little about their bodies and the wonders that take place in them. They are mistakenly told that the menstrual period is a curse that renders them moody and dysfunctional for many daily activities. They are told about premenstrual syndrome but little about the ways they could use this time each month to strengthen the Goddess energy that only they can experience in their own bodies as part of the sacred mysteries unique to females. Young boys are introduced to manhood by competitive or violent rituals, often learned in school athletics, that do little to place their strength and passion in a sacred context. They are not taught the male mysteries that could produce strong spiritual warriors and hunters, men of knowledge and personal power. In other words, we become male or female adults in modern society with little understanding of how that fact, certainly one of the most important in our lives, serves the God and Goddess.

All-male or all-female covens let their members work on these eternal mysteries just as our ancestors did. They provide sacred space off-limits to the other sex. In the privacy and sanctuary of the coven we can find the safety to explore the needs particular to our gender and discover the purpose and meaning of being male or female. These rituals are not about engaging in sexual activities but rather about exploring the power of gender in all things, the yin and yang elements that represent the female and male energy of the universe. In these rituals we learn how to deal with the male and female elements in each of us.

Some gay Witches prefer working in all-gay covens to explore the blend of male/female energies that are unique to all of them. Gay men, for example, have reclaimed the 'fairy' tradition of Celtic lore, which in recent years has played a stimulating role in discussions of gay spirituality. All-lesbian covens use meetings to study and explore the meaning and purpose of lesbian relationships in this same manner, some reclaiming the Sapphic mysteries performed years ago on the ancient Greek islands by priestesses of the Great Goddess.

There is a lot of misunderstanding among people about the role of nudity and sex in Witchcraft. Several years ago, while I was visiting England, a very proper British lady approached me and asked primly, 'Do you run around in the woods naked?' She had read several pot-boiler novels about Witches that sensationalized nude rituals and described lurid sex acts that took place in magic circles. Some novels and popular books on the Craft give the impression that all Witches dance around in the nude and use sex as a source of power in their magic. My coven and circle of friends do not practise in the nude, nor do we engage in sexual acts as part of our rituals. I know that nudity is a way to be close to nature, honour the sacredness of the human body, and express oneself with greater freedom, especially when dancing, and for these reasons some Witches practise 'sky-clad', but my own preference is to use magical robes and ceremonial garments to enhance my magic.

It is important to evaluate each coven and its members carefully. There are many traditions in the Craft and many different types of people, and it may take you a while to find the people and the style of Witchcraft with which you feel comfortable. Because Witchcraft sits on the fringes of society, it has tended to attract eccentric types, which doesn't necessarily mean they are the 'lunatic fringe'. Some of the world's greatest artists and geniuses have also chosen to remain on the edge of society, disengaged from the mainstream. But you do find eccentrics in the Craft, along with more conventional people no different from the hundreds of middle-class and working-class people you meet every week. A survey of the various Wiccan traditions and other neo-pagan groups that are alive and well in the United States today, as well as the types of people that are attracted to them, is Margot Adler's *Drawing Down the Moon*, mentioned earlier.

In judging any coven or tradition do get to know it and what it expects from you. If a coven asks you to do something you think is wrong or to change your life in a way that does not seem appropriate, you are probably in the wrong group. Remember, no respectable coven will ever ask you to do something dangerous or harmful. Neither will they ask you for a fee to join. (This is not the same as a fee charged for a class or workshop; in our capacities as teachers and instructors we have a right to charge for our time and expertise just as an instructor in any other field or discipline.)

You can usually judge a coven by how comfortable you feel with the people in it. They will be evaluating you on the same terms and will require a period of the traditional 'year and a day' before you are formally initiated. They will invite you to join them in some or all of their magic circles for that is where magic is taught. In the new- and full-moon circles you will share magic together. On the sabbats you will learn how the coven celebrates and observes the seasons and honours the Goddess and God. Some coveners may invite you to lunch or to go jogging with them to know you outside the circle. Most fellow coveners are like-minded individuals, sharing common interests, concerns and values. Although each will have had his or her own unique path into the Craft, often similar experiences shaped each one's journey: intellectual questioning, periods of spiritual shopping around, dissatisfaction with contemporary life in some way or another, trying other religious or philosophical belief systems, opening up to their own mystical or psychic experiences.

Be on the watch for covens and coveners who seem to be interested only in power. Witchcraft is about personal power and can attract individuals who interpret power as a way to dominate others. I have seen many people over the years who wanted to become Witches only to satisfy their misguided egos rather than to develop their real selves. There is a difference between the ego and the self. When the self seeks power it is always power from within, never power over others. In all ages religious cults have swallowed up many young people who are either in great need of being dominated by stronger individuals than themselves or who themselves want to manipulate others and play the guru to weak individuals who lack self-confidence. Although we respect Craft elders, we do not consider them gurus. Duties are shared. No one has power over another. And the goal of everyone is to be empowered with knowledge and self-esteem. Those who join the Craft for the wrong reasons usually leave when they realize that in the Witch's circle they must stand on their own two feet and never on the toes of another. Witches respect each other's individuality and operate under the rule of 'perfect love and perfect trust'.

A woman named Linda came to me some years ago saying that she wanted to become a Witch. She took my first class in Witchcraft and disappeared. Shortly afterwards she was seen running around Salem in a black cape, floating up and down the streets, threatening to zap strangers and tourists with her 'magic'. Eventually, her scandalous behaviour began giving all the Salem Witches a bad name, and we decided that something must be done to neutralize her influence. I did a spell to 'change' the situation so that it would harm none and be for the good of all. Four or five days later Linda returned to class waving a letter from a boyfriend in California from whom she hadn't heard in seven years. 'Guess where I'm going,' she announced proudly. We all held our breaths and smiled inwardly. 'San Diego,' she informed us.

She is now happily married, has several children and a good job, and I would suspect is not practising what she mistakenly thought was Witchcraft.

When you have studied and worked with a coven long enough to satisfy them that you are sincere, knowledgeable and have the right intentions, they may formally initiate you into their coven. Not every Witch is initiated into a coven; some solitaries, for example, practise alone, and may even initiate themselves in a special ceremony to acknowledge themselves officially as practitioners of the Craft and followers of the Goddess. Some Witches may meet with a coven (or covens) on certain occasions without being formal members. For most people, however, formal recognition by other Witches is critical because identification with a particular coven strengthens one's personal identity as a Witch.

One part of my initiation ritual is very similar to the dubbing ceremony in knighthood. In our coven each member brings a jar or bowl full of fresh earth from her garden and pours it into the cauldron. A new Witch stands between the high priestess and the cauldron and is dubbed with a sword on the forehead and each shoulder while the priestess says, 'I name you Witch. Return your knowledge and energy to Mother Earth and the cosmos.' The initiate then takes the sword, holds it upright before her heart and head, repeats the phrase and then plunges the sword point into the cauldron of earth. She is then an initiated Witch in my coven, the Black Doves of Isis.

I can see in my Book of Shadows that it took me many years to organize my first coven. Until then I worked alone with my daughters, doing family magic. But the Goddess's ways are always right and correct for each person, and those years were important ones in my own growth as a practising Witch. When the time was ripe, and the right individuals came together, the coven was born; its birth and growth was full of fun and intensity. Today only a few of the original members are still together. Others have moved away with their families or pursued careers that left them no time for coven work. However, many stay in touch and often align their own rituals to coincide with ours and in this way our work is shared by others around the world. One coven member flies to Salem from another state to join us whenever it is convenient for her.

It takes energy and commitment to be an active member of a coven because we become intensely involved in our work and in each other's lives. We are a support group and a second family for each other. We bring tears and laughter, headaches and fun-filled times, joys and hopes to the magic circle. Who we are and what we do become part of our magic, a web interwoven with each member's power and personality. In the coven we gather strength from each other and our lives are enriched. In the last year two baby boys have been born in our coven. For nine months they were part of our magic circles, and all of us helped to nurture them while they were still in the womb. We were all spiritual midwives to these two fine baby boys.

In addition to spiritual and healing work, many covens commit themselves to some form of outside work in the community. The more politically active covens may engage in lobbying for social issues or educating the electorate. Some become involved in demonstrations and protest activities on environmental issues, such as the safety of nuclear power plants or the preservation of forest land; some work for the protection of animal rights. Urban Witches may volunteer time with their city's homeless or at retirement centres or with health and children's services. Members of the Council of Isis here in Salem and others of our friends participated in protesting against the Seabrook nuclear power plant in New Hampshire, and some coven members have joined volunteer efforts to assist beached whales on Cape Cod by staying with them, covering them with blankets, and helping them to return to the sea.

Many Witches socialize with coven members and their families. They have picnics and dinners together or organize public rituals, such as Maypole celebrations in city parks or winter solstice affairs at Yuletide. At Yule the Witches' League invites other Salemites to join in our magic circle to celebrate the season and to contribute new toys for the local children's hospital and family centres. At Samhain, or Halloween, my coven meets on Gallows Hill and leads a candle-light march down to the harbour to commemorate all those who have died for our freedom and rights. Hundreds of marchers who join us do not belong to the Craft, nor do all those we commemorate. It is the spirit of those who died in Salem that moves us, and so we honour all men and women whose lives or deaths inspire others, such as Martin Luther King, Gandhi and others who have died for religious or political reasons.

Some Witches belong to more than one 'circle' and may even say they belong to more than one coven. Belonging to more than one coven, however, is difficult because of divided loyalties. On the high sabbats we cannot all be in two places at once! Some Witches, however, will have their principal coven with which they celebrate the major sabbats and a second, more loosely organized 'coven', or circle of friends, that meets once or twice a month for more specialized spiritual work. In this way a person can belong to a same-sex circle and still be part of a mixed coven. In some areas several covens may join together at the high holy days for a joint ritual or to offer public ceremonies for the larger community, or 'grove', in which they live.

As I flip through my Witch's journal I see the names of people who have blessed my life and my magic circles over the years. Some were fellow coveners, some shared magic with us only on certain occasions. Some are gone now, but as I read each one's name I remember some priceless gift he or she contributed to our work: an energy and spirit, a voice or a sense of humour that enriched our lives. I miss them.

SOLITARIES

Not every Witch belongs to a coven. Often, in remote areas, a Witch will find herself all alone without anyone to practise with. Some Witches choose to work alone even when 'networking' with covens is a possibility. Recently I took a few days' retreat in Maine to get closer to the wild, rural coastline, away from the noisy Salem Harbour and the commotion of tourists. One afternoon as I sat in a small cottage that was the former home of the Witch of Porpois Bay, drinking tea and listening to the gulls and the wind, I heard a soft rap on the door. It was a gentle-looking woman named Janice, a Witch in her early fifties, with grey hair and soft blue eyes, who lived in the fishing village and had seen me walking along the shore earlier that day. Janice had been a Witch all her life and practised alone, using her magic primarily to help members of her family. She had never belonged to a coven. She came just to talk and share ideas about the Craft, and we ended up trading books and herbal teas. We had a pleasant afternoon together. It may be a while before I see her again, but the memory of her, living and practising her ecological and healing magic on the rocky Maine coastline, will always stay with me. Janice is now in my Book of Shadows – a tough but gentle, solitary woman studying the Craft on her own and practising to the best of her ability. There should be more Witches like her.

Some people find it best to practise alone, at least in certain periods of their lives. Even a congenial coven suffers on occasion from the disruptive emotional and personal issues that its members bring to the circle. And as in a close family, one person's problems become everyone's problems. One of the joys of coven work, however, is that it provides a wonderful support group for each member. But there are times when someone may prefer to do magic unencumbered by group dynamics and interpersonal tensions that arise from time to time and unbalance the energies of a magic circle. This is fine, and a Witch who prefers to work alone should not feel like a second-class citizen. We make no demands or write up rules that coerce every Witch to join a coven.

My daughter Penny prefers to do all her rituals and spells alone, but she has a wonderful, creative knack for devising new magic that helps her in her career and personal life. The absence of a coven in her life does not impede her development as a Witch. My daughter Jody, however, is a member of my coven, and all our members benefit from her direct, powerful, businesslike approach to magic.

There will always be loners in the Craft, just as there are loners in all walks of life, and the Goddess needs solitary magic as much as group magic. One of the commendable qualities of the Craft is that it accepts and honours those individuals who prefer to practise on their own. We do not force people to attend rituals or 'worship services' or 'prayer meetings'. A solitary's full-moon sabbats raise power and play an important role in balancing the earth's energies and working for the good of society, just as do those rituals performed by full covens. And when all is said and done I think every Witch should, at some time, face the moon alone, feet planted on the ground, with only his or her voice chanting in the starry night.

THE MAGIC CIRCLE

Casting a magic circle creates sacred space and inaugurates sacred time. For many of us being in a circle is like re-entering the original time or the 'dream time' that existed at the beginning of the world. In the language of fairy tales we stand at the moment when the universe began, the moment we call 'once upon a time'. We experience what Carlos Castenada in his description of Yaqui magic calls 'stopping the world'. We stand in a ring, holding hands, and we are 'between the worlds' of ordinary and non-ordinary reality. All times and all places meet with our circle and it becomes the centre of the universe for us. Like the pentacle, we are the star within the great circle of life.

Circles are powerful places for doing spiritual and healing work. Here we can draw down the celestial energies of the moon, planets and stars, or draw up the vast flows of life from within the Earth Mother. Like Yggdrasil, the Norse people's name for the magical Tree of the World that unites the lower, middle, and upper worlds with its vast roots and branches, the ring of our bodies contains both earth and sky, and all energy flows through our focused and balanced minds. In a circle we meet the gods – the archetypal forces that never die – and in some rituals we draw down the power of the God and Goddess and so become them. By chanting, dancing or rhythmic drumming, our ordinary consciousness shifts and our awareness becomes more god-centred. The human is elevated; we can see more clearly the meaning and purpose behind the cosmos. In these circles where consciousness is sharply attuned, spells are very powerful. The magic works. The results are spectacular.

In casting a magic circle we first purify the space we will use with the four elements of earth, air, fire and water. We walk around the area that will become the magic circle carrying a bowl of salt and water (for earth and water) and an incense burner (for fire and air). As we walk along the path of the circle we say, 'By water and earth, by fire and air, by spirit, be this circle bound and purified as we desire. So mote it be.' Then the high priestess, carrying her wand, walks clockwise around the circle three times saying, 'I cast this circle to protect us from all negative and positive forces and energies that may come to do us harm. I charge this circle to draw in only the most perfect, powerful, correct and harmonious forces and energies that will be compatible with us. I cast this circle to serve as sacred space between the worlds, a place of perfect love and perfect trust. So mote it be.'

Then we invite the animal powers and the spirits to join us. From the south we invite the lion; from the west, the eagle and the salmon; from the north, the boar, bear, wolf, and the white-horned ox; from the east, the birds of the air. We invite these creatures of power, strength, vision, courage and magical wisdom to add their energies to our circle. Next we invite the Celtic Gods and Goddesses: Cernunnos, or Cerne, the Green Man; the Horned God; Brigit, Goddess of Fire, Family and Fertility; Ceridwen, Goddess of the Moon, of Magic, and the Witch of the Gods; Gwyddian, God of Magic and Supreme Druid of the Gods; the Dagda, the Father of the Gods; and Anu, the Mother of the Gods. We ask that they give us the wisdom and understanding of our magical workings so that they will be for our good and for the good of all.

Then we do our magic for the occasion. We cast our spells. We do healing and renewal rituals. We share our hopes and dreams with each other.

Coven rituals are extremely varied. Some are dramatic and powerful experiences; others are dull and boring. It depends on the individual and collective spirit of the participants, the skill and sense of drama that the person conducting the ritual brings to it, the enthusiasm of the occasion, and the ability to invoke and work with the spirit energies that the coven invites into the circle. Psychic energy is heightened by singing, chanting, dancing, or by music played on wind, string or percussion instruments (flutes, drums, tambourines, Pan-pipes and guitars are favourite Craft instruments).

As energy rises in the circle the leader directs the members' consciousness by chant or group meditation to focus on and empower the goal or purpose of the ritual. This might be a personal healing of a covener or healing for someone not present, a social goal such as peace, community prosperity, public safety or an environmental issue, like rain, fertility, balance in nature, healing the earth. In my coven we also use this sacred time and space for each member to read a personal spell (see page 197) or voice individual petitions and sentiments that we wish to share with the group.

In the ritual of drawing down the moon a high priest and high priestess invoke the God and Goddess and draw into their bodies the pure essence of divine power in both its male and female forms. In a typical ritual the woman holds the cup of wine or spring water, a symbol of the womb, fullness and nourishment. The man holds the handle of the athame, his ritual dagger, in both hands, the point directed downwards, which symbolizes male energy and protection. As he places the athame into the cup the couple are ritually re-enacting the union of the male and female energies that are the source of all living things. The man traces a pentacle on the surface of the wine or water with the athame and the drawing down of divine power is complete.

The presence of the God and Goddess incarnated in these two individuals is honoured by all the members of the coven. The two celebrants then become vessels for the total intelligence of the All. Like oracles, or what today are popularly called 'channellers', the two Witches can speak for the God and Goddess and convey knowledge and information to the group. They answer questions about personal issues in the lives of the coveners as well as impart insight and understanding about the spiritual realms. In these rituals the God and Goddess may teach us new rituals and new ways to work magic and do healing or they may advise the coven or individual members on new works and enterprises that they should undertake.

In many rites coveners share the traditional 'meal' of cakes and wine, breaking and sharing bread or cake and passing the cup of wine or juice to celebrate the fruits of Mother Earth. In this way we express with each other our common bond as creatures of the earth and sons and daughters of the Great Ones, upon whom we are dependent for food and nourishment. We also remind ourselves in this sharing that we are dependent upon each other as brothers and sisters, and that we must give of ourselves to each other and to society so that people might live and have abundant life.

When the ritual is ended the high priestess walks counter-clockwise around the circle with her wand, declaring that the 'circle is now open, but not unbroken', and with that our collective energy goes out into the world to do our bidding. When the ritual is ended members usually socialize a bit before departing.

THE WHEEL OF THE YEAR

Covens meet at various times during the year, each coven deciding on when and where to meet so that it is convenient for its members. The usual times are at the new moon and the full moon each month and on the eight great sabbats, or festivals, of the year. The sabbats consist of the four earth holidays Samhain (31 October), Imbolc (1 February), Beltane (1 May), and Lammas (1 August), the winter and summer solstices (around 22 December and 22 June) and the vernal and autumnal equinoxes (around 21 March and 21 September).

No one knows how old these European festivals are. They may have originated around the breeding seasons of animals or the planting and harvesting of crops. The Inquisition claimed that they were always Christian holidays and that Witches perverted them for their own rites. Modern scholars in history and anthropology have proven just the opposite. These were pre-Christian holidays of pagan festivals that the church Christianized. The process of co-opting older festivals is still going on. 1 May was the Celtic feast of Beltane, later becoming the Robin Hood festivals, to be turned into a celebration of the Virgin Mary and St Joseph the worker, and now adopted by the Soviets to honour the worker and Communist military might. As Erica Jong says, 'Holidays tend to layer one atop the other like the remains of civilizations in Asia Minor.'

Most of the old festivals were fire rituals. The Celtic word for fire, 'tan' or 'teine', is still evident today in many British place names, such as Tan Hill, meaning Fire Hill. Fires were built on hills and mounds; celebrants carried torches; participants often jumped across small fires or paraded between large bonfires. Fire gave light and warmth on cold nights and represented for pre-industrial peoples the ultimate in pure energy. In a pantheistic worldview fire would not merely represent divine power but would incorporate it as well. Today Witches' rituals involve the use of candles, lamps and fully built fires whenever practical.

The concept of the Wheel of the Year is based on the insight that time and space are circular. (Modern physics seems to have only recently discovered this.) Hartley Burr Alexander's study of Native American worldviews, *The World's Rim*, explains how the concept of the four directions which mark off the great circle of the horizon follows a certain logic based on the upright structure of the human body. Our four-square frame reflects our sense of body and also our perception of the physical world. In other words, we naturally see space as divided into four parts: before, behind, left and right. As spatial and visual form this scheme is natural for understanding the earth and the passage of time. The four directions – north, east, south and west – parallel the four seasons – winter, spring, summer and autumn, respectively. As Pythagoras and other Greek philosophers maintained, numbers are symbols of order; and so the Wheel of the Year, with its four major divisions easily subdivided by four corresponding points, yields the order of the eight great earth and sky holidays of the Witches' year.

The Celts, however, perceived an even simpler pattern behind the Wheel of the Year: the two fundamental seasons of fire and ice, or summer and winter. In Celtic tradition the new year began on Samhain, 31 October, now called Halloween, which for them was the first day of winter. This day was a very powerful time in Celtic spirituality, for it belonged neither to the old year nor to the new one. It stood between the years. It was a time between time. Not only did it end the old year and begin the new, but it lifted the veil between the worlds. Witches still believe that the boundaries between spirit and matter are less fixed at this moment in time and life flows more easily between the two worlds. Spirits can visit our world of denser matter and we can make forages into their world to communicate with our ancestors and loved ones. The great exchange of energy, so important in keeping the worlds of spirit, nature and the human in balance, takes place at Samhain, as the old year flows into the new. Witches take advantage of this time to communicate with the other side, retrieve ancestral knowledge and prepare for the coming year.

Samhain

Samhain is the Celtic feast of the dead, honouring the Aryan Lord of Death, Samana (the Irish call it the Vigil of Saman). But it has developed into a festival celebrating the spirit world in general rather than any one god, as well as the ongoing co-operation between that world and our own of denser matter. Witches still leave offerings of 'soul cakes' for deceased ancestors, a custom that has been transformed into the giving of treats to the homeless and travellers who wander about on that night. In ancient times it was believed that if the right offerings and sacrifices were not made the spirits of the dead would take advantage of the opening in the seam between the worlds to come and do harm or mischief to the living. The night still retains that threatening

WITCHES' WHEEL OF THE YEAR

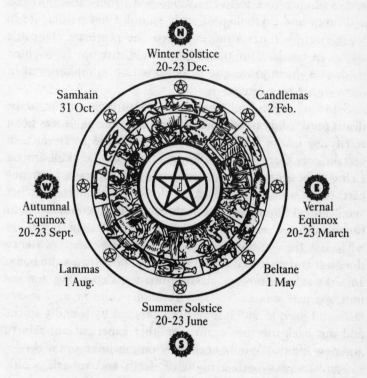

N
Winter Solstice
20-23 Dec.

Samhain
31 Oct.

Candlemas
2 Feb.

W
Autumnal
Equinox
20-23 Sept.

E
Vernal
Equinox
20-23 March

Lammas
1 Aug.

Beltane
1 May

Summer Solstice
20-23 June
S

Every ending is a beginning and for Witches this is Law.
Where they enter in, from there they must withdraw.

air, but most Witches see it not so much as the threat of
unhappy ancestors as the arrival of the powers of destruction:
hunger, cold, winter storms. In the Wheel of the Year,
Samhain marks the beginning of the season of death: winter.
The Goddess of Agriculture relinquishes her power over the
earth to the Horned God of the Hunt. The fertile fields of
summer give way to the bare forests.

To celebrate this magical eve fires were lit on the *sidh*, or fairy mounds, in which the spirits dwelled. Here resided the spirits of ancestors and vanquished gods from earlier periods of history and mythology. People who did not participate in these rites, but nevertheless feared the presence of hostile spirits in the land of the living, would attempt to frighten them away with grotesque faces carved on pumpkins and lit from within by a candle.

Some of these frightening jack-o'-lanterns appear to be death masks, but among the ancient Celts the skull was not a terrifying image but a revered power object. In fact in certain eras there was a widespread cult of the skull among Celtic tribes, and large collections of skulls have been unearthed in archaeological excavations. To modern Witches skulls and skeletons are not frightening but a reminder of our immortality (as well as our mortality) because the bones are what last the longest after death, suggesting that existence does not end once and for all when the spirit leaves the body. In shamanic cultures a classic initiation experience for the new shaman was to 'see' his skeleton while in a visionary state and even to watch it be dismembered by friendly spirits and put back together again – another experience of rebirth and new life that Witches celebrate on this holiest of nights.

Samhain was both a night of death and rebirth. Celtic tradition says that all those who die each year must wait till Samhain before crossing into the spirit world, or Summerland, where they will begin their new lives. At this moment of crossing the little people, the fairies, the spirits of ancestors who still have unfinished business in this world, may appear. Some will help the newly departed leave our world and enter the next; some may come to play and do mischief. Every human life and death is part of the great exchange between the worlds of nature and spirit.

Today many people bob for apples in a large cauldron or barrel, the apple being a symbol for the soul, the cauldron representing the great womb of life. The night is also a time for divination when the future can be more easily seen by those who know how to peer into the coming days. The new life of the coming year is more apparent on this special night. In Salem we not only divine the future, we project it by dressing up in costumes to reflect what we would like to become or experience in the new year. We also wear a lot of orange to symbolize the dying leaves and the dying fires of summer, as well as the traditional black to draw in and fill our bodies with light at this time of year when the days are growing shorter and there is physically less light and warmth.

Yule

The next Wiccan festival is *Yule*, celebrated around the winter solstice. The old pagan trappings of holly, ivy, pine boughs, lighted trees, warm beer and wine beverages (wassail), roasted pigs, enormous Yule logs, songs and gifts are still part of our celebrations. In the northern hemisphere this is the time when the sun reaches its most south-eastern position on its yearly journey. When ancient people noted this they knew that in a matter of weeks they would see it start to rise earlier and slightly further north until six months later it would be rising in its most north-easterly point. In spite of the fact that some of the coldest days and harshest weather still lay ahead, Yule was a time of merriment and gaiety.

Imbolc

On 1 February, Witches celebrate the feast of *Imbolc*, an archaic term for 'in milk'. This is the time when the ewes, if pregnant, began to lactate – an even firmer sign of the coming spring. Most agricultural peoples celebrate some similar sign that winter is almost over: the sap rising in the maple trees, the return of certain birds, the rising of a spring

113

constellation in the winter sky, even the groundhog looking for his shadow. The church honours St Brigid around this time, the Christianized version of the Celtic Goddess Brigid. According to Christian lore, St Brigid was the Virgin Mary's midwife, and of course midwives are a reminder of the new life growing within and waiting to be born.

During the winter, when Stone Age people stayed bundled up in their lodges or caves, they began to realize the need for purification in a more direct way than during the warmer months when life was lived outdoors, close to rain showers, rivers and lakes. Winter purification rites are still with us. Christians celebrate Candlemas on 2 February to remember the presentation of Jesus in the temple and the ritual purification of his mother (according to Jewish law women were considered unclean after birth!). Candles are also blessed at this time and used in throat spells in honour of St Blaize, who was thought to protect churchgoers from illness of the throat, a common ailment during February.

February is the heart of winter, when food supplies run low, hunters may prove unsuccessful, firewood may run out altogether. It is a time of great need for warmth, shelter, clothing and food. In some traditions celebrants spend one last night in feasting and merriment before the following period of fasting and purification. Mardi Gras, Carnival, the old Roman Lupercalia, the Feast of Fools all took place around this time. Witches bring together potluck dinners for their celebrations. We give food to the shelters and soup kitchens. We honour Brigid, not as the Virgin Mary's midwife, but as the Celtic Fire Goddess, who can keep the hearth fires burning during these dark, cold nights.

The Vernal Equinox

At the *vernal equinox* around 21 March (as at the autumnal equinox) Witches celebrate the great balance and harmony that exists in the passage of the seasons and the procession of night and day. This is the time of year when the nights and days are of equal length. The last signs of winter are giving way to spring. Ice melts, rivers run full, leaves begin to bud, grass turns green again, the lambs are born. At this time of year the old tribespeople of Europe honoured Ostera, or Esther, the Goddess of Spring, who holds an egg in her hand and watches a rabbit hop playfully around her bare feet. She stands on the green earth; she wears spring flowers in her hair. Witches empty eggs and paint them bright colours, making talismans for fruitfulness and success in the coming season of summer. We begin our gardens of flowers, vegetables and herbs that will play a part in our rituals, spells and potions.

Beltane

On the first of May the *Beltane* fires are lit and the great fertility ritual of the God and Goddess is celebrated with Maypoles, music and considerable frolicking in the greening countryside. May is a lusty month. The fifth month in the year expresses all the sexual and sensual meanings in the number five; the bodily juices are recharged; we feel our own sap rise; and our five senses are exceptionally keen and acute. Nature celebrates the great fecundity of the earth in rituals of sex, birth and new life. Men and women also share in the exuberance of nature as they yearn to unite and reproduce themselves. In old customs and rituals we re-enact symbolically the coupling of the Goddess and her young Horned God. And we fall in love.

At Beltane we wear green to honour the Celtic God Belenos. We become the 'green people', the little Pan folk with leafy masks, pointy ears, little horns representing the life force of nature, now more evident than ever in the greening countryside. We light fires (Beltane means the fire of Belenos) and leap over them to show our prowess and enthusiasm for the coming season. In agricultural societies May was the time to take the cattle to their summer grazing grounds, and they would be driven between two large bonfires to purify them of winter ailments and to exorcise any evil spirits of winter.

In ritual some of us will play the parts of the young king, the old king and the queen of the magic woods. Our pageants retell the tale of how at this time of year the young king of summer slays the old king of winter to win the hand of his young wife, the Queen of the May. She is the Earth Mother, still young and fresh, but soon to swell with life and bestow a bountiful crop on the land. In Germany, May eve is called *Walpurgisnacht*, the eve of St Walpurga, the Christianized version of the old Teutonic Earth Mother, Walburg.

The sexual forces of springtime abound everywhere, and as the folk songs say, 'we go a-Maying'. Symbolically we celebrate the forces of the season by erecting Maypoles, around which young men and women dance, entwining multicoloured ribbons, weaving themselves together as they wrap the pole in festive colours.

Midsummer Night

In June we celebrate *Midsummer Night*, the shortest night of the year, when Puck and Pan and all manner of fairies and elves are out and about. With such little time to sleep, we confuse dreams and waking reality. These days and nights of the summer solstice are filled with great power and magic. They are times to hold rituals that luxuriate in the season when life is easiest and there are so many hours of daylight that we can accomplish all our tasks with time left over to relax and have fun. It is a time to travel and hold great outdoor festivals, to sleep and cook and eat outdoors. We journey to visit one another and call all the 'tribes' of pagan folk to come and make merry together.

Lammas

As August approaches we see signs of the first harvest and

116

Witches celebrate these first fruits in the feast of *Lammas*. Our ritual circle is an expression of gratitude and thanks to the earth for its bounty, and we ask that all living creatures may share in it. This is the festival of bread and we always place fresh baked bread on our altars for Lammas. We honour the great grain Goddesses like Ceres and Demeter. We wear flowers in our hair, especially yellow flowers to symbolize the colour of the sun while it is at its strongest. In some traditions this is the feast of Lugnasadh, honouring the great Celtic warrior God, Luh. In his honour we play games and hold sporting events. We engage in athletic contests to celebrate the fullness of life and the strength and good health that people enjoy more at the height of summer than any other time of the year.

Autumnal Equinox

With only three more months left in the Celtic summer, pagan folk work hard for the harvest yet to come, whether it be corn and hay from the fields or the personal projects and goals that we planned for the summer months. When the sun crosses the equator and heads south at the *autumnal equinox*, we again celebrate the magnificent balance that the ever-turning Wheel of the Year promises. These equinoxes are great reminders that the bleak days of winter as well as the heady days of summer are temporary, that all things have their seasons, and that none will last forever. The law of polarity and rhythm requires that all things be balanced by their opposites. On these holy days our ancestors aligned themselves psychically and spiritually and balanced themselves in the ebb and flow of life.

As winter, spring, summer and autumn pass by, Witches still reconnect with the ever-moving flow of life; we make our plans and watch them unfold. If some do not come to fruition, we try again. We pass through times of joy and sorrow; little ones are born; the older ones die and pass into the next world. Every event in life is rich in purpose and meaning. Each day, night and season has its own special character. Rituals connect us to both the big and little dramas of the year and to the greater life cycle. We unite with the character and spirit of each passing season and do magic to transform our lives, giving them a depth and an expansiveness that without ritual and celebration we would never achieve. Even the most humble ritual reaps the moment of power and change, and the celebrant partakes in something greater than him or herself. Some would say that in these moments of ecstasy we actually stand outside ourselves, and the God and Goddess within us become brighter and more powerful, and we touch the All.

ALTARS

Every Witch has an altar on which are placed a pentacle, candles, sacred stones, a wand, an athame, incense and burner and other sacred and personal objects. I am often amused when I recall the many different altars I have built over the years. Some were ceremonial altars that were created for circles; others were permanent altars in my home. Every Witch has an altar somewhere in her house. There were times when I lived in small apartments and could not have a permanent altar so I used the kitchen table. Today I have a dresser with drawers and doors to keep wands, candles, parchment and other sacred objects in. In my bedroom I keep a kind of mini-altar on my dresser with a pink candle, a quartz crystal, incense, a wand and a bowl with a crystal garden. This mini-altar is set up to draw in love power and increase self-esteem. Many Witches use a dresser, bureau or a chest of drawers for their main altar, and the mirror over it becomes the Witch's magic mirror. Although the ideal is to have a special altar, sometimes in a room set aside just for ritual, most Witches do not have the space. But any place you designate and charge to be your sacred space will become so.

Incense is a powerful tool of magic for a Witch's sacred place because fragrance is one of the quickest ways to alter consciousness and enter a sacred mode of awareness. Most spiritual and religious groups use some form of it in their own ceremonies. The moment we smell herbal incense, such as frankincense or myrrh, something shifts in our attention and the distractions of the day begin to disappear and we can focus on the sacred work at hand. A sweet fragrance fills the room, purifies the air, creates sacred space. In time you will associate the scent with ritual, just as you may have associated it in the past with a church or temple.

Candles are also important items on the altar. A candle contains all the elements: earth, air, fire, moisture. It is a simple yet powerful tool. Like incense, a burning candle alters the mood of a room. Some traditions say that a candle attracts good spirits.

Candle magic allows us to begin a spell and leave a living, physical presence of it on the altar while we go about our business. The flame is alive, burning through the day and night, sending our intentions out as light that touches other light on all levels and travels to any designated spot or person. Catholics and Anglicans adopted this practice in their churches, and a candle is still a customary way for them to project their intentions long after they have prayed. A candle continues our vigil for us. We choose the colours of our candles according to a table of correspondences to bring in the correct planetary influences. We 'dress' the candle by inscribing talismans, runes or symbols into the wax with a knife, and then we anoint the candle with an appropriate oil. Then we charge it with our intentions.

You can have as many candles on your altar as you wish to

keep your magic working while you are off doing other things. As you pass your altar during the day the candle glow will draw your consciousness back to the purpose of your spell, and the light from the candle will act like a laser to concentrate the energy of your intentions. When charged properly a candle has its own energy to work magic.

On every Witch's altar is an athame, a double-bladed knife with a black handle that is used like a wand. Its point functions much like the top of a pyramid; energy concentrates at the blade tip and runs down both edges to the hand and arm of the person using it. Similarly, it can direct energy out of the body into the atmosphere. Some Witches will not use their athames for anything but ritual work (casting circles, charging the spring water in a chalice, cutting herbs, inscribing candles); other Witches use the athame for 'kitchen' work and, in fact, may use a double-edged kitchen knife as their athame.

The tradition of using household utensils for ritual tools goes back to the Burning Times, when Witches could be persecuted for having magical tools around the house. It was then necessary to conceal our tools by hiding them among household objects or simply using household objects. A broom stick, therefore, served as a wand. One of my Witch friends who lives with her Christian family uses a wooden spoon from her kitchen as a wand. One of my students who is a construction worker carries a special screwdriver with him that he has charged to be his wand.

Wands can be any size from short, pencil-thin wands to great staffs five or six feet long. Usually wands are made of either wood or metal; both are good conductors of energy. Each wood and metal has its own special properties, so you should read up on them before selecting the kind of wand you want to use. I have several wands made out of different materials. A wand extends your arm so that energy can be directed well beyond yourself. A wand acts like a laser in that

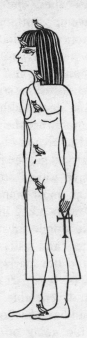

Chakra Points

it concentrates energy and directs it to a specific place. A six-foot staff will direct energy well over the heads of the coveners standing in a circle so that the magic circle is drawn outside the ring of bodies. Some Witches like their staffs to be exactly their own height, and they then inscribe symbols or insert magical stones at each of the chakra points (power spots – see illustration) that align with the chakras of their own bodies.

There is an ongoing debate in the Craft as to which is better, a wand that you find or make yourself or one that you buy in a shop. A friend of mine was going to a local shopping arcade to buy a wand, and after checking all the antique shops and gift boutiques where she thought she might be likely to find one, she gave up. Nothing suited her. When she got back to her car she noticed the door was ajar and remembered that when she had stepped out in a hurry and slammed the door behind her it sounded as if it had not closed tightly. Protruding from the car door was a stick the perfect size and length for her wand. She decided that her 'shopping trip' had been successful. It's just that the wand that came to her was not to be found in the arcade but in the car park. The Goddess will see to it that you get the right wand!

You can buy expensive wands studded with gems and crystals in a Witch shop; most wands are much cheaper. There is nothing wrong in spending money on magical tools. Artists in the Craft make wonderful items and buying them helps support our brothers and sisters. Many Witches hunt through antique shops and flea markets for wands, athames, chalices or incense burners. It is part of our Craft, I believe, to recycle what is old and venerable. The sacred objects of yesteryear are good reminders of who we are and where we come from. It can be fun going on a tool quest. Witches follow their instincts in finding magical tools, hunting down alleys and byways that feel right to them. Witches are connected to the universe in a special way, and the All knows what we need. So we tend to let the tools come to us, in car parks as well as in the woods or in second-hand stores.

CRYSTALS, STONES AND METALS

I am amazed as I glance through my Book of Shadows to see how some Craft traditions and practices have become popular in the last twenty years in the culture at large due to a renewed interest in metaphysics and more ancient forms of spirituality. People used to come into my home in years past and remark that I must really like to collect rocks and crystals. They were usually puzzled by this. Movers once asked me if I had packed rocks in some of the boxes they were loading on the van. I replied that I had, and they shook their heads in disbelief. Today I think fewer movers would shake their heads. Now the same stones and gems that have lain on my altar have become the subjects of popular books, and many people are collecting them. It's gratifying to see this, and to realize that more people recognize that crystals are not just jewellery but conductors of energy, which was their traditional rôle in tribal cultures.

Crystals have been important power objects in every part of the world in which they are found. The crystal is probably the 'white stone' the Druids used in Western Europe. In California quartz crystals have been found in archaeological sites that are thought to be prehistoric burial grounds dating back eight thousand years. Quartz crystals have a long history of being used by shamans and seers to enhance their ability to see spirits, divine the future, look into the past and make contact with the other worlds. A classic Witch experience is to have a high priestess psychically insert crystals into her body for power and protection. In our magic circles, we psychically project crystals to enhance our power. In modern times we've discovered that because crystals contain electrical voltage, they are highly valuable in radio, electronics and computers. You can experience their power for yourself by taking two crystals into a dark room and stressing them by tapping or striking them together with some force. If they connect in the right way, sparks will leap out from them.

Crystals contain the electrical energy that can be tapped into for communication (remember the old crystal wireless sets?), healing, expressing love and preparing us for success in work or life. Many Witches put a crystal into their wands, which enhances the wand's ability to concentrate and direct energy. We also use them in potions and wear them on cords around our necks so they lie about the heart chakra. Crystals make good gifts when selected for a specific person.

Many entries in my Book of Shadows involve experiments that I and other Witches have done with crystals. We have planted them in our gardens in spring and watched unusually healthy and hearty vegetables grow. We've placed them in the four corners of our homes for protection. We've laid them over ill or ailing parts of the body and watched rapid recoveries.

Many Witches wear crystals as jewellery, along with other gemstones that have magical powers. Jewellery is a way to have magic on your body without anyone knowing it but you and others who are wise in the ways of the Craft. In general, Witch jewellery is worn because it directs energies to various parts of the body. Different stones and metals have the ability to heal and relieve pain. Copper, for example, relieves arthritis pain when its healing properties come into contact with the afflicted areas. Copper is ruled by Venus and is used for self-love, which helps us in healing ourselves. Gemstones have always been worn on parts of the body from ancient times. Today people still wear them but without fully comprehending their special properties. A good book on gems and stones will help you make more informed selections for necklaces, earrings, bracelets, rings, pins and belt buckles.

Even without conscious knowledge of stones, each of us is still attracted to certain gems, often because of their colour or shape or texture. When we are asked why we favour such and such a stone, we usually just laugh and say something like 'I've always liked it'. On a deeper level we are attracted to certain stones because we unconsciously know that they meet some personal physical or spiritual need. The custom of carrying 'lucky' charms goes back to this profound truth that the spirit or power in stones can protect, heal or simply make us feel better.

STONE CIRCLES AND OTHER SACRED SITES

Special stones and special arrangements of stones have always held a particular fascination for Witches and magic workers. In olden days Witches designated altars outdoors by a ring of stones around a mound of earth, located on a ley line if possible. Spirit mounds and fairy rings still dot the country-side in Britain and other countries, and even America has some places that have not been too disturbed since pioneer days, when the early settlers, bringing with them old Craft ways, built special mounds or altars. Already here, of course, were the medicine wheels and sacred mounds built by the indigenous peoples from whom the American Indian tribes descended. There has been a recent trend among Native Americans to build new medicine wheels for ritual and earth ceremonies, and non-native Americans have also picked up the practice in a joint effort to reconsecrate ourselves and the earth. Witches also make stone circles or plant crystals in a ring in a wooded area or a garden. On my altar I have many stones from various sacred sites around the world and from special places I have visited.

The whole earth is sacred and has power, but certain places have been recognized from the earliest times as power spots, places of unusual concentrations of energy. Along ley lines and fault lines energy concentrates, and modern science has measured the concentration in the electromagnetic fields around them. Witches make pilgrimages to these sacred sites to do rituals in order to lift the veil between the worlds (often the veil of our own human blindness) and tap into the sacred energy present there. Fields of intense magnetic energy, fault lines and volcanoes – places where the earth is mysteriously active and dangerous – have always attracted humans, whether they were aware of the deities present or not. They are often places of incredible beauty, like Delphi in Greece or Mount Shasta in California or the Black Hills in South Dakota. Today great cities like San Francisco and New York are built on fault lines, and great concentrations of human energy also collect there. Sacred spots and places of great natural power and beauty act like magnets on human sensibilities, stimulating high creativity and spiritual insight.

There is scientific evidence that sacred sites have power on a psychophysical level. Recent investigations have shown that traditional sacred springs and healing waters in the American South-west, for example, contain lithium, a psychopharmaceutical substance that stabilizes moods. Some sacred sites contain rocks with high loads of uranium ore, which stimulates the production of negative ions in the air, giving a person a sense of well-being. Scientists are also finding that when people immerse themselves in strong electromagnetic fields they begin to harmonize with them. Fields that have the same electromagnetic frequencies as the alpha brain waves, associated with creativity and relaxation, have a direct physical effect on our psychic state of being. In some places high concentrations of electromagnetic energy produce halos around mountain peaks, and when you walk through them your hair literally stands on end. You feel charged with energy. Because these places are so empowered with Goddess energy, Witches visit them for inspiration and to connect with our ancestors who worked magic there.

HERBAL MAGIC

Herbs and plants are the basis for most of our medicines today and they have always played an important role in natural healing in every culture. Regrettably, human civilization is destroying the earth's rainforests and woodlands at an alarming rate before the vast majority of medicinal herbs, roots, barks and flowers are even discovered and catalogued, much less before we can discover for which ailments and diseases they might provide a cure. Will our treatment of cancer, AIDS, Alzheimer's disease and other serious illnesses be indefinitely postponed because we are pillaging, burning and looting the cures before they are even found? Not to mention the dire effects our rape of the forests has on the health of the biosphere!

Although the medicinal and nutritional value of herbs has been much discussed in recent years, a Witch's knowledge takes in another very important aspect of herbalism – the psychic power of herbalists to tap into the herb's unseen energy. Every plant has an aura, the invisible charge of energy that exists around all things. It is the refracted and reflected light from electrical impulses, heat and vapour of the object. In other words, it is simply light dancing around, inside and off all things. Each herb has an aura, or energy packet, that can affect people, places and things in various and subtle ways. Ancient wisdom has always seen correlations between astrology and herbs, the planetary influence manifesting as colour and light that interacts with the plant's aura. We say that the herb is 'ruled' by a particular planet because the light that is reflected and refracted from that planet (or planets) is contained in that herb. (See pages 291–292.)

Consider burdock root and saffron. Burdock root is ruled by Saturn, Uranus and Venus. Under the influence of Saturn it can be used for discipline. Under the influence of Uranus it can be used to communicate or publicize something or promote someone. Under Venus's influence burdock root governs sexual love, friendship, money, growth, planting, fertility, and is auspicious for beginning new projects. Saffron, which is ruled by Jupiter, helps attain goals, achieve success, store energy, influence people in high places, and develop our spiritual natures.

Basil, ruled by Venus and Neptune, and found in almost every kitchen, is one of the oldest known herbs used in love potions. Its pleasant aroma and taste is popular in sauces and enhances the flavour of many foods. But the real secret of basil lies in the energy level contained in its aura, which produces a warm, loving sensation in the human body.

In Chapter Seven you will learn more about herbs, how to charge them and use them in potions and spells.

DIVINATION

In my early days of reading Tarot cards I recorded the sessions with clients in my Book of Shadows, noting which readings went smoothly, which were difficult, how they succeeded or failed. I was still learning the art of Tarot reading and how to deal with men and women who came to me with questions about their personal lives. It was a humbling experience to serve others as a channel of information about some of the most important issues in their lives. Slowly I gained confidence in my ability to read for others and learned how to present to them what I saw in the cards without alarming them about the negative aspects or getting them too excited about the positive. We must alert the client to potential harm without projecting the information so that it comes true. Every Witch has a moral obligation to speak the truth and yet protect her clients from undue worry.

When I think of the thousands of people who have come for readings, I am always humbled by the rôle a Witch can play in the lives of so many people. And I am keenly aware that I am just the current link in a chain of Witches that goes back through history to the Ice Age and even further. People have always sought out the 'wise' woman or man in the tribe or village when they were in trouble, when they needed knowledge, when they were filled with fear or doubt. We cast runes or dried stalks, read the omens in the patterns of clouds, heard answers to the questions in the rustle of wind in the trees or the sound of water falling over stones. With the ability to shift consciousness, Witches and seers have unlocked the mysteries of life for many people.

Today the favourite tool for divination is the Tarot deck, which I think of as a computer key to the psychic mind. Although there are many kinds of decks, dating back hundreds of years, they each contain the archetypal images and patterns that speak from the collective unconscious. In spite of regional and cultural differences – and the unique style that each artist brings to the deck that he or she is designing – the Tarot is a collective tool. The meaning or significance of each card has built up over the centuries as it has acquired the collective wisdom of our culture in its many images, colours and shapes. Today each card is an energy packet capable of tapping psychic realms of meaning that lie buried in the unconscious, where past, present and future all meet. Each card creates energy for the client and the reader. Some metaphysical teachers maintain that the Tarot deck contains universal knowledge and is *the* book of life, the only book one needs to solve all the mysteries and divine all the questions about the universe.

Another word for divination is *scrying*. In Celtic traditions it was called 'the sight'. One does not need a deck of cards or a bag of runes to scry. Anything will do, feathers, the flight of birds, a stone, the clouds, ripples in a pool of water, tea leaves in the bottom of a cup, lines in the palm of the hand, the refraction of light in a crystal ball, the flicker of flames, the drift of smoke. Some people are born with the sight; others must develop it, sometimes over many years, by practising the science of Witchcraft.

The technique for scrying is very simple, but not always easy to perfect. While in a slightly altered state of consciousness, the scryer watches for a sign or movement in the stone or water or flames that are being used. Eventually some movement occurs; the scrying object responds with an omen or sign. Beginners may not immediately understand the significance of the sign; it might be a symbol that will require study. There are many fine books on symbols and their universal meanings that are helpful for a beginner. In time, of course, each person learns what the universal symbols mean to him or her and how to interpret them for each client or question. As we record the symbols and meditate on them in a Book of Shadows, their meanings become clearer.

I have begun reading the objects that clients select from a large basket of amulets, containing antique keys, shells, crystals, foreign coins, ceramic scarabs, a green malachite egg, a moonstone, raw copper, a chain carved out of stone and other objects. Each person chooses the objects that tap something important in their unconscious or that seem 'right' for the moment. By scrying with them and looking at the combination of objects while in a magical state of consciousness, I achieve very good readings of the important issues and questions on the individual's mind.

Why do Witches make good readers? Anyone can 'read' cards, but Witches have acquired a much-deserved reputation for it for several reasons. Historically, when the church forbade Christians to do divination work (because it threatened the authority of the clergy), only Witches and Gypsies continued to practise the art of divination. As outsiders to the general culture, their consciousness was not as conditioned by mainstream thought. Their thoughts transcended the commonplace. Often it takes a slightly detached perspective to see the deeper significance in the events of a person's life as they appear in the cards or runes or tea leaves.

Another reason is that Witches are well trained in using symbols – in spells, rituals, magical tools and spiritual practices. The basic talent required in reading cards or runes or the I Ching is a working knowledge of symbols. We believe that all knowledge is attainable because it manifests by means of symbols and metaphors that act as a kind of key to the vast realms of information and wisdom stored in the unconscious. There are many keys, and a Tarot deck is one of them.

Witches are also adept at handling the flow of events through time. We know from our experiences in visionary states that past and future do not exist except in the present. (I will discuss the scientific reason for this in the next chapter.) Only the present has power for us. Reading Tarot cards is a away of concentrating the past and the future into a present moment and space where the clients' questions find their answers. When a client comes with questions about the past or future, we deal or spread the cards, confident that we can see the information the client seeks. We also know that the client already knows the answers, too, and that we are merely the catalysts that will help the client draw that knowledge out of his or her deeper mind, where it lies waiting to be consciously known.

Tools, magic circles, bags of herbs, spells written on parchment, a candle burning silently on my altar – the Craft of the Wise is a constantly changing kaleidoscope of magic and power. And yet, underneath all the accoutrements the Craft is always about real people living their lives, sometimes easily and successfully, sometimes with effort and struggle. The advantage of the Craft, as I am always reminded by reading through my Book of Shadows, is that I am never alone. I am surrounded by tools of magic, symbols and talismans of the Goddess and God, the love and concern of my sisters and brothers in the Craft. We are all doing the Great Work, each in our own way. In the next chapter I will show you how and why our craft really works.

· 5 ·

THE SCIENCE OF
WITCHCRAFT

In the mid-1970s *National Geographic* sent one of their top photographers, Nathan Ben, to shoot a story about summer on the New England coast. He stopped in Salem. It was June, the time of the summer solstice. Nathan asked if we would allow him to photograph our coven's solstice ritual, something we had never allowed before. We told him he could provided he kept the camera outside the circle and shot only from the perimeter. He agreed, and so it proceeded. At the conclusion he asked us to step back for a group portrait. So we opened the circle and he stepped into the area that we had charged with energy from the sun and the planet Jupiter.

The developed photographs revealed a startling phenomenon. Each of the thirty-six frames shot during the ritual showed areas of blue light, increasing in scope and intensity with each frame. On the final group shot the blue light branched into twelve radiant streams, each leading up to a member of the coven. Over the next two months the Kodak Institute sent investigators to ask me if I could explain what we had been doing. I could because Witchcraft is a science based on cause and effect. Unfortunately, as modern researchers programmed not to believe in magic as part of life, they failed to recognize the controlled process of our ritual and hence failed to understand it. What they heard was hocus-pocus. And, of course they scoffed at my explanation.

What I told them was this. At that solstice the sun had been aligned with the planet Jupiter, and we had gone into an alpha state to cast a spell that in the coming year more people would understand the true nature of Witchcraft as a science that can be put to use to heal the planet. We were hoping that the Jupiter energy, which rules people in high places, would influence men and women who have the capacity to make significant reforms. We held hands in a circle, transferring Jupiter's blue light into our bodies so that we, too, would have more influence. As a kind of answer to our spell, Jupiter's blue light appeared in the room and was caught on the photograph. That is what happened and what I told the Kodak people. In our terms it was simple cause and effect. They were confused by their preconceived notions of what is real and what is fantasy. Weeks later, however, they returned and asked me to explain it again.

Eventually Nathan dropped by to show me the photographs himself and to say that the film had undergone every conceivable test to determine if the blue light had been static electricity. It was not. For it to be some form of electrical interference, climatic conditions would have to have been dry and cold, much like Antarctica – not the muggy, humid summer day in Salem. After intensive examinations the experts concluded that the blue light was actually in the room. The running joke at the Kodak Institute was, 'Well, what are those Witches hiding under their robes?'

Most people are very resistant to accepting magic because they have been conditioned from childhood by a rational, left-brain worldview in which the old ways of magic make no sense. At *National Geographic*'s editorial offices a dispute erupted over whether to print the photograph with the royal-blue light. One faction of editors argued against it on the grounds that the prestigious magazine should not validate what they called 'black magic' and 'satanic ritual'. A second group carried the day, arguing that the photograph made history and should be included, but to appease the sceptics the text for the photograph included the usual media disclaimer: 'The Witches *claim* that the light is in the room.'

Since then scientists have 'discovered' that Jupiter emits its own light. In time they will discover that it is blue.

LIGHT

I failed to convince the investigators from the Kodak Institute – ironically an industry based on the principles of light energy! – that my coven works with the same principles. In fact much of what I said to them has been thoroughly discussed by physicists and science writers in such books as *The Tao of Physics* by Fritjof Capra and *The Looking Glass Universe* and *Synchronicity: The Bridge between Matter and Mind*, both by F. David Peat. These are just three of the many excellent books dealing with the exciting new discoveries in subatomic physics and written for the average lay reader. One of the most valuable books on the subject, which I list as required reading for all my students, is *Stalking the Wild Pendulum* by Itzhak Bentov.

In all of these works, the physical universe as described by contemporary physicists and the spiritual universe as described by mystics and sages in every century are shown to be remarkably similar. In short, what we are discovering is that the physical universe and spiritual universe operate on parallel principles that, in the final analysis, may be identical. As F. David Peat explains, the latest scientific discoveries suggest that matter is not mere matter. He writes, 'Rather than nature being *reduced* to the material, the whole notion of the material has been extended into regions of indefinite intangibility' (Peat's emphasis). In other words, there are intangible qualities, such as pattern and meaning, behind what appears to be solid matter. And underlying both the material realms and mental realms are patterns of information. The conclusion to this amazing discovery is that there is a vital unity in the universe. Peat says, '. . . there unfold harmonies that spread out across the mental and material realms in the form of meaningful patterns and conjunctions that act as intimations of the essential unity of all nature.'

The question, then, is how to access and work with these patterns of information. And the answer is by means of light. The discovery that on the subatomic level all material things are composed of energy and radiation reinforces what Witches have always known about physical things – namely, they radiate energy. They emit auras. Herbs, stones, cloth, water, animals, the entire earth, moon and galaxy radiate energy. Everything emits, refracts and reflects light. By 'light' we don't mean just that spectrum of light visible to the human eye but X-rays, ultra-violet, infra-red and radar, the same electromagnetic energy found in television and radio waves. The point is that light energy is everywhere, and science is discovering that everything that exists is composed of light. Outside of light nothing exists.

Another mind-spinning discovery by twentieth-century physicists is that the universe is a shapeshifter. According to quantum theory, subatomic energy exhibits the characteristics of both waves and particles *but not at the same time*. Although the two manifestations of energy seem to be contradictory, they are not. They simply indicate the shapeshifting nature of reality. As Fritjof Capra says, these 'concepts of quantum theory were not easy to accept even after their mathematical formulation had been completed. Their effect on the physicists' imagination was truly shattering.' I imagine it was! The results of their studies required a radically new definition of the universe. Einstein himself was stunned by the implications. He confessed, 'It was as if the ground had been pulled out from under me, with no firm foundation to be seen anywhere, upon which one could have built.' The bottom line is that solid matter does not exist as it appears to us. The particles of which objects are made do not behave like the solid objects of classical physics, like a chair or table, for instance. Subatomic particles are abstract entities, and the way they appear and behave depends on how we look at them. Sometimes they act like particles, and sometimes like waves. The determining factor is *how our consciousness perceives them*. And this dual nature is also exhibited by light and all other forms of electromagnetic radiation.

An even more recent revelation is the quantum field theory, which completely replaces the traditional notion that solid particles and the space surrounding them are separate and distinct. The quantum field, according to Capra, is 'the fundamental physical entity: a continuous medium which is present everywhere in space'. Solid objects, then, are only temporary condensations of energy that come and go in that field. This is very similar to what the oriental sages say about 'form' and 'emptiness' being the same thing. What looks like an empty void can produce an object that is made up of the very stuff of the void in which it appears. And consciousness is such an integral part of this process that some physicists, like Geoffrey Chew and Eugene Wigner, wonder if consciousness might not be essential for the 'self-consistency of the whole'. In other words, intelligence becomes not just a human trait but an essential aspect of the entire universe.

At last physicists support and confirm an understanding of the universe that Witches have always had, and in so doing they make it immensely easier for us to explain our magic. As Peat puts it, 'The universe springs from a creative source . . . out of which the orders of consciousness and the material world unfold. The heart of this movement and hierarchy of

136

levels is meaning' or knowledge. Consciousness in all its forms – human, animal, plant, spirit – lies at the heart of the universe. Consciousness lies at the heart of magic and is the reason that the power of magic really works. In other words, a Witch's consciousness can effect changes in the physical world (or mental and emotional worlds) because, based on what we know from subatomic experiments, *what* we see and *how* what we see behaves depends upon our participation, our effort, our involvement. Formerly it was assumed that scientists were merely observers of the universe who watched and reported what they saw. The new physics disproves that. Scientists are active participants even when they think they are just observing. As physicist John Wheeler says, 'The old word *observer* simply has to be crossed off the books, and we must put in the new word *participator*. In this way we've come to realize that the universe is a participatory universe.'

The human mind is truly powerful because it is a participator, not a mere observer and recorder. The new physics has disproved Descartes' notion that has dominated scientific thinking since the seventeenth century – that mind and matter are two separate and distinct realms. They are not. As Capra says, the universe is 'a dynamic inseparable whole which always includes the observer in an essential way'. There is no discontinuity between mind and matter, and no discontinuity between humans and nature. For these reasons the Witches' belief that thought can be projected out into the universe and impact on external reality makes perfect sense. Thought projections can become external realities because there is no separation of mental reality and external reality.

Our minds can draw in information from anywhere in the universe because all things emit light. Even black holes appear to emit particles of light, according to Cambridge physicist Stephen Hawking. Although nothing can escape what is called the 'event horizon' of a black hole, Hawking claims that there is light at the core of this seemingly utter darkness. And so as all things display their patterns of information and meaning as they radiate energy and give off light, we 'observe' and we 'participate', and as we participate we share the energy, the knowledge, the meaning inherent in every created thing. All things are interconnected, just as the sages and mystics in every religious tradition have been saying for thousands of years. By our active involvement in nature we determine what nature is; we take physical things and turn them into energy; we take energy and shape it into material things. In other words, we do magic.

THE LAWS OF WITCHCRAFT

Not everyone has caught up with the new physics, and this includes many scientists. (Peat laments, 'Paradoxically, scientists have not yet caught up with the deeper implications of their own subject.') Many people still think that science and magic are opposed to each other, science being hard, practical, real, and magic being soft, fanciful and imaginary. Yet nothing could be further from the truth. To the wise, to Witches versed and trained in the old ways of our ancestors, magic and science are equal threads of power, woven through the same fabric of life. It has always been so. Magic and the natural sciences are allies, and together make up the science of Witchcraft.

The new Science Tradition that I founded and have been teaching in Salem for twenty years draws on both ancient wisdom and the latest developments in theoretical physics. It blends the new science with the old laws of magic, now largely forgotten and certainly not taught in twentieth-century educational programmes with their bias against what is old and sacred. Using science as an approach to Witchcraft gives my students a solid grounding upon which to stand. Some teachers in the Craft present our practices and beliefs in terms of art or religion or psychology or mythology, and these have their merits, but at some point the student wants to know 'how magic works'. Science is our country, it is where we feel at home. In spite of the dazzling, almost unbelievable discoveries on the subatomic level, science describes a world that makes sense.

The Science Tradition is based on the Hermetic principles that parallel the principles of the new physics. They have their origins in the teachings of Hermes, known to the Egyptians at Thoth, and to the Romans as Mercury. Neoplatonic philosophers referred to Hermes as the 'Logos' or Word-of-God-Made-Flesh, and Christians applied images long associated with Hermes to Jesus. Actually Hermes seems to have been a universal Indo-European god who taught astrology, alchemy and the many magical practices that are at the heart of Witchcraft. He seems to have taught the universal truths everywhere, for he even pops up among Native Americans as the trickster gods Raven, Coyote and Hare. From the intellectual seeds that he sowed in human consciousness so many centuries ago have grown the modern sciences of astrology, chemistry and physics.

Pythagoras was versed in Hermetic principles, as were the Druids. The Romans thought that the Druids had received their instruction in the Hermetic Laws from Pythagoras, but it was probably just the opposite. More recent evidence indicates that Pythagoras had been instructed by the Druid priestesses of Thrace. In the Middle Ages the God appeared as Hermes Trismegistus, the Triple Wise One, and it is through this incarnation that we derive the Seven Hermetic Laws.

It is not surprising to me that modern physicists are verifying the old Hermetic principles because all Witches know that the relationships of earth, mind and spirit, as taught by Hermes, are grounded in scientific fact. Scientists, who don't incorporate their psychic abilities into their work along with their rational skills, have had to plod along for centuries to rediscover in their own terms the laws of the universe that Witches know intuitively or have been taught by elders in the Craft.

When I speak of Witchcraft as a science I use the word *science* in its strictest form. Witchcraft is a system based on hypotheses that can be tested under controlled conditions. Magical spells are step-by-step experiments that produce statistical results from which we can derive our success rates. The physical sciences maintain that a 32 per cent success rate establishes the validity of a hypothesis. When I teach the science of Witchcraft based on the Hermetic Laws, my students' experiments show a 50 per cent and often a 75 to 90 per cent success rate. In other words, we can verify how often and under what conditions psychic diagnosis can be performed, how often a love potion works, what effect a wand or crystal has on the outcome of a spell or ritual. We take into account the physical ingredients used, the date and time, weather conditions, astrological considerations and the psychological state, or mood, of the person casting the spell because the experimenter is part of the experiment and, as the new physicists attest, affects the outcome of the experiment.

The seven Hermetic Laws are the basis of Witchcraft. Like the laws of physical science, the Hermetic Laws form a system that can be studied by anyone who is willing to put in the effort and take the time to practise.

The Law of Mentalism: The first Hermetic principle is that of mentalism, which states that the universe is mental, or Mind. As explained in *The Kybalion* (a clear and concise treatment of the Hermetic Laws written by three anonymous Hermetic philosophers), mentalism means that 'all the phenomenal world or universe is simply a Mental Creation of THE ALL . . . and that the universe . . . has its existence in the Mind of THE ALL.' Another way to put this is that everything exists in the mind of the God or Goddess who 'thinks' us into existence. All creation is composed of the Divine Mind, for creation first began as an idea in the Divine Mind, and it continues to live and move and have its being in the Divine Consciousness. F. David Peat tells us that scientific discoveries now suggest something very similar, that 'behind the phenomena of the material world lies a generative and formative order called the objective intelligence'. In *Stalking the Wild Pendulum*, Bentov says, 'The universe and all matter is consciousness in process of evolving.' Witches would say that this objective intelligence, this evolving consciousness, is the Mind of the Goddess.

Subatomic physicists have discovered in their laboratories that the basic 'stuff' of the universe – matter and energy – is really information. It is what Peat calls 'active information', or information encoded in the DNA structures that form and shape all created life. And so we find laws, principles and information encoded in every crystal, plant, rock, drop of water or flicker of candlelight.

All knowledge exists in the Divine Mind, which constantly flows in and out of our own minds because our individual minds are not separate from the Great Mind that created us. Of course we are not aware of 'all knowledge' at any given moment because it would be too much for us to handle. We would go berserk. The five senses and the human brain act as much as filters as they do as sources of information. They block out a great deal of daily stimulation to prevent us from being overwhelmed by all the knowledge that bombards us minute by minute. Without filtering out many of the sights, sounds, smells, even ideas, we would not be able to concentrate on the specific tasks at hand. But under the right conditions we can slow that filter process down or even turn it off, and in those moments of altered consciousness (explored in Chapter Six), universal knowledge becomes available. We open up to the Mind of the All. We let knowledge in. We let light in. We are enlightened.

The Law of Correspondence: The second Hermetic principle is the law of correspondence. 'As above, so below; as below, so above.' This is one of the most important principles of Witchcraft because it reminds us that we live in more than one world. We live in the space–time co-ordinates that we perceive in the gross physical plane, but we also live in a spaceless–timeless realm independent of the physical universe. Both mystics and physicists know this. Our earth-bound perspective often keeps us from realizing the other realms above and below us. Our attention is usually so focused on the microcosm that we are unaware of the immense macrocosm around us. The principle of correspondence tells us that what is true on the macrocosm is also true on the microcosm and vice versa. Therefore we can extrapolate knowledge and wisdom from the known to the unknown. We can learn the great truths of the cosmos by observing how they manifest in our own lives. Similarly, we can learn about ourselves by studying the whirling worlds on any other level, be it the subatomic level of matter and energy or the spirit level of angels and divine epiphanies. Whether we look up into the vast reaches of outer space or down into the vast inner spaces between subatomic particles, we discover the same basic truths and principles.

Physicists are discovering the law of correspondence in the holographic nature of the universe. A hologram is a photo created by the light of two laser beams: one bathing the object to be photographed, the second bounced off the light of the first. The interference of these two beams is captured on film. When the developed film is illuminated by a third laser beam, the original object appears in three dimensions. In other words, a hologram is created by the swirling interplay of lasered light. The remarkable feature of a hologram is that if it is broken into any number of pieces, no matter how small, the original picture is not shattered but *duplicated* into as many pieces as there are. Each hologram is smaller than the original, but it has not lost any details. Each part contains a complete but smaller whole.

The new definitions of space and time derived by modern physics indicate that every particle of matter contains all others. As astounding as this may sound, it merely confirms the law of correspondence: in every particle (every microcosm) is the rest of the universe (the macrocosm). Thinking about holograms has led physicist David Bohm to suggest that at some deep level of reality, particles do not exist as separate entities but are merely extensions of the fundamental substance of the universe, which is holographic and indivisible. Mystics and some poets have intuited this long before modern physics. William Blake wrote:

> *To see a world in a grain of sand*
> *And a heaven in a wild flower,*
> *Hold infinity in the palm of your hand,*
> *And eternity in an hour.*

Holograms may eventually help us understand ghostly apparitions. A ghost may simply be a hologram – an image trapped in a particular place, like a mirage, without the physical substances that make it up. Once I was travelling in Death Valley and saw an old train go hurtling across the desert, coughing up big billows of black smoke. It was one of those old 'iron maidens' that haven't been used for generations. What was more remarkable was that there was no set of tracks there. It was a ghost train. I know I wasn't hallucinating in the hot desert because the fifteen people I was with also saw the train. Somehow the image of a real train from years ago got caught in that particular time and place and became visible to us on that particular day. 'As then, so now' is another application of the law of correspondence.

Historical events can imprint themselves in the quantum fields in which they take place. A particular time, space and event can get 'caught' or 'photographed', as it were, in the universal energy fields. Later the image of that event in that time and place can reappear when the same configuration of light energy recurs in the spot where it was first imprinted. General George S. Patton, for example, could see and hear battles fought centuries ago when he walked across old battlefields. It's possible that manifestations may not be bound to their original spot. If the universe is as fluid and interdependent as modern science suggests and operates in a holographic manner, any event could reappear in any place where the original light energy was reactivated, or 'conjured up' to use a magical phrase. With practice the trained mind can do precisely that, usually using a tool such as a crystal ball or Witch's mirror to focus the seer's attention and concentrate the energy. By gazing into a crystal or mirror (or any other medium that reflects and refracts light) we can capture images of events transpiring in other parts of the world and in other warps of time.

The law of correspondence also directs Witches towards the most appropriate tools and ingredients for 'seeing' and for casting spells. While energy and information are reproduced on all planes and levels of existence, and all infinity is contained in every flower, as Blake would say, specific information and specific power tends to concentrate in those places for which they have a natural rapport. In other words certain herbs, gems, places, activities and tools activate the specific light energy with which they are naturally associated. In herbal lore, for example, certain plants and herbs contain specific ingredients or qualities that correspond to specific purposes. Colour is one of those correspondences. Yellow flowering herbs are ruled by the sun, and its energy heals ailments that require sunlight. Purple and lavender are ruled by Uranus, rose and pink by Venus, red by Mars, and so forth. The powers associated with those planets can be activated by using the appropriate colour. Witches use a table of correspondences to find the correct components (colours, herbs, gems and other ingredients) for spells and rituals. (See table of correspondences, pages 291–292.)

But even without a table or list, we can discover the correct correspondences from nature herself. Plants can tell us their secrets because patterns of information are encoded in them. Information radiates outwards from the plant in its aura or energy field. A sensitive Witch or herbalist can draw that intelligence into his or her mind.

George Washington Carver could do this. He had an astounding rapport with plants and was renowned for being able to heal ailing plants. When asked how he performed his miracles, he answered, 'All flowers talk to me and so do hundreds of little things in the woods. I learn what I know by watching and loving everything.' Carver would get up at 4.00 a.m. to roam the woods, listening to the plants because he thought the 'still dark hours before sunrise' the best time to engage in dialogue with nature. Much of his technical knowledge as a horticulturist and chemist came from his ability to elicit the scientific truths from the plants themselves. One evening he asked the peanut plant, 'Why did the Lord make you?' In a visionary state the answer flashed across his mind: 'compatibility, temperature and pressure'. From this Carver went on to discover the many uses for the humble peanut plant.

Once Carver was asked how he became such an astute student of nature. He answered, 'The secrets are in the plants. To elicit them you have to love them enough.' When asked 'Who besides you can do these things?' he replied, 'Everyone can if only they believe it.' Carver understood the law of correspondence: in simple everyday things lie the wisdom and knowledge of the universe. The truths are above us and below us if we would but look. 'When I touch that flower,' Carver once said, 'I am touching infinity ... Through the flower I talk to the Infinite ... This is not a physical contact. It is not in the earthquake, wind or fire. It is in the invisible world. It is that still small voice that calls up the fairies.'

Is it fairies? Is it plants? Is it the stars? Or the voice we hear in the wind? Seers and diviners differ on what tools they use, but the underlying holographic principle is the same: they, like Carver, allow knowledge or information to surface into consciousness. They work with a holographic mind and a holographic universe, discovering that what is known above can be known below.

The Law of Vibration: The Hermetic principle of vibration states that everything moves and vibrates with its own rate of vibration. Nothing is at rest. From solar systems to subatomic particles, everything is in motion. In *The Tao of Physics*, Fritjof Capra explains that all the material objects of our environment are made of atoms and that the 'enormous variety of molecular structures ... are not rigid and motionless but oscillate according to their temperature and in harmony with the thermal vibrations of their environment'. Matter is not passive and inert, as it may appear to us on the material level, but restless with rhythm and motion. It dances.

Scientists have measured vibrations in the laboratory with sensitive instruments that can detect radiation patterns, but lay people have performed simple experiments on their own by means of dowsing with a pendulum. The English writer Colin Wilson explains in *Mysteries* that a pendulum will swing in a greater or lesser arc depending on what kind of information it is picking up. The famous English dowser T. C. Lethbridge calculated how many inches a pendulum would swing for various qualities and then located these on a map of concentric circles. Eventually he plotted the arc lengths for both material things and abstract concepts, such as love, hate, silver, sulphur, gold, even death and time. Wilson, too, suggests that events imprint themselves on a particular place and a skilled dowser will pick up the vibrations from those imprinted events or objects even years later.

Matter and energy not only emit vibratory motion but, according to modern scientists, they *are* vibratory motion. Because of this, electromagnetic rates for molecular structures can be calculated, including the brain waves in various states of mental activity. Brain waves correspond to various states of consciousness. Alpha, for example, represents a rate of fourteen to seven waves per second, which occurs when we dream, meditate or do trance work. Beta waves correspond to states of alertness and intense mental activity. Theta waves occur during deep, dreamless sleep. We will look at the importance of brain waves in regard to Witchcraft in the next chapter.

Kirlian photography is another way of measuring the vibrational field around objects. The energy field around plants, rocks, even the human body, can be captured on specially developed photographs. Studies in Kirlian photography have revealed an interesting phenomenon about these auras. A plant that has recently been pruned will continue to emit the aura of the missing limb or leaf, which indicates that some vibrationary disturbances in the field around an object remain even after the physical object is gone. In other words the physical object imprints its unique concentration of energy into the field that surrounds it. Perhaps this is why General Patton could hear and see clashing armies in empty battlefields and why a dowser's swinging pendulum will indicate fear and death in a spot that once witnessed violence. The intense emotional and physical energy expended in the course of slaughter imprints itself on the evironment. No event is lost in the universe. The vibrations given off are eternal. As Itzhak Bentov says in *Stalking the Wild Pendulum*,

'We are pulsating beings in a vibrating universe in constant motion between the finite and the infinite.' There is some evidence that the more intense the emotional energy, the greater impact the aura will have on the energy field around it. For example, Kirlian photography shows that the aura around the hands of healers intensifies during a healing session.

Witches have always known that objects give off energy. We also believe that vibrations and auras affect the minds and bodies of others and influence situations. The old hippy concept of 'bad vibes' and 'good vibes' was not just fantasy. We do send messages and information by the energy we radiate. I believe that studies in parapsychology will eventually show that the basis of all telepathic messages is this transfer, or movement, of knowledge from mind to mind via invisible light waves.

The Law of Polarity: Polarity is the key to power in the Hermetic system. As *The Kybalion* puts it, everything is dual; all truths are half-truths; everything contains its opposite; extremes meet; and every pair of opposites can be reconciled. Knowing this is the key to making the universe work for you instead of against you. In the words of *The Kybalion*, 'Opposites are really only two extremes of the same thing with many varying degrees between them.'

Modern science works with this same principle. Capra calls the unification of opposites 'one of the most startling features' of the new reality. On the subatomic level particles are both destructible and indestructible; matter turns out to be both continuous and discontinuous; and energy and matter are simply different aspects of the same phenomenon. Scientists, as well as lay people, have had to rethink their definition of reality to incorporate the fact that what appears to be irreconcilable can in fact be reconciled.

Physicist Neils Bohr calls this the principle of 'complementarity', which states that energy must be described as *both* particles and waves. Each description is correct but only partially correct, and both are needed for a complete picture of reality. Bohr himself often suggested that the concept of complementarity would be useful outside the field of physics. Certainly it has proven useful in expressing the great spiritual truths of the ages. Only by paradox have the great spiritual teachers been able to convey their profound insights. Jesus said that the first shall be last and the last shall be first, and that only by losing your life will you save it. Lao Tzu wrote:

> *Be bent, and you will remain straight.*
> *Be vacant, and you will remain full.*
> *Be worn, and you will remain new.*

Witches use the principle of complementarity, or polarity, as it manifests in positive and negative charges. We know that the charge on anything can be altered. Nothing is fixed. All objects, moods and states of mind have positive and negative poles, much like those in electrical circuits, between which energy passes. Many spells are nothing more than the transfer of positive and negative energies directed by consciousness. We are simply working with the laws of nature in the most intense and intimate way.

It is liberating to know that life's energy flows on a continuum between poles of opposites and that you are never stuck in any one spot on the continuum. You have the power to advance or retreat, turn hate into love, fear into courage, doubt into faith. By learning to 'walk in balance', as Native Americans say, we can keep our lives from being dominated by any extreme. In time we come to recognize the midpoint between extremes and to centre and balance ourselves. 'In the middle is virtue' says an old Roman proverb, and the Latin word *virtus* actually means strength. The middle is a strong position because it contains both poles. It is where we experience the reconciliation of opposite forces, and reconciliation is the gateway to experiencing the oneness with all things. Nothing is stronger than that.

The Law of Rhythm: We know from physics and the Hermetic Laws that everything is in constant change and constant movement and that reality is composed of opposites. The law of rhythm gives us an important insight into *how* these opposites move. They move in circles. Like waves in the ocean, the linear movement that appears to advance actually contains millions of individual drops of water turning in circles. Again the paradox of opposites. Things are not as they seem!

Things move back and forth, up and down, in and out. They ebb and flow. But they also turn in wheels and spirals. Rhythm is the measured motion between extremes. As the oriental sages teach, all opposites flow together and into each other, everything continually becoming its opposite. As the Greek philosopher Heraclitus put it, because everything is in perpetual change, everything is in a continual state of 'becoming', a *cyclic* interplay of opposites. Chuang Tzu, the Chinese philosopher, said that the very essence of the Tao was the fact that the 'that' and the 'this' cease to be opposites at 'the centre of the circle responding to the endless changes'. The poet T. S. Eliot called it 'the still point of the turning world'. But the 'still point' is hard to achieve, for as *The Kybalion* tells us, 'the pendulum of rhythm . . . swing(s) ever toward first one pole and then the other.'

Some creation stories tell us that the creator breathed the breath of life into matter and so life began. This is not just a metaphor, for astrophysicists are now talking about the expansion and contraction of the universe. The entire universe breathes in and out, slowly, over aeons of time. Breathing is a circular process, measured by the rhythm of inhalation and exhalation. The law of rhythm assures us that each cycle seeks its completion, that the Great Wheel of Life, although forever turning, is always completing a cycle. Witchcraft trains us in finding our place in that flow and teaches us how to direct its energy. It is a cardinal tenet of Hermetic philosophy that the human will can override the forces around us, even as we work with them. *The Kybalion* says, 'The pendulum ever swings, although we may escape being carried along with it.' But the secret is to learn to direct our own energy and master ourselves first.

To understand the three laws of vibration, polarity and rhythm, an analogy might be useful. Consider the flow of blood through the human body. Vibration is the pulse or rate of flow measured by how much blood passes a given point every so many seconds. Polarity is the direction in which the blood flows at any given point, that is, away from the heart or back to the heart. Rhythm is the cyclic nature of the flow that always assures complete cycles.

Witches live intimately and in harmony with the great natural rhythms: the alternations of day and night, the ever-changing weather patterns, the gradual shift of one season into the next, the unending movement of life through birth, growth, decay, death and rebirth. Capra informs us that 'the rhythm of creation and destruction is not only manifest in the turn of the seasons and in the birth and death of all living creatures, but is also the very essence of inorganic matter.' The very essence of reality, we might add. As we live with the Great Wheel of Life and Death on the macrocosm, we know that it is also turning in the microcosm of each molecule. Since there are no passive observers, our observing of seasonal changes is also active participation. We observe and participate with the phases of the moon; we witness the rise and fall of the earth's tides and feel the tides in our own bodies. We meditate on the crystalline structure present in everything and know that each phase of growth leads to stabilization and ultimately decay. And out of decay comes new life.

There was a time in my life when I did not live by these three laws. I was fed up with the injustices and the evil that I saw all around me, and I thought that being 'out of sync' with society was the only honourable way to live. So I withdrew from society, and I used my black clothing and my magical life-style as a Witch to build walls between me and the outside world. In other words I cultivated my own rhythm so that society could not affect me. I succeeded, but I knew that something was terribly wrong. To live a personally satisfying life I needed to be of service to others, which meant being in harmony and communicating with society. I needed to find a way to be 'in the world but not of it', as the saying goes. So I decided to integrate the rhythm of my life into society's rhythms. I could no longer live as a polar extreme from what I saw around me. I began teaching and offering my services as a healer, teacher and counsellor. The only way I could be effective was to tap into society and neutralize whatever harmful vibrations I could. So I made the wheel of my life turn out rather than in. I managed to achieve a kind of dynamic balance, which is still my ideal. But as all things contain their opposites, so too does my dynamic balance.

The Law of Gender: The Hermetic principle of gender states that everything has both masculine and feminine components. This law is an important application of the law of polarity. It is similar to the principle of the anima and animus that Carl Jung and his followers have popularized, namely, that each person contains both masculine and feminine aspects regardless of his or her physical gender. No human being is totally masculine or feminine. Although developed as personality theory, these insights have proven enormously useful in other areas.

The law of gender is really about force and energy. In all things there is a receptive or feminine energy. In all things

152

there is a receptive or feminine energy and a projective or masculine energy, which the Chinese call yin and yang. According to the law of polarity, all things contain their opposites, and according to modern physics, there is a dynamic vitality between those opposites. Therefore masculine and feminine energies are in a constant cosmic dance. We are not locked into a static gender rôle no matter what our sex or how hard we try to live up to culturally determined myths about 'real men' and 'real women'. It is important for Witches (and all magic workers) who work in various states of consciousness to understand this fundamental polarity in the human psyche and factor masculine and feminine energies into their work as they are needed.

Magic is creative work. Creativity studies indicate that androgyny is an important component in the creative individual. A person who recognizes and appreciates the androgynous nature of his or her personality, and can express it, stands a better chance of being creative than the person whose perspective is narrowed or limited by his or her physical gender.

Creation legends from around the world attest to the importance of androgyny in the creation of the universe. Often they recount how an androgynous divine or supernatural being created the world, usually with the feminine or maternal aspect dominating and manifesting as a goddess or Great Mother. In some of these legends the original androgyne is split in two, and thus males and females in every species are destined to pursue each other to recreate the original union. In other tales the androgyne remained intact and brought culture to the earth and served an important rôle in mediating between the sexes and the worlds of spirit and matter. In many of these cultures homosexual people were honoured as healers and spiritual leaders because they represented the original androgynous god/goddess.

A Witch must learn to respect the feminine and masculine

elements of his or her nature, even though one or the other may not operate on a fully conscious level. By ritual and magic we can bring the unconscious element closer to awareness. A female Witch nurtures her animus; a male Witch woos his anima. For many Witches the anima and animus become psychic guides. All acts of generation, regeneration and creation, such as spells, enchantments and meditation, involve these two principles. By knowing how they work and following their guidance, we can unlock many of the mysteries of life.

The Law of Cause and Effect: In its traditional form the law of cause and effect states that nothing happens by chance, that for every effect there is a cause, and that every cause is itself an effect of something else. Modern science has shown that on the molecular level the law of cause and effect ceases to operate as it does on the macrocosm. The new physicists talk about probability rather than predictability. But the realities of the subatomic world do not eliminate the law so much as redefine it. As Peat explains, the '. . . *chain* of causality . . . is in fact a complex *network* of causation. And the more the limits of this network are extended, the more it is seen to stretch out over the entire earth and ultimately the universe itself.' This remarkable observation leads him to conclude that if any event or phenomenon is examined closely enough, it will be revealed that 'everything causes everything else'! In a holographic sense the whole is in every part, and everything interpenetrates everything.

So the old Hermetic principle that everything has a cause and is itself a cause of something in return is really more sweeping and exciting than it appears at first glance. The implications are truly astounding. We are not describing billiard balls bumping each other or rows of dominoes collapsing. We are not isolated individuals leading isolated lives except for the occasional encounter with someone or something else. We are literally and figuratively plugged into the entire universe. What happens on the other side of the globe effects us. Our actions have cosmic repercussions. It is as humbling as it is awe-inspiring to realize the influence we possess and the incredible responsibility to use our powers wisely and for the good of all.

The hard data behind the law of cause and effect is, as Capra puts it, that the universe is not a collection of physical objects (as it might appear to our limited vision) but rather 'a complicated web of relations between the various parts of a unified whole'. In other words, a corollary to the theory that 'everything causes everything else' is that everything can interface with everything, everything can influence everything. What Witches call 'projections' – thoughts and intentions directed from the mind to the external world – make a definite impact. They have an effect. They influence external events. From our brief overview of modern physics this should not be hard to understand. Of course the techniques for influencing others by mental projections must be learned and mastered. We must learn how to slip through the natural barriers that prevent our minds from continually running amok throughout the universe! If everyone could be in everyone else's mind all the time, it would be chaos!

But similarly, because the human mind can take an active part in the unfolding of events, we cannot surrender to the chaos of our own individual lives. We cannot excuse ourselves or complain about our lives on the grounds that nothing can be done. As Witches we know that is simply not true. There is a solution to every problem. A Witch can move from a lower plane to a higher plane, from being stuck in troubles and difficulties to a more exalted vantage point where she or he becomes an active agent in the web of relationships that can change any situation.

Some Witches think that by using the law of causation

they can make anything happen that they wish. But I must caution you about grandiose visions of power. A Witch's power, like anyone else's, is checked by the realms of power and energy above, below and around her. While she may be a master of events on one plane, she does not escape the principle of causation. She is merely a link in the unending flow of power that permeates the universe. She is answerable to energies higher than herself.

The law of cause and effect, like the other Hermetic principles, suggests a worldview that is at once comforting and exhilarating. The Hermetic Laws show the orderly unfolding of life. No event ever really 'creates' another event out of nothing. Each is a crossroads or an interchange in a web of all that went before and of all that will come after. Each of us is the current 'still point' in a bloodline whose splayed roots grow deep into the past and whose branches extend far into the future. We are part of the unending flow of knowledge and wisdom, configurating here in a specific moment of time. But our consciousness is not limited by time or space. It contains all time and all space. As the Greek philosopher Proclus put it, 'All things are in us psychically, and through this we are naturally capable of knowing all things.'

.6.

ALPHA

In a banquet room on the ground floor of the Hawthorne Hotel on Salem Common a Christian renewal group meets on a Sunday morning after their church service. On the first floor thirty people gather to learn the principles of Witchcraft. They are beginning their second day of my course, the Science of Witchcraft. They are a varied group: a mother and daughter from Australia, a mysterious woman from Michigan, a married couple from New Jersey, a young man from Maine, a poet who lives in the Hudson River Valley, individuals from New Hampshire, New York City and the greater Boston area. Some are Witches and have been practising alone or in their covens for years. Others are here out of curiosity, to see what it's all about. On this particular morning they will all do something they have never done before – they will locate and name a medically diagnosed disease in someone they have never met and about whom the only information they will have is name, age, sex and place of residence. Each person will do three cases. Most will get at least two out of three correct; a large majority will solve all three.

Susan, a waitress from New York, works with Frank, her partner for the day, a computer programmer for a Boston-based advertising firm. Susan has filled out a case form regarding her sister Connie. The form is on her lap as she sits across from Frank, who has closed his eyes. Susan counts Frank down into alpha with the Crystal Countdown, which the group learned the day before. When Frank is ready Susan reads from the form: 'Connie Walters, age forty, female, Cincinnati, Ohio.' Frank allows Connie to appear on the screen of his mind. His eyes still closed, he raises his hands a few inches before his forehead and 'touches' Connie's hair, feels the shape of her head, the texture of her skin, the slope of her nose. He begins his analysis:

FRANK:		SUSAN:
Short hair.		Correct.
Curly.		Correct.
Light brown.		Right.
High cheekbones.		Correct.
Thin face.		Yes.
About five feet four inches tall.		Pretty close.
Oh, a little taller.		Yes.
A lot of energy near her forehead. Does she work with her mind?		Yes, she's a reporter.
Arms feel good. Wait a minute! One is broken.		

Susan then gives the agreed–upon response for 'no'. She says, 'I don't have that information.'

'Are you sure?' Frank persists. Susan starts to say 'yes', then stops. She remembers something. 'Oh, well, she did break her arm ten years ago.'

FRANK: I thought so.	SUSAN: Yes.
Left arm?	

Letting his hands explore his image of Connie, Frank feels her back, examines her legs, heart, lungs and stomach. Nine out of ten times he gets a correct answer from Susan, or occasionally, when he misses a point, Susan will tell him to look 'more closely' or 'look again'. He does. Often he sees what he missed the first time.

FRANK: She has problems near her lower stomach and pelvic area. It feels hot there.

SUSAN: Yes, keep looking.

Frank pauses to explore that area further. He hesitates. A frown crosses his face. He knows that what he sees and learns in alpha is correct, but he's still new at this. It's hard for him to trust himself, but he does.

'She has cancer.'

'Yes, she does,' confirms Susan.

And around the room other pairs are concluding their first cases with the same results.

Bleeding ulcer?	Right.
Arthritis.	Yes.
AIDS-related pneumonia.	Yes.
Slipped disc?	Right.
Alzheimer's disease.	Correct.

And then from every corner of the room I hear people saying 'I can't believe it!' and 'I didn't think I could do it, and I did it.' And everyone wants to do another case. I'm not sure what the Christian renewal group is doing downstairs, but in my Witchcraft seminar, day two of a long, intensive weekend, ordinary men and women from all walks of life are learning something very important about themselves and the universe around them: everything is connected; we are all one.

Psychic diagnosis is performed throughout the world by

psychic healers, Witches, shamans and native medicine people. Over the last three or four hundred years, however, it has fallen into disfavour in many places because medical science has come to dominate the health-care field with rationalistic, left-brain-dominated procedures that have proven remarkably successful in the limited sense of repairing the physical body. This 'fix-it' approach seldom addresses the mental, emotional and spiritual suffering that accompanies physical illness. In general the Western-educated medical community has demeaned the psychic aspects of healing either by ignoring them altogether or by explicitly speaking out against them, telling patients not to trust any diagnosing or healing procedure not based on the Western medical paradigm. Over the years many psychic healing techniques were lost. Nevertheless, much healing wisdom has survived, particularly among village healers in the Philippines, Indonesia, Australia and the Soviet Union. A growing number of people are enrolling in courses and workshops to learn alternative healing systems, as they are currently being taught under such names as Reiki, Therapeutic Touch and Mariel Healing, to name only a few.

The fascinating questions about psychic healing and parapsychology in general have led to academic programmes and several chairs in parapsychology at a handful of research universities. Among them are Syracuse University, University of Vermont, University of California at Davis, City College of New York, and in institutions in Canada and overseas. Researchers like Lawrence LeShan, Stanley Krippner, Bernard Gittelson and Jean Achterberg have written extensively on the visionary mind's ability to facilitate healing, even in cases of cancer.

Psychic diagnosis and psychic healing can be done by most men and women, given the proper instruction and the right intention. Studies with a random selection of subjects who represent a cross-section of the population indicate that, as Bernard Gittelson and Laura Torbet say in their survey of psychic phenomena, *Intangible Evidence*, 'just about everyone has some measurable psi ability'. My own classes and workshops confirm this.

What amazes so many people is that psychic power can be controlled and directed, pulled out of your pocket, as it were, and used when needed. We have been led to believe that psychic power is elusive, coming and going on its own, temperamental and terribly unreliable. Certainly many investigations by sceptical scientists, who are often determined to prove it a hoax, have been unable to locate psi power or explain it adequately. It's quite possible, of course, that since experimenters always influence the results of their experiments, a sceptical attitude, picked up by the psychic being tested, interferes with a successful demonstration.

Witches, however, firmly believe that psychic power is reliable. We use it in spells, divination, magic circles and rituals. Psychic power – or magic – is based on science and can be taught to others. It has been studied and researched scientifically along the lines that J. B. Rhine pioneered at Duke University in the 1930s. Rhine showed that experiments in psychic functioning could be simple, easily controlled, standardized, repeatable and subject to professional statistical analysis. Since then other researchers, such as Keith Harary, Charles Tart, Stanley Krippner and Russell Targ, have developed those fifty-year-old research techniques in new and exciting ways. There is a growing respect in the scientific community for this kind of research and its findings.

ALPHA: EVERYONE'S ALTERED STATE OF CONSCIOUSNESS

The science of Witchcraft is based on our ability to enter an altered state of consciousness we call 'alpha', where brain waves register at seven to fourteen cycles per second. As mentioned earlier, this is a state of consciousness associated with relaxation, meditation and dreaming. The faster fourteen to thirty cycles of the beta state occur when we are mentally alert, awake and engaged in physical activity. They also accompany excitement, fear, tension and anxiety. The slower theta waves, four to seven cycles per second, are associated with drowsiness, euphoria, and deep tranquillity. Delta waves of one to three occur in deep, dreamless sleep.

In alpha the mind opens up to non-ordinary forms of communication, such as telepathy, clairvoyance and pre-cognition. Here we also may experience out-of-the-body sensations and psychokinesis, or receive mystical, visionary information that does not come through the five senses. In alpha the rational filters that process ordinary reality are weakened or removed, and the mind is receptive to non-ordinary realities. Itzhak Bentov says, 'The general underlying principle . . . is an altered state of consciousness . . . which allows us to function in realities that are normally not available to us.'

The reason information not ordinarily available becomes accessible in alpha is that the brain is itself a hologram. Stanford neurophysiologist Karl Pribram was the first to call our attention to this. His studies in the 1960s led him to suggest that the brain stores memories in a holographic manner. Brain scientists had known for years that memories are dispersed throughout the brain, but no one could explain the mechanisms that would account for the whole-in-every-part aspect of memory storage and retrieval. Pribram applied the concept of holograms to the brain and argued that nerve impulses web across the entire brain just as laser patterns web across an entire piece of film. Since all information in the universe is in our minds to begin with, it is simply a matter of putting the brain into the proper state to retrieve that information, much like retrieving a memory. Alpha is that state, and the trigger for retrieval is light energy. As Bentov says, 'The universe is a hologram and so is the brain a hologram interpreting a holographic universe.'

162

Almost all cultures have used altered states of consciousness, such as alpha, for communal religious rituals, personal spiritual rites, divination and healing work. The famous Oracle of Delphi, for example, entered a trance state before she could answer the questions presented to her by petitioners. In northern Europe priestesses of the Norse Goddess Freyja practised a similar kind of spiritual counselling in which falling into a state of ecstasy was essential for receiving information. Only in the trance state could they answer a supplicant's questions. Among the Sami people of northern Scandinavia trance journeys to the other psychic realms or spirit worlds were taken in a state of ecstasy supported by ritual chanting by a choir of women. Among the Kung people of Africa all-night healing sessions involve dancing and chanting to maintain an intense altered state of consciousness until, as they say, the energy 'boils'. Native American medicine people use ritual drumming and chanting to focus their consciousness in an alpha state while they perform healing ceremonies or seek personal visions.

In an alpha state wonderful changes take place. Our egos are less dominant so that we can process information in terms other than our own personal security and survival. The holographic potential of the brain/mind comes into full play: memories are more accessible; connections between different pieces of information come readily; contact with unconscious materials and images occur spontaneously. Imaginative possibilities are more sharply focused. Insights are clearer. We are less aware of the time-space categories that we use to process experience. As Einstein said, 'Time and space are modes by which we think, not conditions in which we live.' Alpha alters our perceptions so that we are freed from those time-space constructs and can draw in experience from other times and places. For all these reasons Witches do most of their magical work in alpha.

It is my belief that all information and all non-ordinary

experiences come to us in alpha because all information in the universe (and all phenomena in the universe) consists of light energy. Light enters the pineal gland, or Third Eye, located in the centre of the head between the eyebrows, where many psychics say they experience physical sensations when they receive extra-sensory information. In some trance states a person's eyes naturally roll upwards, gazing at this power spot above the eyes.

Situated in the centre of the head under the hardest and thickest bone in the skull, this master gland would seem to be too deeply buried to receive light. For many years researchers knew that daylight affected the pineal glands of animals, regulating hibernation and oestrus, for example, but they doubted whether light had any effect upon the pineal glands of human beings. But recent scientific research indicates that light does affect the human pineal gland, regulating on a daily basis its ability to secrete melatonin, a hormone that has an important effect on the production of other hormones. In the autumn of 1985 the first international conference on the pineal gland was held in Vienna to draw attention to the importance of light on this master gland.

Furthermore, the term 'Third Eye' is not just a fanciful metaphor conjured up by Witches and psychics to sound mysterious. Anatomists believe that the gland is indeed a remnant of a third eye that never developed in the course of evolution. From the oldest times, sages, magicians and Witches have spoken of the Third Eye as the doorway to all knowledge. Ancient peoples have intuitively understood the importance of this power spot and honoured it in various ways. In the Orient it is one of the seven chakras. Egyptian monarchs wore a cobra-headed ornament at the centre of the forehead. In India a red dot is placed over the Third Eye. Celtic priestesses painted the area blue. Cultures that use ritual face make-up often single out this area in front of the pineal gland for special attention.

From the experiences of hundreds of people in my workshops, I believe that not only does the pineal gland draw in visual information, but that it also perceives sound that is undetectable to the ear. Both kinds of information travel as light energy. It is my belief that light and sound cannot be separated. When light arrives so does sight and sound. This is why the information we receive in alpha can be either visual or auditory. Some people are more prone to one than the other: some see visions, others hear voices. At the beginning of this chapter we saw how Frank received most of his information about Connie's condition visually, but some in the group arrived at their diagnoses by hearing information as much as seeing it.

As Witches we believe that we are meant to know how everything works – earth, air, fire, water, stars, planets, spirits. This knowledge is available to us. Furthermore, we are *responsible* for knowing how everything in the universe works because we are responsible for the universe. Our mission is ecological; we are here to balance energies, reconcile opposites and right wrongs by mentally projecting that all things be corrected. It is our responsibility – and yours – to promote health and life in all its forms.

This is what we do on every major holiday in the Craft. Our observance is truly 'an observing'. In alpha we examine the fields, the gardens, the harbour waters, the streets of town. We attend to our 'crops' – the crops of children, the elderly, parents, politicians, business leaders, not just those crops planted in the fields. We enter alpha and observe every area of human life that is important to us so we can offer help where it is needed, nurture what requires growth, teach and serve those less able to care for themselves.

We often think of psychics as being gifted and rare because they can tap into this wisdom of the universe, but the gift is not rare. Everyone has it, and each of us can relearn – or remember – how to use it. It may take time, however, just as it was necessary for each of us to learn to crawl before we could walk and run.

THE POWER OF COLOUR AND NUMBER

In Salem I teach a very easy method for going into alpha and seeing with the Third Eye. I call it 'the Crystal Countdown', a method based on Pythagorean principles of number and colour. Pythagoras, whose work was based on the Hermetic Laws, is one of the few universally acknowledged wise teachers of science *and* spirituality.

Pythagoras was born between 600 and 590 BC. He was versed in the Eastern and Western mysticism of his day and was initiated into the Egyptian, Babylonian, Chaldean and Eleusinian mystery schools. He also studied the Mosaic traditions with Jewish scholars, as well as the Essene Brotherhood. At Crotona, a Greek colony in southern Italy, he set up his academy, where he taught his unique brand of philosophy and science based on mathematics, geometry, music and astronomy. Pythagoras considered these subjects absolutely necessary for understanding human existence, nature and God, whom he described as the Supreme Mind that pervades the universe both as the cause of all things and the power within all things. Similar to the theories of modern physics, Pythagoras' teachings posited that God (i.e. the universe) was circular and composed of the substance of light (or energy). He also taught that the nature of God (i.e. the universe) was the substance of truth, which, as some contemporary physicists would say, is the pattern of objective intelligence that underlies all phenomena.

Pythagoras' philosophy is based on numbers, with the numbers one to ten constituting the sacred *decad*. Each number contains power and meaning in a wide range of human experience. For example, the number one stands for that which is separate, whole and stable; it is the beginning and end; it is mind. Two represents death, science, generations, all that is dual, and all opposites. Three is peace, justice, prudence, piety, temperance and virtue. Four encompasses harmony, strength, virility, impetuosity and is called 'the fountain of Nature'. Five governs reconciliation, alternation, cordiality, vitality, health and providence. Six represents time, panacea, the world and sufficiency. Seven is the number of religion, life, fortune and dreams. Eight is love, law and convenience. Nine stands for the ocean, the horizon, boundaries and limitations. Ten is age, power, faith, memory and necessity.

According to Pythagoras, the amazing harmony in the universe, whether musical or moral, can be explained and experienced as numbers. Over the years I have come to prefer Pythagoras' system because mathematical harmony, when coupled with the harmonies of colour, balances and centres the mind, making it more receptive to the external harmonies of the universe. I strongly encourage my students to study Pythagoras' system more extensively and learn the mathematical foundations of all existence.

By closing our eyes and breaking light into its component colours, as in a prism, and by counting down from seven to one, we can lower our brain waves from beta to alpha, the slightly altered trance that we slip into during the day when we are 'lost' in daydreams, doodling on a pad of paper, running, listening to captivating music or meditating. In all these states we spontaneously visualize, see pictures or hear information. In alpha we can diagnose illness, send healing energy to others, draw in important knowledge, check on loved ones no matter where they live, travel back or forwards in time (for the mental categories of time and space are suspended in alpha), and create change in the material world as long as it is for the good of all and harms no one.

Society has fabricated taboos about this kind of work, and

most people grow up with powerful cultural inhibitions about doing it. For example, we are told that it leads to 'losing touch with reality', which is true in a certain sense, but not frightening when we realize that we are just giving up contact with one kind of reality momentarily so that we can tune into other non-ordinary realities. We are also programmed to dismiss any state that appears to us as 'mindless'. Zen monks, on the other hand, teach that a state of 'no-mind', as they call it, is not an empty void but a void filled with unlimited potential. Most of us educated in Western school systems were taught primarily, if not exclusively, left-brain skills characterized by alert, mental, linear analysis. We have neglected to develop skills based on intuitive, spontaneous, non-linear perceptions typical of right-brain thinking processes.

In general we have been conditioned not to value, appreciate or induce the kinds of activity that foster alpha states: staring blankly for a period of time, daydreaming, letting the mind wander, observing silently without the incessant internal dialogue that chatters and comments about everything we experience. We rarely remember, record or review our nightly dreams. I find some people very reluctant to learn alpha and explore its potentials because of these societal attitudes. In time most people get over them when they realize the value of alpha.

We go into alpha states automatically anyway at various times of the day and night, so it is our responsibility to learn to use alpha correctly. The tendency today is to shirk responsibility in many areas of life. And I suspect that some people's inhibitions about learning this work come from their unconscious realization that alpha brings with it responsibilities. Our ancestors, however, knew differently. They knew they were responsible for planting the crops *and* the weather that would ensure their growth, responsible for crafting their hunting tools *and* for calling the animals who would die for them, responsible for the group or clan *and* those individuals who were ill, orphaned or too old to care for themselves.

Although it should never be used frivolously, there is no need to fear the responsibility that comes with using alpha. The ethical law of Witchcraft – like that of other major religious systems – is to harm no one. Do what you will and harm none. The powers of alpha are serious, but there is nothing wrong in enjoying yourself while using them. In fact they can be fun.

After I had determined I would no longer hide the fact that I am a Witch, my daughter Penny and I were one day in a Salem restaurant when other customers began casting dirty looks and muttering nasty remarks about my black robes and the fact that we were Witches. Penny was only eight at the time and had had a rough week from schoolchildren who taunted her about being a Witch. As the customers began to giggle I could see Penny's face grow longer and longer. I pretended not to notice the insults, hoping she would ignore them too. When that didn't work I proposed that we do 'something magical'. Since it was a beautiful summer day, I suggested, 'How about making snow?' Her eyes twinkled. Sitting in front of our salads, we closed our eyes, went into alpha, invoked the elements and charged that when the snow arrived it would do no harm and be for the good of all. Then we ate our lunch and went home.

Later that afternoon a friend rushed into my house after she got off work. 'You did it, didn't you?' she accused. 'You made it snow in July.' Penny and I had not even seen it, but it had snowed off and on, here and there, all afternoon in downtown Salem while the sun continued to shine. At times we need to see magic work like this in dramatic, fun and surprising ways. It proved to Penny that 'what her mother was up to' was real, no matter what kids at school or strangers in a restaurant may think. Summer snow in Salem didn't upset any grand cosmic scheme and, according to the newspaper accounts, everyone enjoyed it. It harmed no one and provided a lesson in the Craft for a young Witch child.

Some people dabble in Witchcraft thinking that once they acquire magical powers, they'll be able to ignore or even subvert the physical laws of the universe to their own selfish ends. What a rude awakening they receive when they learn that to be wise in the ways of magic entails working with the physical laws as well as the higher. During my first months in Salem, when I had very little money, I had to find ways to earn money to pay the rent. I could not expect a spell to absolve me from that necessity. Last year, when I ran for mayor of Salem, I astounded the local political leaders by proposing that we clean up the polluted water of Salem Harbor by hiring Japanese technicians specially trained in reversing environmental damage to urban waterways. I could not expect a spell to absolve the citizens of Salem from shouldering the responsibility for their harbour. 'Why the Japanese?' people asked. I answered, 'Because they are good at it.' Nothing psychic about that!

Those who are drawn to Witchcraft must first be well grounded on the material plane and understand and respect the natural laws of life. It is an ancient law of Witchcraft (and a modern discovery in Western physics) that spirit and matter are one. They cannot be separated. It is not possible to live solely on the spiritual level, but the wonderful thing is that we don't need to. We are always living on both planes. You never have to forsake the spiritual level when you become grounded on the material plane. Witches believe that in the final analysis all is spirit or energy. As Witches or scientists we must be grounded in both matter and spirit.

THE CRYSTAL COUNTDOWN

Alpha is the springboard for all psychic and magical workings. It is the heart of Witchcraft. The alpha state is the scientific basis for magic. In order to develop your own psychic powers and learn the ways of the Craft, you must learn to control alpha. The following exercise will teach you to do just that. It is simple but extremely important. You must master it first before proceeding to any other spell, ritual or exercise in this book.

Read through the entire directions for the Crystal Countdown several times before you attempt to do it. Make sure you are familiar with all the steps before you begin because you won't be able to stop in the middle to look something up in the book.

To put yourself into alpha find a quiet place, sit down, get comfortable, close your eyes and spend a minute breathing deeply and relaxing.

When you feel centred, or balanced, keep your eyes closed and with your Third Eye – your mind's eye – visualize an empty screen (like a television screen) about one foot in front of you and just above your eyelids. Actually, the screen on which the Third Eye projects images encircles your entire head like a helmet, but most people see images on only the front portion.

You may notice your eyes fluttering a bit even though they are closed. They may even tend to roll upwards, as if that would help you see the screen better. It is an automatic reflex because you have been trained to 'see' only with your eyes open and fixed on the object you are viewing. Now it is time to train yourself to see with your mind. In time the fluttering will stop. Keep in mind that in alpha you do not need to 'see' with your physical eyes. You are looking through your mind's eye.

Next, picture on the screen a red number seven. If this won't appear easily, try seeing just a seven or just a red field. If you have difficulty splashing the colours on the screen, recall some object that is the colour you want to envision and see it in your mind's eye – for example, a red fire engine, an

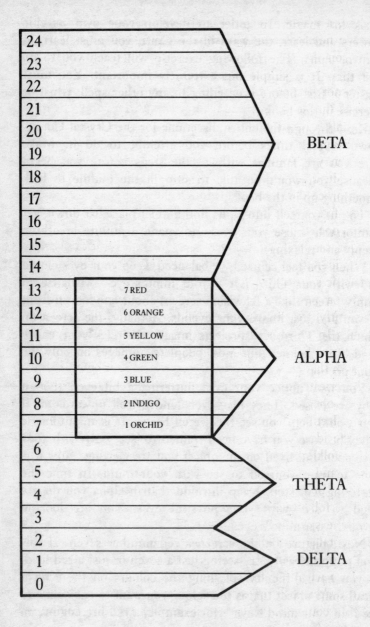

orange, a yellow banana. Practise this until you are able to see the field of colour. In time you will be able to put the seven on the red field and eventually you will see the red seven.

Do not become discouraged. Remember that society has told us that it is not natural to 'see' with our eyes closed or that only dreams and hallucinations – things that are not 'real' – appear when we close our eyes.

When you see the red seven hold it for a moment and release it. Then bring up an orange six, hold it, and release. Then proceed downwards through the spectrum of colours: a yellow five, a green four, a blue three, an indigo two and an orchid one.

This sequence of colours is a universally acknowledged scientific reality. It appears in the rainbow and in every prismatic splitting of light. This colour spectrum or rainbow is also a powerful archetypal image in all cultures. It is frequently a symbol for other magical realities and new worlds. In Genesis the rainbow is a sign of a fresh start for human society after the flood – a promise from the wrathful Yahweh that he wouldn't do it again. The Rainbow Coalition in American politics promises a new age of racial harmony and co-operation. Native Americans have seen the rainbow as a reflection of the oneness amid the multiplicity in nature and the ideal of peace and balance among all creatures. In Celtic folklore the rainbow indicated the presence of elves, fairies and a possible pot of gold. Norse myths tell of a rainbow bridge, Bifrost, which only the gods can cross. In modern folklore the rainbow separates the banality of Kansas from the splendours of Oz. In my tradition the rainbow is the crystal gateway into alpha.

The indigo two is a deeper colour and lower level than you need, so when the lighter orchid one appears you will sense your awareness lifting ever so slightly. When you settle into orchid, count down from ten to one without colours to deepen the alpha state. Then mentally say to yourself with conviction, 'I am now in alpha, and everything I do will be accurate and correct, and this is so.'

At this point you will perform the task you decided upon.

Keep in mind that the alpha state is not like being asleep. Even though you have counted down, feel relaxed and have your eyes closed, you are still in total control of what happens to you. You will hear sounds around you and you will be aware of the room you are in. Anytime you feel as though you want to come out of alpha, you may. In fact, anytime you feel that you want to start over again, you can.

When you have finished your task and wish to return to what science calls the beta level of brain waves, or normal waking consciousness, erase what is on the screen with your hands. Then, while still in alpha, and with your eyes still closed, give yourself total health clearance in the following way: place your hand about six inches above your head, palm downwards. Then in one smooth swoop, bring your hand down in front of your face, chest and stomach while turning your palm outwards and pushing away from you. Say to yourself, 'I am healing myself and giving myself total health clearance.' This must be done every time you prepare to come out of alpha. By this simple procedure you will clear away any harmful energies that are present, and you will project an image of yourself as strong and healthy.

Next count slowly up from one to ten, then one to seven. You do not need to see colours as you count up since you are returning to the full light and the colours will converge on their own as you open your eyes. You can, of course, 'snap out' of alpha by simply opening your eyes, but I do not advise it. Being startled out of a deep sleep or dream is always disorientating, and something similar occurs when you come out of alpha too quickly. Count up, slowly open your eyes and gradually realize your presence in the room.

This basic procedure for entering alpha is the key to all

future work in the Craft. Practise it (and the following meditation) every day for at least five weeks in order to perfect it. As you grow more comfortable and proficient at counting down to alpha, you will enter alpha quite easily and feel at home in it. And you should, because alpha is a natural state, one you enter every day or night in dreams and reverie. The only difference is that with the Crystal Countdown you are controlling it and using the state consciously for psychic work.

THE APPLE MEDITATION

There are many tasks you can carry out in alpha, but for beginners the Apple Meditation is good practice. The apple is sacred to Witches in the Celtic tradition because the apple tree flourishes in paradise, which in Welsh lore is called 'Avalon' or 'Apple-land'. When you cut an apple in half you will find the seeded pentacle at the centre: five brown seeds forming a five-pointed star. Interestingly, the Christian tradition chose the apple to replace the nameless 'Fruit of the Tree of Knowledge' that Eve offered to Adam, a decision that further connected the wisdom of the Craft with evil. A more recent version of using an apple to link Witchcraft with evil is the Walt Disney film *Snow White and the Seven Dwarfs*. The evil queen turns herself into a wicked Witch and poisons an apple to give to Snow White. It is time to redeem the apple as the sacred fruit it has always been in Celtic lore.

Go into alpha as explained above. When you are firmly grounded see the screen and bring up on to it an apple. Bring it clearly into view, look at it carefully, notice its size, shape, colour, the stem, any leaves, smudges, bruises, worm-holes. Then reach up with your hands (slightly above your eyebrows in front of you) and feel the apple with your index finger and middle finger. These finger-tips contain acu-pressure points that activate the Third Eye. The blind, whose tactile sensitivity is extremely heightened, can often 'see' or 'read' colours, shapes and forms using only their fingers. The tip of the index finger is for 'seeing' and 'reading'. The tip of the middle finger helps you to memorize and recall.

So feel the apple's shape, note its temperature, texture and degree of firmness.

Next visualize the apple cut in half. Examine it closer. See the pentacle of seeds.

When you have finished keep your eyes closed and with your hands erase the apple from the screen. Then count yourself back up and open your eyes.

When I teach this meditation in my classes each student describes a different apple, the reason being that each is a *real* apple that comes from somewhere beyond the mental screen. Often sceptical students think they are merely imagining apples. If you harbour a little doubt at first, don't worry about it. As you continue to do this meditation and the following one, you will gradually realize that what you experience in alpha is just as real as ordinary reality. You are in fact seeing a real apple. As you continue to do this exercise for the first few weeks, you will notice that it is not the same apple that appears each time. The size, shape, colour and age of each apple may vary considerably. You are not making this up. You are tapping into the presence of a real apple that exists in time and space.

MIND TRAVEL

This exercise will help prove that the information that you receive in alpha comes from the external world and that you are not just making it up.

176

Go into alpha using the Crystal Countdown.

When you are relaxed bring up on to your screen a shop you have never visited before in your town or city. Choose a real shop on a specific street or in a specific location in a shopping arcade. It is easier to use a small one-room shop or boutique rather than a large store with several departments.

See yourself in your mind's eye standing outside the shop. Then walk in. Look all around psychically. See the floor plan. Notice where the counters are and what is on them. Observe the colours in the store, signs on the wall, where the cash registers are, any free-standing displays in the centre of the floor. Use your hands to feel and see the items in the store. Of course, you may not see everything on your first psychic visit. You may get only a few impressions, a few shapes or colours. Do not make up details just so you will have a complete picture. Let come what comes. Remember, your mind does not have this information prior to your psychic visit. The information comes into your mind *because* you are psychically present in the store.

When you feel you have seen all that you are going to see today, erase the shop with your hands and count yourself back up and open your eyes.

Then write down what you saw or draw a diagram so you won't forget it. When you have the time visit the shop you saw on your screen and confirm how many of the details are accurate. Don't be disappointed if they are not all 100 per cent perfect. Keep in mind that you saw the shop at a particular hour on a particular day. It may have changed between then and your physical visit. For example, you may have seen on your screen a milk-shake and wondered what it was doing in a clothing boutique. Perhaps a customer had carried it in. You might have detected a bright red colour behind the counter that isn't there when you visit physically. Maybe the sales assistant that day was wearing a red sweater.

Psychic work takes practice. It will take a while to learn

how to evaluate your experiences. Always notice how many 'direct hits' you have and be glad even if you had only a few. I think you will be surprised to discover that you are usually about 50 per cent accurate.

THE EGYPTIAN SUN MEDITATION

This meditation is wonderful for renewing your physical and psychic energies. After a long day of work I often use it to revitalize myself before an evening of teaching or meeting with my coven. You can also do it first thing in the morning before the business of the day begins.

Do the Crystal Countdown into alpha.

When you are ready see a bright psychic sun shining about six feet over your head. Notice how its golden energy pulsates. See the power of the sun leap out from it, eager to share itself with all living things.

In time you will notice six beams of lasered sunlight that seem directed towards you. They will leave the fiery globe and descend to six areas of your body.

The first beam enters your head and travels to the pineal gland, your Third Eye.

The second ray enters the throat chakra, where the thyroid is located.

The third beam streams through the heart.

The fourth beam penetrates the solar plexus between the rib cage and the stomach.

Next raise your hands, palms upwards, as in an Egyptian prayer pose. Each hand should be at shoulder level, the fingertips pointed outwards to the right and the left. Now let the fifth and sixth rays penetrate the centre of your palms.

When the six rays have entered your body feel the golden rays flowing through your blood, your nervous system, up and down your spinal column, to every cell in your muscles, to every internal organ. Eventually you will feel a tingling sensation in your fingertips. It may feel icy or warm. Touch your feet together and cross your hands over your chest. With your eyes still closed, hold the light within you. Bathe in its warm glow, letting it renew your energy as long as it is comfortable. Repeat over and over to yourself, 'The sun gives me physical and psychic energy.' Sit like this for about ten or fifteen minutes and you will feel completely energized in body, mind and aura.

INSTANT ALPHA

The deepest alpha states require the Crystal Countdown in a quiet place. Unfortunately, this is not always possible. Here is a method for going into alpha instantly for quick tasks when you cannot close your eyes, such as while driving a car or walking through a crowded grocery store. Instant alpha is great for finding a parking space or getting a table at a restaurant. But before attempting instant alpha practise the Crystal Countdown and the three exercises above for a couple of weeks until you feel comfortable and confident using alpha.

First you must programme yourself for instant alpha, and this of course requires going into a deep alpha state with the Crystal Countdown.

When you are in alpha cross the middle finger of your left hand over the top of the index finger and hold it. This will activate the pineal gland. You may even feel a sensation of energy in the area of your Third Eye while you hold your fingers crossed. Repeat to yourself that by crossing your fingers you will trigger the instant alpha state. Say, 'I cross my fingers and I am in instant alpha.' The mind is like a computer, and once you have programmed this command into it, you will be able to go into alpha at a moment's notice with your eyes open just by crossing your fingers and making the intention to enter it.

Then count yourself back and you are ready to use alpha whenever you need it at a moment's notice.

A good use of instant alpha is for finding a parking space. About two streets away from your destination cross your fingers and on your mind's screen visualize an empty parking space. (Never see a car leaving a spot. That is too manipulative.) When you arrive a parking space will be waiting for you.

Once I was going to lunch with three other Witches and we arrived at the restaurant to find all the parking spaces on the street and in the car park filled. We laughed when we realized that none of us had bothered to arrange for a space. We each thought one of the others would do it. So while we drove around the block each of us used instant alpha to get a parking space. When we circled around to the front of the restaurant, there were four parking spaces waiting for us all in a row! But we only used one.

THE PINK STAR MEDITATION

Self-esteem and proper self-love are at the core of successful magic and successful living. The Pink Star Meditation is a prerequisite for all spells – health, wealth, love, protection, success – because it will strengthen your belief that it is correct to have these things. Self-esteem is basic to Witchcraft because magic can be done only by people who know they are worthy of it. If you have self-esteem, you will not feel guilty about having material things or about your ability to create and possess your own fortune. After all, you can't contribute to the good fortune of others if you don't have anything to share. Use the Pink Star Meditation to clear your mind on these matters and remove the mental obstacles that prevent successful magic.

Lie down, close your eyes and count yourself into alpha. Visualize the sky and the cosmos. See the light of the universe, the God/Goddess, the Force, the All, or whatever you choose to call the Source of all living things. See white light coming from this source entering each foot.

Next allow the light to travel up your body, stopping momentarily to empower each chakra. See the seven chakras as coloured crystals in the same sequence as the colours in the Crystal Countdown. The feet are red, the spleen orange, the solar plexus yellow, the heart green, the throat blue, the forehead indigo, the crown orchid.

As the white light exits through the crown it becomes a silver lotus flower opening out into the solar system. Your consciousness can travel on this flower, its petals softly and gently propelling you through space.

Travel past the sun and all the planets. Soar out among the stars and planets we have not discovered yet. Enter new and unknown solar systems far beyond the range of earthly telescopes and radar systems. As you look ahead you see a bright pink star, its ways extending far out into space. Travel towards this pink star, and as the first rays from it touch you, feel its power drawing you into it, further and further to its centre. You feel warm and exhilarated by the pink light. It surges through every part of your body. The rays fill your entire being and emanate as wings. You feel total self-esteem and total self-love. You are now one with the entire universe, the All, the God/Goddess. You and the cosmos exist in perfect harmony and perfect love.

While still inside the pink star reach out and grasp two handfuls of pink light and make the decision to return to earth. With the pink light in your body and in your hands, float back to earth, noticing the planets, suns, stars and other celestial bodies as you pass them. Return to earth and re-enter your physical body through the crown of your head.

With your eyes still closed, see two people to whom you

would like to give a gift of self-love and picture them on your mental screen. Take one hand of pink light and speak the name of one individual while placing the light inside his or her solar plexus. Then watch the person's body turn into pink light as it spreads throughout the body. Do the same for the other person.

Then give yourself total health clearance and count yourself up into beta.

MEETING YOUR ANIMA/ANIMUS

As we saw in the previous chapter, the Hermetic principle of gender tells us that each of us is both male and female. Physically we contain both X and Y chromosomes and both male and female hormones. Psychically or spiritually we contain both male and female energy, as does every created thing, as does the Creator/Creatrix. Usually our anima or animus – the opposite of our biological gender – remains relatively hidden and unconscious. And yet magic requires that we incorporate both male and female energies consciously into our Craft. This means that we must meet our anima or animus and develop a viable relationship with him or her. Here is a meditation for doing just that.

Lie down, close your eyes and count yourself into alpha. On the screen of your mind see a natural opening into the earth, such as a cave, a hollow tree trunk, a small animal hole, a well or a spring. It helps if this opening exists in ordinary reality and it is one that you have seen yourself at some time or other. It should also be a place where you feel comfortable. But if you do not know of such an opening, let any one appear on your screen just as you let an apple appear.

Spend a few moments looking at the opening, noticing what is around it. Be as sensory as you can: see objects and colours; note the smells; feel the air, the temperature; listen for any sounds or noises. Next enter the opening by letting your consciousness descend into it. Once inside you will be in a tunnel. Proceed down the tunnel, noticing the atmosphere, the texture of the walls, the amount of darkness or light. Shortly after you begin your descent you will see a light. Head for it. Notice what colour it is. When you pass through the light you will leave the tunnel and be in a room.

Find a chair and sit down. Look around the room. Notice the furnishings and objects, the colours, the walls, the amount of light. On one wall you will see a closed door that opens out on to a balcony. Go over to it, open it and step out on to the balcony. You will be looking out into the universe, as if you had stepped out on to the platform of a starship. Peer as far into the universe as you can. Become aware of the tremendous power, energy and light that pulsates through the cosmos. Take a few deep breaths and let this energy enter your body. Then step back inside and close the door.

Go back to your chair. Sit down. Ask your anima/animus to come to you. Be patient. In a few moments the door will open and your anima/animus will come in.

Offer her/him a chair and get to know each other. You may want to spend a few moments just looking at the spirit body he/she will have. Notice how he/she is dressed. Look at the face, the hands, the general shape of the body.

Ask the anima/animus for a name that she/he wants to be called. Tell him/ her that you need his/her energy in your magic. Ask the anima/animus what it needs from you. Talk over these things and get to know each other.

When you have finished the anima/animus will get up, go back out on the balcony and shut the door. When you next open the door he/she will be gone.

When you are ready to leave look around the room for the coloured light that marks the entry to the tunnel. Go into that light and pass quickly up the tunnel until you emerge at the opening where you began.

Then erase your screen, give yourself total health clearance and count yourself back up into beta.

I suggest you take this journey to your anima/animus about once a week for several weeks, using each session to get to know each other and to create a working relationship. Find out from him/her how you can introduce his/her energy into every aspect of your life. Most people discover that the anima/animus is their first spirit guide. He or she may introduce you to others.

Most spirit guides, whether they be an anima/animus, a power animal, an angel or a mythical character, need us as much as we need them. Many Witches and shamans claim that they did not find their spirit helpers but the spirit helpers found them. Guardian spirits are eager to find us; power animals will hunt us down and befriend us if we stay receptive to the natural world and do not clog our senses and minds with the frivolous distractions of modern life. A Witch keeps her animal familiars around because they attune us to the natural world and the spirit that pervades it. Keep looking and listening. There are faces and voices in the clouds. The starry sky at night is alive with laughter and song.

Establish a reciprocal relationship with your spirit helpers from the start. Be aware of how you fit into their mission and purpose, and do your best to be a partner or companion to your spirit guides. We must prove to them that we understand the reciprocal nature of the universe – that we are all related.

A REMINDER

Magic is the ability to change consciousness at will. It is more than just wishful thinking, however. The laws of Witchcraft are the laws of magic. They derive from the seven

Hermetic principles that scientists are now discovering operate on the physical plane. I would suggest that if you want to become adept in the ancient ways of our ancestors and in the most modern scientific practices, you should meditate on the seven Hermetic principles and practise the meditations and exercises in this chapter. Only practice will make you a competent Witch. Start with reasonable tasks for a beginner, like finding parking spaces or looking for lost objects, communicating with other people or caring for your health and the health of your family. Don't expect lightning bolts to flash out of your fingertips yet and don't imagine that you will ever change the physical laws of nature.

CODA: THE SCIENCE BEHIND
ALL RELIGIOUS PRACTICES

I am often asked how people can practise the science of Witchcraft and still retain membership in mainstream churches. Some of the Salem Witches are practising Catholics, Protestants and Jews. A few are even Zen Buddhists. But this is not unusual. For example, there have always been Christian Witches. The fate that befell indigenous people in North and South America, Africa, and Polynesia befell pagan culture in Western Europe as well – Christian missionaries 'converted' pre-Christian peoples and the magical practices were blended. Christian magic and Pagan magic worked hand in hand, and only the missionaries were fooled into thinking that baptism wiped away the old beliefs and practices. During the Burning Times many Witch families officially joined the church and followed the Christian calendar of holy days but still kept the old magic at home: the herbs, knots, bindings, oils, candles, spells and occasionally a magic circle beneath the moon. Wise women who preserved the old knowledge and rituals often practised in secret.

185

Even today many Christian people still rely on the remnants of once-powerful Craft spells and practices. They bury an opened pair of scissors by the door to send enemies away or hang a horseshoe over the door or bed to neutralize harmful energy. Women hang dried herbs and pieces of medicinal bark in their kitchens without really knowing why. To many individuals these are just old superstitions that 'make them feel better'. When done without a knowledge of the science behind them, they only partially work.

My course in the science of Witchcraft does not proselytize. I don't want people to give up their religions. They can learn the Craft and apply it to their own forms of prayer and ritual in their churches and synagogues. The Hermetic Laws are universal and are the underpinning for all serious spiritual work: Pagan, Christian, Buddhist, Muslim, Jewish. For example, if Catholic prayer, novenas, Masses, litanies, rosaries, holy cards, candles, statues, medals, incense and other religious articles work, it is because the Christian uses them in alpha. All sacred tools work if we are in a sacred state of mind that allows light to enter the pineal gland, shift consciousness, and link our thoughts and intentions with the mind of the universe.

Those who deride moon worshippers, sun worshippers and the efficacy of sacred objects, prayers and rites overlook a crucial scientific fact: light energy is the source of life, intelligence and all knowledge. When we open the pineal gland by shifting our consciousness into alpha, light enters and brings knowledge and understanding. This is the basis of all religion – to let the light in, to let Divine Wisdom in. Mystics in every religious tradition speak of alpha states of consciousness and the lure of Divine Light, although they do so in their own metaphors and images. In their own ways they have learned how to enter alpha as they pray or worship. They learn how to become enlightened.

Religious people without alpha skills merely recite their

prayers from rote or rely on priests and ministers to do their rituals and praying for them. When their spiritual questing fails to give them answers or produce results, they seek out oracles or readers to give them information about the most pressing issues of their lives. Nine out of ten people who come to me at weekends for readings at my daughter Jody's Witch shop, Crow Haven Corner, are Christians looking for answers that they could find for themselves if they had spiritual teachers in their own religious communities who could teach them practical techniques for going into alpha and then going directly to the source as Witches do.

The Higher Intelligence (under whatever name we call it – the All, God/Goddess, the Tao, the Force) knows more than we do. It alone sees the big picture. It *is* the big picture. Even though alpha opens our eyes to a greater chunk of the picture, we can never see the totality in this life. People of every religious persuasion can ask for knowledge and understanding. But for Witches asking is not enough. We must also *work* for it in alpha. We must use the physical as well as the metaphysical laws to enhance our lives and to enlighten our understanding.

· 7 ·

A WITCH'S LIFE:
EVERYDAY MAGIC

A Witch's life is filled with magic and power. We don't reserve our Craft just for certain days of the week or certain seasons of the year. Most of us live the life of a Witch completely and totally, day in and day out, and through the nights whether awake or asleep, for even our dreams have power. Every hour and minute is filled with magic and meaning and there is nothing that happens to us, good or bad, that is not part of the Craft. A Witch's life is filled with enchantment. In this chapter we will look at the everyday magic that enhances a Witch's life: magical spells for health, prosperity, protection and love. In the next chapter we will consider the common milestones of life: marriage, birth, raising children and death.

BASICS

There are basic guidelines and principles that apply to all magical workings. Learn these first and they will provide a sound foundation for all your Craft practices. They are simple steps but necessary for successful magic: setting up an altar, casting a circle, charging tools, writing out a spell, determining the best times of the month for spells and brewing a protection potion.

Setting Up An Altar

If possible, position the altar so that when you are standing in front of it and facing it, you are also facing north, the direction of mystery and constancy. Some Witches prefer to face east, the place of new light, freshness, rebirth and beginnings. Whichever direction you face, know what powers and meanings it holds. It is important to ground yourself geographically by the way your altar is positioned and constructed. Whether round, square or rectangular, the altar sits in the centre of the four directions and each direction should be represented on it in some way.

Traditions vary as to which elements, colours, animals, or spirits guard the four directions and which symbols or talismans should be used to represent them. I set up my altar with earth in the north, fire in the east, air in the south and water in the west. The archangels are Uriel in the north for earth, Michael in the east for fire, Gabriel in the south for air and Raphael in the west for water.

All the elements and spirits abide in each direction geographically, and the seasons of the year and times of day occur in each quarter also. Remember that on a subatomic level as well as in a mystical state of consciousness, time and place do not exist as we know them; the altar in the magic circle stands outside of time and place. There is more than one way to set up the quarters of an altar, and you need not fear that if you miss something, you upset cosmic forces. What's important is that each Witch's altar embodies all four elements and the space-time energies that are important for her or his personal magic.

One way to represent the elements on the altar is with stone or oil for earth, a candle for fire, incense or an air plant for air and a bowl or chalice of water (naturally) for water.

Place a pentacle on the altar to define the centre. The point should be positioned upwards towards the north. Above the pentacle place a thurible for burning incense. Place a black candle to the left of the pentacle and a white candle on the right. The altar is a power spot, a conduit or circuit in touch with energies that pervade the universe, and the black and white candles are used to direct energy. Witches believe that energy enters on the left and exits on the right. This is true of the human body as well as an altar – energy enters through the left hand, for example, and exits through the right. A black candle will draw in energy just as it draws in all the colours in light. A white candle reflects all the colours of light energy and will thus function like a transmitter, sending out the energy from your altar.

Stones, herbs, colours and talismans on the altar should also reflect this basic left–right circuit. Every item corresponds to the purposes for which you are working. Charge them (see below) either to draw in or send out energy and place them to the left or right of the altar. For example, if you are working a spell to enhance your career or get a better job, you might charge lapis lazuli, cinnamon or cloves for this purpose and place them on the left. These ingredients are associated with Jupiter, the planet that rules careers and jobs. On the right side would be turquoise or purple amethyst, charged to send your spell out into the world where the energy will do your bidding. (You could also put a royal-blue candle on the left and a turquoise candle on the right.)

Place protection items such as black coral or sea salt on each side of the altar. The need for protection around an altar is often misunderstood. We are not worried about monsters or demons who will try to interfere with our magic. Magic is never performed in a state of fear but joyously and with a sense of wonder. Rather we protect our work from energies and forces that might be conflicting with our

190

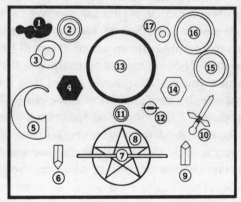

1 Black Coral
2 Goblet
3 Protection Potion
4 Black Beeswax Candle
5 Bull's Horn
6 Quartz Crystal (pointed towards you)
7 Wand
8 Altar Pentacle
9 Quartz Crystal (pointed away from you)

10 Athame
11 Statue of the Goddess
12 Bell
13 Incense Burner
14 White Beeswax Candle
15 Ash Pot
16 Incense Pot
17 Altar Oil

intentions, such as astrological influences that are not synch-ronized with our spell, or other magical work occurring in the area that is at cross-purposes with our own. Sometimes we ourselves bring contrary moods or intentions (usually in the form of mental distractions) to our circle or altar, so we use protection items to neutralize their influences too.

Charging Tools

A Catholic chaplain at a Boston hospital came to me for instruction because he spent a great deal of time anointing the dying and he felt the Catholic Church had not told him enough about spiritual tools, such as the holy oils, frank-incense, myrrh and candles he used in the last rites. Witchcraft has powerful techniques for charging sacred objects, and I showed him how to charge his oils and candles to make them more effective conductors of both sacred energy and his own. Today he feels that his work with the dying and their families is much more satisfying for all involved.

Charging a tool is a method of transferring energy from you and from the cosmos into an article that will be used for magical purposes. The first tool to be charged is the wand or staff with which you will cast magic circles. It's a Catch-22 situation, however, because all tools must be charged within a magic circle, yet the circle should be cast with a wand, sword or athame. If you have friends who are Witches, you could ask them to cast a circle for you to charge your wand. Or you can cast a special circle with sea salt, which can be purchased in a supermarket or health-food store, or from your local Witch shop.

The Sea Salt Circle

Before casting the circle set up your altar (along with your wand and all the tools you will need) inside the area where you intend to create the circle because you cannot step outside the circle once it is cast. If you do, you break the circle's energy and will have to begin again. This includes even a hand or elbow that may protrude, so be sure your circle is large enough for the work you need to do.

To cast the traditional nine-foot circle take a cord four and a half feet long and secure one end of it in the centre of the space where you want to cast your circle. When you stand at the free end of it and use it as a compass, you can outline a perfect nine-foot circle. Find magnetic north with a compass and begin dropping the sea salt in a circle, walking clockwise. After completing one full circle make another circle about one foot inside the first, and then a third one a foot inside the second. You must have your altar set up and your wand and all the tools you will need inside the circle before you begin.

When you have the circle cast with sea salt, hold your wand in your hand, go into alpha (eyes closed) and examine the wand psychically for any incorrect energy. Even if your wand has been recently made from new materials, there may be energies that are inappropriate for magical work – not necessarily harmful energies, just inappropriate. Look at the wand's aura to determine the energies to be removed. Seeing an aura is very similar to seeing the apple in the Apple Meditation. Let the aura appear on the screen of your mind. Some people find it helps to think of their screens as computers on which they bring up a file called 'aura'. An aura will look like a light radiating around the physical body or object.

With your eyes still closed, hold the wand in both hands and with alternating motions of both hands push out the unwanted energies while you say, 'I neutralize any incorrect energy in this wand'. Then put a small dab of protection potion (see pages 201–2 for recipe) on the wand. Hold the wand in both hands again, close your eyes and see your own aura. Allow it to travel around and into the wand. Watch your aura mingle with that of the wand. Notice how they both become brighter and stronger, extending outward into the space around you. Then say, 'I charge this wand to catalyse my every thought and deed by my will. I ask that this be correct and for the good of all. So mote it be.'

This procedure is basically the same for charging any tool, herb, article of clothing or jewellery or any object that you want to fill with your own energy so that the tool becomes a magical object capable of carrying out your spells. Go into alpha and look at the object for incorrect or inappropriate energies. If the object is small enough, hold it in your left hand and cover it with your right hand. Push incorrect energy out with the right hand and send it out to dissipate in the cosmos, where it will have no harmful effects. (Incorrect energy is harmful only in the sense that it is in the wrong place or object. Once removed, energy is simply energy.) Then check the object's aura again to make sure it is purely its own, that it contains no interference. Close your eyes and watch your aura and the objects mingle, becoming one. When the combined auras are strong and bright, state the purpose for which you are charging the object and say that this energy is now fixed and shielded from any contrary energy that could work against the object's purpose.

An alternative way to neutralize any incorrect energies in a tool or object is to place a dab of protection potion on it before charging it for the specific purpose.

Charging Herbs

Herbs must first be charged or catalysed before using them in potions or philters. A catalyst is any agent that induces or increases the rate of interaction between a substance and other agents. In herbal magic the aura from your mental energy acts as a catalyst upon the aura around the herbs, roots or flowers. The herb's aura is like a light packet that contains information from one or more planets. When you charge herbs, roots or flowers to perform a specific magical intention and then blend them together in a potion, you create more power. The energy of the combined auras empowers your magic.

The way to catalyse the energy of a herb is to take a pinch of it (or the desired amount), hold it in your left hand and sit quietly with your eyes closed. Go into alpha and then visualize and say aloud what you want this herb to do. Then direct that mental image into your hand and the herb by focusing your consciousness there. See in your mind's eye the aura of your own body around your hand, and then visualize the two auras mingling together. Focus on the person, place, or situation that you would like the herb to influence. After seeing everything completed in your mind's eye, the spell is done. Repeat out loud the magical intention you wish to bring about and then say, 'I ask that this be correct and for the good of all people. So mote it be.' Your spell will last four days if you have charged herbs, leaves or flowers. Root, bark, wood, seeds, beans and berries stay charged from three months to a year. Gums and resins stay charged for years.

You may use these charged herbs, roots or flowers by carrying them with you in cloth bags of the appropriate colours or you may burn them on charcoal as incense to release the energies. Or leave them in an open bowl in your home or workplace to send out or draw in what you want. While it is true that many herbs may be taken internally for medical purposes, the magic potions and philters in this book are not to be ingested in any way. The herbal magic discussed in this chapter is to prepare herbs only for carrying or wearing outside the human body, kept in the home or burned as incense. As you become more skilled in your craft, you may want to charge herbs in a Witch's magic circle and in conjunction with the correct planetary hours and days.

Casting A Circle
I explained the method for casting a circle in Chapter Four,

but here are the basic steps outlined to help you remember them:

1. Remove all animals and small children from the area and any furniture that you do not want to be inside your circle.
2. Set up your altar before you cast the circle.
3. Locate magnetic north with a compass and, holding the wand out from your body, go into alpha and see the wand's aura extending out from it, especially at the tip.
4. Visualize the tip of the wand creating a circle of light and energy, like a laser, as you walk clockwise three times around the area. The circumference drawn by the wand's tip will be the edge of your circle. Project white light out from the wand to create the circle of energy. In your mind see the circle as geometrically perfect and say to yourself that it is.
5. Walk around the circle the second time and say out loud, 'I cast this circle to protect me/us from all negative and positive energies and forces on any level that may come to do me/us harm. I draw into this circle only the energies and forces that are right for me/us and the most correct for my/our work.'
6. Walk around the circle the third time and say, 'I create sacred space. So mote it be.'
7. Invoke the four directions and the energies of the elements, angels and powers that reside in them by using the athame, wand, sword or index finger to draw an invoking pentagram as you face each direction. Use a ritual spell of invocation or one you write for yourself.
8. To open a circle hold the wand out over the circumference of the circle and, beginning at magnetic north, walk once around the circle counter-clockwise as you say, 'I send this circle into the cosmos to do my/our bidding. The circle is undone but not broken.'

Writing Spells

A spell is a mental projection, either spoken, written or thought. It is sent out into the universe to effect some change. In my coven we always write our spells down first and spend a few moments reading them to each other before casting our circle. If a member reads her spell in the circle and it is different from what she read to us before, we stop her and point out to her that that is not the way she had agreed to read it. It is very important that a spell is worded correctly because you will get exactly what you ask for so you must be careful. Otherwise, what you get may not be what you really want.

For example, a Salem Witch who was a former bank vice-president wrote a spell to get rid of all her bills. She worded it 'to get all my bills paid'. Shortly after casting the spell she started to receive bills she had forgotten about, such as an old college tuition bill for several thousand dollars, a medical bill; even a friend from whom she borrowed money several months before dropped by to remind her of her debt. She was swamped with bills and had to take out a loan to pay them off. She got what she asked for, but not in the way she wanted. So it is important to see your spell written out and to consider the way it is worded very carefully.

Write spells on parchment paper or on loose, unlined, unbonded sheets about four by five inches in size. Do not use recycled paper because whatever was written on it previously will be brought into your circle and it might contain energy that conflicts with the purpose of the spell. The formula we use is 'I ask in the name of [Goddess/God or the All] that I [state your name] be granted [here state your desire] . . . I ask that this be correct and for the good of all people. So mote it be.'

In the place for the name of the Goddess or God you can choose whatever name or form of the divinity with which you work. Since my coven is called the Black Doves of Isis,

197

we write our spells in the names of Isis and Osiris. Using these names does not mean that we are worshipping the old Egyptian gods. We use these terms in the Hermetic sense of uniting the forces of gender, both masculine and feminine, similar to the yin and yang. For us the names of the Goddess and God are energy forces that we draw in to do our bidding through the spell. Because we also work with Celtic Druidic traditions, we sometimes use the names Ceridwen, Cerne and Brigit. The important point is that you connect your intentions with the universe, the All or Total Intelligence in whatever form you know it.

Sybil Leek used to add a little verse to her spells that went 'In no way will this spell reverse, or place upon me any curse.' Often we write out our spells in simple rhymes to aid us in remembering them later on and because a spoken spell that rhymes carries with it the power of chant or song, which impresses upon our consciousnesses the potency of what we are saying. Here is a simple rhyme for a spell to bring pleasant dreams to a lover:

> *Falling star*
> *In a streaking path*
> *Destroy and dissolve*
> *All wrath.*
> *Sprinkle stardust,*
> *Shed your beam,*
> *Give my love*
> *A pleasant dream.*

Rhyming spells do not need to be great poetry. Use images and rhymes that sound powerful to you. Don't worry if a spell doesn't have perfect metre.

In the circle we read our spells out loud because sound is a tool of manifestation. Then we either burn the spells in an ash pot, used only for burning spells, or we carry them with us after we leave the circle. Sometimes we also charge a talisman, stone, candle or herb to reinforce the spell and to carry with us as a reminder.

In the spring near the feast of Beltane (1 May) we put the ashes collected over the previous year on our foreheads. The darkened area draws more light into the Third Eye. This ancient custom of anointing the forehead with ashes in the spring was co-opted by Christians and moved to Ash Wednesday as a reminder of their mortality. We do this in the spring to remind us of new life and rebirth.

Timing

You will be doing spells and magic circles at different times of the month and year. Certain times are more auspicious than others for certain types of spells and rituals. In general, the month has two halves – the time of the waxing moon and the time of the waning moon. The waxing moon is the best time to do a spell for growth, beginning, nurturing, initiation and enhancement. During the waning of the moon do spells to banish evil, lessen or remove obstacles or illness, neutralize enemies and remove harm. The three days after the new moon appears in the sky as a tender sliver just after sunset is the most powerful time to do a spell for growth and beginnings. The days just before the moon is fullest are the most powerful time for spells for fruition amd completion. The black moon or the dark of the moon – the three nights when the moon is not visible – is the most propitious time for banishing and neutralizing spells.

It is also wise to consult an astrological calendar to determine which signs the moon will be in during the month or which planets it will be near. If a spell is performed during a time when the moon is in a sign or in conjunction with a planet that is favourable or compatible with the purpose of the spell, you have a greater chance of the spell working.

What happens in the macrocosm happens in the microcosm. Outer space is also inner space. The great celestial movements correspond to movements within us. The archetypal patterns in the stars share the same power as the archetypal images in our personal unconscious and the collective unconscious. In other words there are common symbols in the mind, in the sky, in the earth. In a holographic universe there is a great unity of objects and symbols, and we do well to take account of these in our spells and rituals by performing them under celestial patterns that reinforce our intentions.

Astrological patterns always influence the effectiveness of magical workings, so the more you know about astrology and can make use of it in your spells and rituals, the better they will be. In an emergency, of course, you can do a spell at any time. To make up for a lack of knowledge about astrology, a Witch can ask that only the most correct and powerful astrological influences will come into a circle and that any that are harmful will be kept out. A powerful Witch whose magic is pure and focused will have success regardless of the signs, planets or phases of the moon.

Notes On Some Ingredients

Here are a few brief descriptions of some of the less familiar ingredients you'll use in your potions:

Witches use *vervain* to heighten psychic power by carrying it in a magic black bag and sprinkling it around candles on 2 February to ensure power for the next year. Vervain tea was once sipped to slow excessive bleeding.

Wolf hair is used for protection. In medieval times the scent of it when it was carried in a magic pouch would keep other animals in the woods from coming near. Also, Witches know that the wolf is a clannish animal that protects its own, so we invoke its spirit to guard us in our work.

Patchouli is a herb that has an aroma of fresh soil and deep jasmine. It is used by many Witches as a perfume potion. It brings love as well as protection.

Cinquefoil is a plant that has five-lobed leaves. It symbolizes the pentagram.

Goldenseal root and powder is ruled by Jupiter. Witches carry it and often use it in spells to become admired by people in positions of power. Witches also hang the root in their homes or offices to bring fortune. Goldenseal is also a healing herb, still used to seal wounds.

Often Witches put *mustard seeds* in their cash-registers at work to bring money. Carry them and keep a few in your wallet.

Witches use *camomile tea* to cure a sore throat or a heavy cough; we also charge our camomile tea bags in a circle to bring material comfort.

Heather is always grown in a Witch's herb garden, then dried and hung upside down in the home to bring riches. A little *cinnamon* in your morning coffee does the same thing.

Mistletoe was called 'heal all' by the Druids. My ancestors cut it down from the sacred oaks in England and let it fall on fresh cloth. It is used year-round but it is charged at the winter solstice to retain its full power. It is a plant of the sun and brings health and wealth and power.

Hibiscus flowers are dried by Witches into powder and used in letters and packages to loved ones far away. It is said that hibiscus and red poppy will bring a moon goblin to whisper sweet things in your lover's ear while he is sleeping, and he will dream of you as the moon goblins whisper your name.

Protection Potion

You should always have protection potion on your altar. I use the following ingredients for mine.

    2–4 cups spring water
      1 tablespoon powdered iron or iron shavings
      1 teaspoon vervain

2 tablespoons sea salt

2 tablespoons myrrh

2 tablespoons frankincense

1 pinch of wolf's hair *from a live, shedding wolf* (ask the keeper at the local zoo)

OPTIONAL: a pinch of graveyard dust. (Take the dirt from the top of a grave of someone you revere for courage or bravery; do not use a shovel or you could be arrested for disturbing a grave; always replace any sod that you pull up.)

Charge all the ingredients and put them in an enamel or iron pot that you use solely for brewing protection potion. Bring to a slow simmer. Go into instant alpha and move your hands clockwise over the potion while saying, 'I charge this potion to protect me [and anyone I designate] from any positive or negative forces that come to do harm.'

Keep protection potion in a sealed bottle or jar. When you need it place a dab on both your wrists, your forehead and behind your neck. You can also dab it on the tyres of your car before a long journey or on your doors and windows to protect against intruders.

Important Reminders

Keep these seven points in mind when doing spells:

1. Do all spells and rituals in a magic circle.
2. Do all spells in alpha.
3. Always ask the God or Goddess that each spell or ritual be done in a way 'that is correct and for the good of all'.
4. Be careful of what you project for because you will get it, but it may not come in the form that you had intended. For example, don't simply project for a million pounds. You might receive it as a settlement for a car accident that leaves you paralysed. Always state that what you are

asking for is correct and for the good of all. You may also stipulate that the spell be totally acceptable to you in every way and that the money come in a safe and correct manner.

5. Some people try to 'negotiate' with a higher intelligence in order to make their spells work. 'Oh, God,' they pray, 'if I win the £500,000 premium bond, I'll never want anything else.' Yes, you will! Never limit yourself. A Christian mother once prayed every Sunday in church that her son could get into college, promising her God that she would take up three jobs if he did. Her projection came through and her son went off to college. And true to form she took on two part-time jobs in addition to her regular job to pay for the tuition. After one month the boy dyed his hair green, dropped out of college and hitch-hiked to California to live in a nudist commune. The mother was stuck with the three jobs to pay off the term's tuition fees. Although this woman would not have considered her prayers a form of black magic, she was trying to manipulate someone else's life without knowing if the projection was really correct or needed. Her prayers were not said in a spirit of correctness and for the good of all. The woman's son never wanted to go to college and she never wanted to have three jobs. Witches would say that she interfered with her son's karma.

6. Often we don't have to do a spell to project for money because what we want might be available to us without buying it. For example, if you want to live in a better house, project yourself living in it rather than receiving the money to buy it. You may not need money. You may meet and marry someone with such a house. Or you may find a lodger who will help with the rent. Or you may win a house or be able to buy one with no money down. And don't rule out the unexpected gift. Sometimes by psychically projecting for something it just comes to us as a gift from someone or out of a situation that we never

dreamed would occur. Once I wanted to go to England but didn't have the money. Shortly after casting a spell that I would somehow get to England, a British chemical company hired me to do some psychic diagnoses of their employees to determine if they were engaged in substance abuse or stealing from the company's stock. They paid my way to England.

My ex-husband was once helping friends build a flight of stairs and needed three more bags of cement to finish the job. But since it was a holiday they could not go to the hardware store for the additional bags. As they took a break from the hot sun he said, 'If we only had three more bags of cement.' Moments later an elegantly dressed woman drove up in a Cadillac, opened her boot, and said, 'I saw you working over here so I brought over these three spare bags of cement that have been sitting in my garage for months. I'll never use them. Maybe you can.' My ex-husband thought I had 'zapped' for them, but they were really a projection from his own desires.

7. Jealousy is a green-eyed monster that can dilute and block even the best spells. It has no place in magic. Even unconscious envy of others' good fortune can ruin a spell. Occasionally I have discussed my projections or achievements with other people and have felt their jealousy. Others who are envious can neutralize or weaken our magic, as can our own jealousy and envy. Be discreet in discussing personal ventures or achievements. Don't brag or boast. Others working magic for the same thing might work against you. And if you do magic against someone else's goals, you are practising black magic.

PROTECTION SPELLS

All living creatures have ways to protect themselves: fangs, claws, thorns, camouflage colouring, speed, acute senses of vision and hearing. The Goddess's plan is that as long as a species has a purpose, it will survive. She has not abandoned any plant, bird or animal to live in a hostile environment without the means to survive. Even human beings can protect themselves from harm, evil and danger. Whereas our bodily structures are often not as powerful or sensitive as our brothers' and sisters' in the animal kingdom, we have the intelligence and ingenuity to shape our environments and create the tools necessary for survival: fences, homes, door locks, weapons. In addition to the instinct for survival, we have been taught as children how to fend for ourselves and stay out of harm's way. Most of us learned not to speak to strangers, run out in the street without looking, venture into dangerous neighbourhoods alone, go out in the cold weather without bundling up. Some of it is common sense; some of it the traditional wisdom passed down from generation to generation.

Most of us, however, were not taught how to protect ourselves through magic, how to work with the higher forces to keep our lives in harmony and balance, how to shield ourselves from harmful attacks, both physical and psychic. Witches know that we are responsible for our safety and well-being. We also know how to promote our own welfare and defend ourselves without causing harm to others. People in the Craft do not share the widespread beliefs found in some religious and ethical systems that human beings are vulnerable and helpless, that our lives are determined by fate or a devil or forces too great for us to comprehend. We view some suffering as an inevitable part of life, but we do not resign ourselves to suffering the ills that befall us as if they were divine will. And we don't accept suffering as being a kind of karmic punishment for the evil we did in past lives.

Witches do not turn the other cheek. Nor do we have itchy 'trigger fingers'. Instead we use 'active resistance', a method of neutralizing harmful energy and polarizing a situation so that no one can do us harm. We actively resist efforts to hurt or thwart us; but we avoid hurting others in return. The Witch's law is that whatever you send out from you comes back threefold. That applies to both good and bad energy. Once one of my students was divorcing her husband of twenty-seven years and she told me she was 'sending back the bad energy he's sending me to teach him a lesson'. I was horrified, although I could sympathize with her needs and her anger. But I told her that none of us knows what lessons another person is here in this life to learn. We have trouble understanding the lessons we ourselves are supposed to learn! We cannot second-guess the Goddess about anyone, no matter how well we know that person.

Neutralizing Harm

There are several methods of neutralizing another person's harmful energy. The simplest way is to go into alpha and see the threatening person or situation with your Third Eye. Then see yourself painting a huge white X over him, her or it. Repeat this until you have blocked out the harmful scene. Say, 'I neutralize this' as you 'x' it out.

Another method is to use alpha to visualize the harmful person and see yourself binding his or her body, head, arms and legs with a beam of white light. Always ask, however, that this projection be done correctly and for the good of all. I use this technique when I see terrorists or murderers on television newscasts or when I read about similar atrocities in the newspapers. It is an excellent way of being involved magically in the welfare of your town or county or even in national affairs. It is similar to the projections done by prayer groups who meet and pray for the release of hostages or the capture of a criminal or an end to the drug problems in their neighbourhoods. Of course, we can't take on the problems of the entire world. We need to be selective and focus our energy. Usually Witches neutralize harm and do healing work on a rather personal and local level – their families and friends and neighbourhoods.

The Bottle Spell

This spell can be used to neutralize the power of those who intend to do you physical harm, or hurt your reputation, or in any way pose a threat to your security. You will need:

4 tablespoons frankincense or myrrh
4 tablespoons black powdered iron (available at pottery shops where ironstone is made)
4 tablespoons sea salt
4 tablespoons orris-root powder (or oak moss)
1 white candle
1 bottle with a cork or lid
mortar and pestle
parchment paper
black ink or black ballpoint pen
black thread

Mix the sea salt, orris-root powder and iron in a bowl. Then cut a piece of parchment to fit inside your bottle and write on it with black ink, 'I neutralize the power of [name your adversary] to do me any harm. I ask that this be correct and for the good of all. So mote it be.'

Roll up the parchment, tie it with a black thread to bind it and place it in the bottle. Fill the bottle with the dry ingredients. Then take the white candle and, while turning the bottle counter-clockwise, drip wax over the cork to seal it. Finally, secretly bury the bottle in a place where it will not be disturbed and no animal or person will dig it up. This spell is like a genie in a bottle. It should never be unleashed or the power of the spell is lost.

207

Polarity Spell

Often we sense that there is some energy imbalance in a room or home or situation but we are not sure what it is or what to do about it. When this happens use this Polarity Spell to balance the situation. Go into alpha and visualize a white candle burning before you. Stare at the flame carefully and notice if it begins to fade out, move, duplicate itself or change in any way. If it burns steadily and with consistent brightness, the energy is balanced. However, if it changes in any way, imbalanced energy, possibly harmful, is present. To correct it picture a rod with a sphere at each end. The rod is in an upright, vertical position. Place the imbalanced energy in the top sphere, visualizing it as a colour or a texture that you find unpleasant. In the bottom sphere place its opposite image, which will be balanced energy. Mentally turn the rod 180 degrees while saying to yourself, 'I polarize the energy [in this room, space etc.]. It is now corrected and balanced.' Remove the rod from your mental vision and see the candle again. It will remain still and bright.

The Protective Shield

In my course on the science of Witchcraft I teach my beginners a method for protecting themselves wherever they are and from any kind of physical or psychological harm. It is the most basic protective spell in the Craft but do not underestimate its efficacy. We call it the 'protective shield'.

Go into alpha and at your innermost level envisage a protective shield around you that resembles an egg. It is clear, shining, crystalline. See it grow brighter and stronger around your entire body until it is so large that it will always be well beyond the reach of your fingertips regardless of the direction in which you extend your arms. When you see the egg-shaped shield clearly, repeat the following several times: 'This shield protects me from all positive and negative energy and forces that come to do me harm. I ask that this be done correctly and for the good of all. So mote it be.'

I always put a protective shield around my car or any car I travel in, in addition to one around myself and others in the car. I firmly believe that I have avoided terrible collisions on several occasions when cars seemed to pass through each other instead of crashing. You can put shields around the members of your family, your home and surroundings. Periodically go into alpha and inspect the condition of your shields. Although the shields will remain, they occasionally need reinforcing. You can repeat the following affirmations periodically at an alpha level to reinforce your protective shield. If these do not suit you, use them as models for creating your own:

'Incorrect or harmful thoughts or suggestions will have no power over me at any level of mind.'

'Undesirable memories no longer affect me in an incorrect way.'

'I am protected in a correct way from all positive and negative energies and forces that may come to do me harm.'

Protective shields guard you in many ways. In addition to being a real barrier to physical danger, knowing that you live within an egg of safety makes you more attuned to danger on all levels. Once in secondary school I stayed a weekend with a girlfriend in Las Vegas who spent her evenings joyriding through the desert with some of the boys in her circle of friends. It was the trendy thing to do in those days! I joined them the first night I was there, a clear, fully moonlit night. As they got out on to the desert flats they turned off the headlights. I was jammed in the backseat on someone's lap and could not see where we were headed, but I suddenly felt sick with a strong sensation of danger. I pleaded with the boy driving the car to stop. He did, with some snide comment about my being a 'scaredy-cat'. But when he stopped and switched on the lights, we saw that we had stopped barely twenty feet from a gully that dropped down fifteen to twenty feet.

A Witch from Salem was once driving to visit a friend in Maine. As she drove along she felt someone or something tap on her shoulder. She slowed down to see what it could be since there was no one in the car but herself. This happened several times. At one point she pulled over on to the side of the road for a few seconds just to check out the backseat and calm her nerves. Nothing there. She got back on the motorway and started up a steep incline, driving slowly because she was anticipating the ghostly tap on her shoulder. As she drove over the top of the hill she saw a fourteen-car pile-up where a juggernaut had jack-knifed. Fortunately, she was going slowly enough to avoid being car number fifteen. Not only does the protective shield keep harm at a safe distance from us, but it can psychically trigger information for us, as in this case, so that we can pick it up, pay attention to it and use it in ways that will assure our safety.

Amulets And Talismans

Since the earliest times human beings have used amulets (fetishes of animals, birds, plants, parts of the body) and talismans (geometric shapes) to protect themselves from harm. We find them in the remains of ancient cultures and still see them dangling from charm bracelets today. Some of these are part of one's culture. The Italians, for example, wear a charm in the shape of a horn that represents the spiral chakra energy of the body. Arabs use many talismans, a common one being the 'Hand of Fatima', a representation of the hand of Muhammad's daughter Fatima with an eye on it. The Turks and Greeks wear blue glass beads to symbolize eyes staring out at the world, watching protectively. In our culture a rabbit's foot and a horseshoe are amulets. Other talismans and amulets are personal and have meaning only for the individual who uses them.

Traditionally, Witches have found protection in a variety of amulets and talismans, the pentacle being the most common and important. Another favourite is Solomon's Seal, two superimposed triangles, one pointing upwards, the other downwards, inside a circle. This talisman represents the mechanical dynamics of the earth and protects its structures. It is especially good to protect cars or any equipment that operates on motors.

Solomon's Seal

The Tetragrammaton

Another talisman I use for protection is the tetragrammaton, a yellow equilateral triangle inscribed with the Hebrew letters for the fourfold name of God. If you draw a tetragrammaton on the floor in chalk and leave it for four days, you will be forewarned about harm heading your way.

Usually I have found that the warning comes verbally when someone alerts me about gossip or unfriendly conversation. It can also indicate the course of this harmful talk.

Protecting Your Home

Witches take great care in protecting their homes. This was true even before the Burning Times, but it took on added urgency during those fearful centuries. I often wonder how many more Witches would have been captured and executed had they not protected themselves. Whether we live alone or with our families, safeguarding the sanctity and security of our homes is very important to us. The lucky horseshoe originated because of the protective properties of iron, which is ruled by the planet Mars and diffuses harmful energies. A traditional practice was to hang the horseshoe over a door or in a barn with the open end up, so that harmful energy would come in one end and turn around and exit through the other. In tearing down old colonial homes in New England, workers have discovered horseshoes hidden in the walls, probably put there by the original owners who feared they would be discovered practising Witchcraft if they displayed them openly.

Iron nails also diffuse harm. Old railroad nails or hand-made nails from earlier times make wonderful protection nails. Charge them first and drive three of them into a window frame, one in each lower corner and the third in the middle of the top to form a triangle. This will protect the window. If you are building a new house, lay four charged nails in the corners of the foundation of the house. Or if you live in an older home, simply place four charged nails in the four corners, either in the attic or in the basement. Your home will then be 'nailed tight' against any harmful forces.

Another effective home protection spell uses a mental

212

representation of the Cheops pyramid, which Witches have long recognized for its magical powers, as did the Egyptians who built it. The triangular structures are hailed even in physics for their strength and power. Go into alpha and visualize the pyramid with its four equal sides made of brilliant white light or clear quartz crystal. Position the pyramid over your house with one wall aligned with magnetic north. Ask that this pyramid of light energy protect you and your house and keep you safe. Ask that it be done correctly and for the good of all.

I add a little extra power to my home protection spells by visualizing a sleeping dragon with its shiny green body curled up around my house. It waits and will awaken when someone comes to do harm. In ancient legends the sleeping dragon guarded the treasure hoard in the mountain or castle. Today our treasure is our family and loved ones. I know Witches and others who prefer some other animal spirit to the dragon. You can use any animal power that comes to you or that you summon for this special purpose.

On the inside of my kitchen door I have a protection philter that has kept harm away for years. (A philter is like a potion except that the ingredients are not brewed.) Here are the ingredients:

    5 drops patchouli oil
    3 drops frankincense oil
    6 parts sandalwood powder
    1 part wolf's hair
    2 parts cinquefoil leaves
    4 parts powdered myrrh

Mix the dry ingredients, then bind them with the oils. Place the philter in a black muslin bag and hang it on your door. Be sure to keep in out of the reach of children and animals.

Psychic Attack

Nearly every day I meet people who are convinced that someone has 'hexed' them with an evil curse. They interpret all the natural disasters of their lives in terms of someone else's evil-doing. Unemployment, illness, loneliness and troublesome relationships are seen as the result of psychic attack or a family curse from the old country. Unethical psychics may even encourage this fear, telling their clients that someone has indeed cursed them and their families, but for an exorbitant fee the psychic will light a candle or do whatever is needed to remove the curse.

Very few people know what psychic attack really is. Despite the images created by film-makers and the tremendously popular novelists of the horror genre, most of us are not in any danger from psychic attack. People are far more likely to be harmed by their own unguarded thoughts than by evil curses from foes and enemies who use malice or stick pins into dolls. Hexes, curses and evil sorcery do exist, but unscrupulous practitioners who are versed in these forms of abuse are few and far between. Most of us will go safely through life without ever encountering them.

What we should really be wary of are our own thoughts and actions (and those of others) that can unwittingly project harmful situations into our lives. Most people's malicious wishes are not meant to do harm, and as a matter of fact they prove to be harmless. This is because very few of our thoughts are absolute and focused. Contrary feelings of guilt or love dilute the mind's harmful intentions and thus dilute the hostile energy. However, a strong, absolute thought and a strong evil intention can actually do harm.

The best way to protect yourself from psychic attack, whether in the form of a curse or a harmful thought projection, is to be aware of the possiblity, refuse to accept it and then do something positive to counteract it. Neutralize your 'enemy's' power by psychically painting over it with a big

214

white X, as you learned earlier in this chapter. Trigger your psychic shield when someone says something harmful about you. Also, visualize the protective energies that your pentacle draws into your body and your mind when you hear or see something evil.

There are many ways to protect yourself psychically, but if you think that you are still in real danger, seek the help of others. Ask your coven members to help or other Witches to work a spell for you or to send you protection from their magic circle. They can also make you a special talisman, philter or amulet. And by all means do not overlook the most obvious way to protect yourself from physical harm – call the police.

Not all psychic harm comes from others. We must take responsibility for misfortune if it befalls us and not look outside ourselves for scapegoats. It is always easier to blame someone else for our difficulties than to take personal responsibility for our own lives. In some cases where you are the cause of your own problems, you may need professional help to get your life back into shape. An outside view from a Witch, a psychic, a therapist or a counsellor may be what you need. Often we stand too close to our own problems to see them for what they really are – us 'zapping' ourselves.

WEALTH AND PROSPERITY

Witches need to be prosperity conscious. Wealth and personal prosperity are essential for a happy and fulfilling life. While I never advocate that money becomes the primary focus of life – it certainly is not the primary *goal* of life – we cannot live a fully human and productive life if we have to continually scrimp and worry about where our next meal will come from or how we will buy clothes for our children or send them to school. Many Witches mistakenly believe that since so many of our traditions come from poor, rural areas of Europe, we must continue to live a lifestyle that reflects our ancestors' poverty. I disagree. Those who want to model themselves on our forerunners should remember that many wealthy people practised the Craft too.

Some spiritual traditions value poverty or the spirit of poverty as an ideal. I agree with the underlying message of these beliefs in that the primary goal of life is spiritual, not material. For some very dedicated people a life of actual poverty or self-renunciation may be the right path for them at certain times in their lives, and their example can serve as an inspiration for others. But not everyone should feel called to live a life of poverty, especially the abject poverty that cramps the development of our talents and our ability to serve others.

It is very difficult to balance spiritual and material needs. The Law of Polarity suggests that either extreme wealth or extreme poverty is not natural. Obsession with both wealth and self-imposed poverty can strip the human spirit of its ability to develop and evolve. As Witches we try to live somewhere in the golden mean. It is just as wrong to give away your last penny as to give away nothing at all. Each of us is at a particular place on a spiritual path and each of us must live in a material world at the same time. We must each strike the proper balance so that we can flourish as both spiritual and physical beings.

Many years ago I worried about charging a fee to people who enrolled in my Witchcraft classes. Like many others in the Craft, I thought that accepting a fee was somehow compromising my moral responsibility to share my knowledge with others. At the same time, however, I spent many sleepless nights worrying about how I would pay my bills. After struggling financially for some time I realized that if I wanted to continue teaching, I would have to charge money. A surprising thing then happened. My students seemed to value the classes more and took them more seriously. They also demanded a better quality of teaching since they were paying for it with hard-earned money. I became a better teacher, more keenly aware of the exchange being made between my students and me. They paid tuition; I taught the Craft. Furthermore, my self-esteem was heightened when I realized that people were willing to pay money for what I had to offer. My tuition fees have never been exorbitant, but I am always touched by some students in every class for whom the fee is a real sacrifice. For them it is worthwhile, and I realize my responsibility to make it worthwhile for them.

Read through the following statements about wealth and money. Many of them are part of our so-called folk wisdom. Notice your immediate, intuitive response to each one. Don't spend too much time analysing them. Just read each and see if you agree or disagree with it.

'Money seekers are hedonists.'

'Money corrupts.'

'Money is the root of all evil.'

'You don't need money to be happy.'

'The best things in life are free.'

'Rich people tend to be corrupt and selfish.'

'To walk a spiritual path you should give away your possessions.'

If you tend to agree with these comments, you may be creating psychic roadblocks to prosperity. You may be rooting yourself in attitudes that will prevent you from moving ahead in your job, receiving financial windfalls or simply making enough money to live comfortably or provide for your family. You can neutralize these attitudes and reprogramme your thinking. Money magic and prosperity spells will project the material comforts and the wealth that you need and at the same time teach you to accept them. In the meantime repeat the following affirmations until they become part of your consciousness. Soon they will draw into your life whatever you need to improve your financial situation:

'Money enables us to obtain the goods and services that we need and helps us provide these services to others.'

'Money is an acceptable form of exchange throughout the world.'

'Money is neutral and can be used for good.'

'I create my own financial situation.'

When we hang on to beliefs that we don't deserve a better car or home, or that we are not qualified for a promotion, we project those beliefs into our lives and they come true. On the other hand, if we can use alpha to get a parking space, we can use it to increase our income or get a better-paid job. If you deserve a parking space, and the All arranges one for you, how much more do you deserve a good job? Most of the things we never seem to get in life elude us because we have convinced ourselves that we do not deserve them and then we stop working to acquire them. There is no real difference in manifesting a parking space or a million pounds. The only limits to your Witch magic are those that you impose yourself, and I have come to the conclusion, after dealing with all kinds of people over the years, that all our limitations come from a lack of self-esteem.

Once again self-esteem and proper self-love are at the core of successful magic and successful living. The Pink Star Meditation (page 180) is a prerequisite for all money spells for it will bolster self-esteem and create a strong self-image. It will strengthen your belief that it is correct to have personal wealth and health and to share them with others. Remember that every 'I believe' must be turned into an 'I know'. It is one thing to believe something, another to actually know it.

Sometimes projecting for needed money can work apparent miracles. Years ago, when my daughters and I moved to our new home, money was tight. We stopped in a restaurant for lunch, and when I looked at the menu I realized that we would not be able to afford lunch because I would be about £5 short. Jody, who was around nine years old at the time, felt sorry for me and I could tell by the question in her eyes that she wanted to help. I told her we would need £5 more if we were going to order. She looked down at her plate, and I knew that she was projecting for the money. Suddenly a £5 note floated down out of the air and on to her plate. The waitress who was standing there saw the note and our surprise at it, but she said nothing. We looked around to see if someone had dropped it by mistake, but we were sitting at a table in the middle of the room and no one was near us.

A Magic Wish List

To make a magic wish list sit back and think about the material things you need for about fifteen minutes. Evaluate them carefully, discarding what is not truly necessary, selecting only those that you must have. Then write out a spell, asking in the name of a higher source for the items you need. List them and read the list over out loud. By reciting the list you are charging your intentions with vocal vibrations and the projection is fortified with magical energy. Burn the list or carry it with you or keep it in a place that holds magic for you.

The Crystal Moon List

If you project a wish list in conjunction with the phases of the moon, what I call a Crystal Moon List, you will have an even greater chance of seeing your dreams come true. Begin the spell on the first full moon after your birthday each year. Compile the list of only material objects that you want or need. (Intangibles like love and happiness can be projected by using other meditations.) Recite the list aloud, asking in the name of the Higher Intelligence that makes sense to you to grant your requests.

Years ago I was doing psychic consulting work for a large corporation in England, during which time my daughter Jody had projected for a Rolex watch on her Crystal Moon List. When I arrived back in Salem there was a package waiting for me from the corporation. Since I had already received my salary, I wondered what it could be. It was an extra gift – a Rolex watch. Since I have never been able to wear watches because my psychic energy always seems to break the timing mechanisms, I decided to give it to Jody as a present, not knowing that just days before she had projected for it on her Crystal Moon List. How happily surprised we both were!

Herbal Prosperity Spells

Herbs ruled by Jupiter will draw money and prosperity. (See list of plants, page 291.) Cloves and cinnamon can be charged for a spell and sometimes added to foods. Skullcap and tonka beans are not edible but can be carried or worn in a royal-blue or purple bag to bring luck, money and influence. Valerian root will attract money; red clover tops draw customers to your business; and mistletoe wins success, fortune and gold.

Crush cinnamon, cloves, sandalwood, mustard seeds and tonka beans into a powder using a mortar and pestle. Sprinkle the powder anywhere money is kept, such as in a purse or wallet, cash-register drawer or a safe-deposit box. Or carry the powder in a gold lamé or bright blue pouch.

Herb and Crystal Spell

The following mixture can be used in spells to bring prosperity and gain money in unexpected ways. Ingredients include:

    4–5 tonka beans
      1 goldenseal root
      1 teaspoon mustard seeds
      3 cups sea salt
      1 clear quartz crystal

Cover the crystal in sea salt for twelve days, then run it under tap water to recharge its electrical force. Place it with the other ingredients in a bowl and hold it in your left hand. Go into alpha and charge the crystal and the herbs to bring you money or wealth in a way that is for the good of all. Then place all the ingredients in a gold lamé bag.

A Money Perfume

The following money potion can be dabbed on your wrists, forehead and solar plexus to strengthen your spells. It also helps to dab small amounts on bank deposit slips, job applications and any correspondence that deals with money. Mix the ingredients in a stainless steel or enamel pot. (Do not use an iron pot except for protection potion. Iron will neutralize and diffuse the energy. An aluminium pot will poison the liquid.) Charge each of the following ingredients:

    2 cups spring water
    $\frac{1}{8}$ oz heliotrope oil
      heather herb or heather oil
      cinnamon sticks
      gold jewellery (not gold plate) or silver jewellery
    2 tablespoons sea salt
    1 camomile tea bag (so leaves stay filtered)
      red clover (in unbleached muslin bag)

Put all the charged ingredients into a saucepan and mix them together. Bring the mixture to a slow simmer, then turn off the stove. (If possible, use a gas or wood stove, for electrical stoves can interfere with the energy.) If you have a large denomination note, such as £50, place it on the stove next to the pan, but don't let it catch fire! Sometimes you have to spend money to make money, but you should not have to *burn* money to get money! Etch the word *money* or *wealth* on the side of a gold, yellow or bright blue candle and, as the potion is warming, hold the burning candle over the note. Or place the candle in a holder and pile money around it. When you finish you will have a potion that can be dabbed on your wrists, forehead and solar plexus. Wipe the jewellery clean and wear it as usual. The jewellery helps to charge the potion and in turn is infused with the energy of the money spell. Wearing it will bring prosperity.

You can also pour the potion, once it has cooled, over a charged crystal. Seal the potion in a jar and place it on your altar, or if you have made the potion for someone else's use, give it to him or her as a gift.

A Money Philter

Here is a recipe for a money philter that can be used to attract wealth, food, clothing and all necessary goods.

- 1 tablespoon yellow mustard seeds
- 1 tablespoon mistletoe
- 1 tablespoon safflowers
- 1 tablespoon cloves

Add:
- 10 drops sweet orange oil
- 10 drops sandalwood oil
- 10 drops jasmine oil

Bind the ingredients together with:

1 teaspoon myrrh
1 tablespoon frankincense

Mix all the ingredients together and focus your intentions on the purpose of the spell. Cup your hands around the ingredients and charge the mixture by stating whatever you want it to accomplish. Say, 'I charge these herbs to bring [state what you want]. This spell assures that changes will bring gain and benefit. I ask that this spell be correct and for the good of many people. So mote it be.'

Colours for Prosperity

Certain colours of the spectrum attract abundance. Blend these colours into your wardrobe, home furnishings, office or car. The following colours are especially good for prosperity:

Royal blue, purple and turquoise – the colours of Jupiter – trigger success and influence people in high places. They also bring good fortune.

Gold and yellow – the sun's colours – bring health, wealth and promote success and winning. The element gold brings physical strength. Yellow brings news, information and sometimes gossip.

Green, pink and copper are the colours of Venus and money, and represent growth and fertility. These colours bring prosperity and growth to business and professional endeavours.

Candle Money Spell

An effective candle spell for wealth and prosperity utilizes two black candles since black draws in all colour and energy in the universe. Etch your name and the words *money*, *wealth*, *riches* and any other words of power along the sides of the candles. Then light the candles and grasp them firmly in your hands until you feel your pulse throbbing beneath your fingers – a sign that your aura is mingling with the candles' auras and that your intentions are firmly grounded in the candles. Project for what you want, saying, 'These candles bring me wealth and riches.' When finished, extinguish the flame with a spoon, candle snuffer or your fingers (not your breath, which will change the spell). Begin this spell on Sunday, Thursday or Friday as these days honour the sun, Jupiter and Venus respectively. Relight the candles every night until they are completely burned down. Daily repetition will increase the spell's effectiveness and your own prosperity consciousness.

Magic and Gambling

A word about gambling and magic. I have always enjoyed playing the Massachusetts state lottery, but I have never won 'megabucks'. It is exciting to take part in an event in which thousands of people are projecting for the same end result. A large number of participants evens out the psychic odds and makes the game fair. Lotteries and other games can be fun ways to use your energies to manifest money; they should, however, be played in moderation. Also, I don't believe in luck. The people who win do so for a purpose. Everything comes about from self-directed energy and spells and is for a specific purpose, even though we may not always know what that purpose is. Witches don't have any monopoly on the lottery and to my knowledge are not cornering the money market. Most of the people who win are not Witches, but their winnings come from their own projections just as in magic. When it comes to important things in life, like financial security, we can all project powerfully. The only guidelines I would advise for gambling and games of 'chance' is to use moderation and never bet money that you or your family need for necessities.

LOVE

Love is the most magical part of human life. Falling in love is like coming under a spell. Being in love is a kind of enchantment that transforms our lives and makes us feel so

224

good that we hope against hope that the feeling will never end. When we are in love we experience the great cosmic link that binds us not only to the one we love but to all others. When we love our hearts expand and we feel our love reaching out to the boundaries of the earth, to the furthest corners of the universe. Love is something we naturally want to share, and in that universal sentiment we know deep in our hearts that love is the ultimate power or force in the universe. It is what we call 'God' or 'Goddess'.

Because love is the very stuff of magic, a Witch's magic has always been sought out by those who are looking for a lover, or need help in attracting a certain someone, or are searching for ways to improve and strengthen relationships. Every week the majority of men and women who come to see me at Crow Haven Corner for Tarot or amulet readings or psychic counselling have questions about their love lives. And with every person I always begin with the basics – self-love and self-esteem. As with wealth, so with love: you cannot perform magic or acquire what you want and need if you don't first have a healthy self-love. Self-respect and self-confidence are necessary for successful magic just as they are necessary for a healthy psychological outlook. The two go hand in hand. Without them we cannot throw ourselves into a rich and rewarding life. If you do not love yourself or consider yourself lovable and attractive, others will not find you attractive either; nor will they fall in love with you. The old folk saying that all the world loves a lover is true. Love is contagious. Love yourself and others, and love will spread.

Too many people are desperately seeking the right potion, spell or charm without knowing that the power behind any potion, spell or charm lies right in their own hearts. My daughter Jody calls these people 'love junkies', trying all sorts of magical aids, and eventually becoming addicted to the mechanics of love magic without ever discovering the secret – namely, the self-love and self-esteem that only they can cultivate in themselves. Most love spells last for only four days. When a 'love junkie' comes into Crow Haven Corner for his or her third week still looking for the right herb or incense, Jody usually suggests another tactic. Either the desired 'Mr or Ms Right' just isn't suitable or the individuals need to do magic on themselves first to become more attractive, more desirable and more lovable.

Love is a choice, one we make each morning. We either make the decision to love ourselves and everything in the world around us or we do not. We must start with ourselves and let our love flow out to the universe around us, and only then will love act as a kind of net to catch the right individual. No true lover will ever drain us of love. If he or she does, I suspect you have found a 'love vampire', not a real lover. We will always have more love than any one individual can consume, and knowing this gives us a position of power to work from. Loving yourself and the world is the cake; the love of a lover is the icing. If an affair ends and you are left alone, you are still encircled and protected in a blanket of self-love and universal love from which you can derive happiness and the strength to go on with life, perhaps even seeking another partner.

Magic Mirror Exercise

Self-love means looking at yourself and saying that you love what you see. The best magical tool for this is the bathroom mirror that you face every morning when you get up. Fairy tales, legends and folklore are filled with mystical and magical mirrors, and Witches continue this tradition of gazing into magical mirrors as a daily ritual of knowing and focusing on who they are and what they want to become. A bathroom is not too mundane for this purpose. Charge the mirror. Place a talisman, amulet or charm on it. Transform it by giving it another daily purpose in addition to helping you comb your hair, shave or put on make-up.

Go into instant alpha as you brush your teeth or splash your face with water. Then look at your reflection straight in the eye and say out loud, 'I love you. You are terrific. You are beautiful. You can do anything you want to do. You are special. You are absolutely perfect.' Of course you can rewrite these if you wish, but you must *not* dilute them! No matter how silly they sound or how foolish you think you sound saying them, you must say them with full intention and purpose, with meaning and conviction. If you are self-conscious about other people overhearing you, close the bathroom door or turn up the radio. Let your self-consciousness be a warning of how much you need to do this exercise because one of the goals is to overcome this self-consciousness, which is probably hindering your ability to radiate the qualities that will make you attractive and lovable to others. Practise this Magic Mirror Spell every day. Never stop it, even after you find a lover. This daily reinforcement will strengthen all your relationships. As you become more self-loving and self-appreciative, all your relationships will become more loving. The time you invest in loving yourself in a healthy and constructive way will manifest in others investing their time in loving you.

A Love Philter

Here is a recipe for a spell to attract love into your life in general. It is to be carried in a philter.

    1 tablespoon patchouli leaves
    1 tablespoon hibiscus flowers
    1 tablespoon yarrow
    1 tablespoon passion flower
    1 tablespoon strawberry leaves
    1 tablespoon damiana
    1 tablespoon motherwort
    1 tablespoon red poppy flowers

  4 Adam and Eve roots
  1 tablespoon lovage-root powder

Add:
 20 drops or more of rose oil
 10 drops strawberry oil
  8 drops musk oil
  5 drops patchouli oil

Blend with:
  2 tablespoons orris-root powder

Mix all the ingredients together and catalyse the intentions of your spell by saying aloud, 'I ask that a lover or companion be attracted to me and that there be love between us. I ask that this be correct and for the good of all people. So mote it be.' Either visualize the specific person you wish to attract or the kind of person you seek. Be specific about what you do *not* want to draw in before you do the spell. Carry this philter in a red or pink cloth bag. Remember, it is the energy and aura of the herbs, not the scent, that attracts.

It's always important to project for a person who is *correct* for you, even though you may not know exactly what 'correct' entails. For example, if you project for a specific person, you will get him or her along with, perhaps, drinking problems, miserable in-laws, a bitter ex-spouse, nagging children or money problems. And the person's family will have you in their lives also. You may become an interference in their lives. We can never see completely down the path we walk, so we must tread carefully. Part of doing successful love magic is the ability to be detached enough to give up our heart's desire if need be in order not to encumber our lives with all the lover's problems or the lover's life with all our problems. We must always try to view things in the long term. So always project for someone who is correct for you in every way.

Beauty Magic

Beauty may be only skin-deep, but magic goes to the centre of our being. When the two are blended we have the perfect combination for attracting love. Both men and women use some type of make-up as a form of magic in Witchcraft. We are not alone in this. Native Americans, Polynesians, the ancient Egyptians, the Chinese and Japanese and African tribal peoples have also used make-up and body paint for magical purposes. The use of colour affects our behaviour and emotional dispositions.

The origins of tattooing came from ancient magical practices of painting designs and talismans on the skin either for temporary ceremonial purposes or permanently. Drawing and painting are themselves magical acts, and the image that is put on the body attracts and reflects light energy that activates the magic. You might use standard symbols such as stars, moons, suns, the male and female logos, or write a spell somewhere on your body where no one will see it (for now!).

Outlining the eye emulates the Goddess, who is often portrayed with large, distinctive eyes, capable of seeing through space and time as well as into our innermost hearts. Ishtar, the Goddess of Light, was known in the ancient Middle East as the Eye Goddess because the light she brings from heaven to earth illuminates the world. The Egyptian Goddess Maat originally possessed the All-Seeing Eye, which later was transferred to Horus. In Syria the Goddess Mari had large, strong eyes that could see deep into the human soul. The Goddess's ability to see and know all things became a terrifying concept in patriarchal times, and her mystical eye was turned into the 'evil eye', associated during the time of the Inquisition with Witches. During the Burning Times, Witches were forced to enter courtrooms backwards so they would not have the advantage of being able to cast a spell on the judges by an 'evil glance'.

But the tradition of outlining the eye to honour the Goddess of Love and to make one's own eyes more radiant and mysterious is a time-honoured custom. Green, rose or copper eyeshadow or eyeliner draw in energy from Venus, the planet of love and romance. Pink eyeshadow, blusher or lipstick will strengthen self-esteem. Glitter refracts and reflects light and will send out light to others. Affixing jewellery to your body or face is also powerful. Remember to charge your make-up, jewellery and body paint before you use them, catalysing them with the specific intention of your spell.

Pay particular attention to how you adorn your forehead where the Third Eye is located. East Indians wear a red dot over this chakra point; ancient Druids wore crowns with a band of jewels in the centre of the forehead; the African Berbers use black make-up to tattoo their faces with stars, moons and other magical symbols. A quartz crystal worn across the Third Eye can be particularly powerful.

Magical Dress

Anyone seeking a lover should pay attention to how he or she dresses. Not that you have to dress to the hilt every day, but other people do evaluate us, at least initially, on our clothes. While clothes do not *make* either the man or the woman, they are the first indications we get of who the person inside those clothes might be. As you become more self-confident about your personal identity and know your strengths and weaknesses, you should dress to send out the right signals. Clothes and fashions project our personas. If you feel drawn to 1930s fashions, or hippy garb from the 1960s, wear them, but know why you do so. Know what it is about you that enjoys dressing this way. Whether you dress according to *Vogue* or delight in rejecting trends and setting your own, you are expressing and using your magical power in doing so. Colours are also important: they reflect mood; they suggest seasons and times of the year; they can highlight our best features or tone down unflattering ones. Design and pattern play similar rôles. By our dress we make statements about ourselves. We cast spells. We announce what we want by announcing who we are – even if just for the night.

Don't overlook talismans such as feathers, beads, ribbons or headbands and armbands that can be inscribed with runes, magic words or love symbols. Braid feathers or ribbons into your hair, charging them for whatever love intention you require. Wear a special piece of jewellery for your intentions.

Magical Scents

Scientific studies are showing that scent plays a much stronger role in sexual attraction among human beings than we have previously thought. We always knew that animals are strongly stimulated by scent, but the latest research in the perfume industry indicates that men and women also respond strongly to scents. The way to a lover's heart may be through the nose! So the alluring advertisements are not just fantasies. Perfumes and colognes work. A Witch can use commercial perfumes and colognes, but we usually feel more powerful with ones we make ourselves. We know what has gone into them, and we know that the ingredients have been magically charged to do our bidding, that is, to get what is good and correct for us. While the manufacturers' perfumes may get us a partner, he or she may not be the correct one.

My favourite love potion to add to commercial perfume consists of:

$\frac{1}{4}$ oz patchouli oil
$\frac{1}{4}$ oz styrax (benzoin oil)
$\frac{1}{4}$ oz lotus oil

$\frac{1}{4}$ oz heliotrope oil
$\frac{1}{4}$ oz orris oil
$\frac{1}{4}$ oz olive oil

Charge the ingredients and mix them together. Add a few drops to your favourite perfume or cologne.

A bewitching, organic perfume can be made from the right combination of herbs and spices. Simmer any three of the following ingredients in a cup or two of spring water with a tablespoon of sea salt: apples, cloves, cinnamon, lovage-root powder, yarrow flower, strawberry oil, patchouli oil or musk. Let the scent permeate your house or add a small quantity to your favourite cologne or perfume. You might also put a few drops on your lover's desk, pillow, car, doorknob or clothes. Even though the scent will eventually fade, the magic stays and will work for the traditional four days.

The Golden Star Love Spell

The Golden Star Love Spell that my daughters and I created years ago is a wonderful and powerful spell to protect your lover while you are apart. The materials you need are one gold pentacle, one piece of black velvet big enough to drape around a jar or a small, black, velvet draw-string bag, a one-quart glass jar, and a three-foot length of thick, black silk cord. Go into alpha and hold the pentacle in your hand while repeating this rhyming enchantment:

> *A golden ring around a star*
> *Placed in black velvet and hung in a jar*
> *Will keep you, my love,*
> *When you are afar.*

Visualize your lover on the screen of your mind as you recite the spell. Then suspend the pentacle from the silk cord so that it dangles freely in the glass jar. Secure the cord with the lid and wrap the jar in black velvet or place it in a black velvet bag and hang it close to the ceiling.

Crystal Love Spell

Here is a love spell using a crystal. Get a clear or rose quartz crystal. Bathe it in sea salt and spring water and wrap it in a white cloth until you are ready to perform the spell. This will cleanse it and neutralize all unwanted vibrations and energies. Charge it by holding it and asking the powers of the Goddess to bring you a lover who is correct and good for you. Carry the crystal in a bright pink, red, copper or green satin or lamé bag. Instead of a bag you can cut a square of coloured cloth, place the crystal in it and tie the corners together with a string of the same colour.

Love Feasts

One of the most powerful spells a Witch can perform is to transform an entire evening into an enchantment for the recipient of the spell. In this section we will look at the ingredients for a Love Feast, but a dinner or party can be used for other purposes as well: a dinner for your boss to enhance your career; a health feast for someone recovering from an illness or operation; a prosperity feast for friends or relatives who are down on their luck. And, of course, the many happy, celebratory feasts, such as anniversaries and birthdays, that have become part of our dominant culture. In each case the goal is to create an enchanting atmosphere with ingredients and magical objects that will work their special magic on the guest of honour.

Here is how I would prepare a dinner to make a lover more amorous and responsive. Of course, you must add your own personal magic so that a romantic night that begins with a meal ends up the way you envisage it!

Dress your table with pink and/or green, the colours of Venus, planet of love. The centrepiece could be roses, poppies or bunches of hibiscus, the flowers of love. Scent the room with the aroma of a love philter or potion made from rose and strawberry oil. Dab it on a candle, mix it in with a potpourri, rub it on to the edge of a wooden table. Put a few drops on a ribbon and tie it to a door; put a few drops in a pan of water and boil it on the stove, allowing the fragrance to vaporize in the room. And don't forget yourself – mix several drops in with your bathwater or add it to your perfume or cologne.

For a summer love meal begin with cold strawberry soup sweetened with honey and a touch of cinnamon for success. In winter serve cream of mushroom soup flavoured with a few nettle leaves to encourage thoughts of love. Basil and a small amount of catmint could also be added to the soup.

Basil has long been a traditional herb for love potions, philters and love meals. When magically charged, the herb's aura produces a loving sensation within the human body. Directing its energy to the one you admire will stir a reciprocal feeling in him or her. Add a little to any recipe that can accommodate it.

A tossed salad can include the flowers and leaves of dandelion, as well as rose petals if they have not been sprayed with pesticide. Season with a dressing of mayonnaise, poppy seeds, brown sugar and rose vinegar. Blend to taste.

For the main course serve chicken with apricot or peach jam or fish baked or steamed with tomatoes, basil and oregano. Mustard (for luck) and basil leaves (ruled by Venus) will enhance the spell. Bake fresh bread with caraway seeds (for lust).

Beer is always appropriate for a love feast because it is the potion of Isis. Hops come from barley, ruled by Venus. Apple juice, which enhances self-love, is also a traditional love drink. You can make a rose-petal wine by picking rose petals that are in full bloom, washing them, and placing them in a decanter filled with rosé wine and letting it sit overnight in the refrigerator. A delicious non-alcoholic alternative is a fruit punch made by mixing cherry, strawberry or apple juice with spearmint. Or try a hot lovage-root or hibiscus tea.

For dessert serve a fruit salad of sliced peaches, apples, cherries and strawberries, or a strawberry or cherry sorbet. A magical spice-cake flavoured with hints of cinnamon, cloves, dried nettles, dried strawberry leaves and a quarter of a teaspoon of lovage-root powder is usually very popular. Or serve rice pudding. Rice represents purity of mind and encourages longing and desire. Dust with cinnamon.

Remember to magically charge each ingredient in a magic circle with the energy of your aura before you prepare the meal.

Soul Mates

One of the major issues that I am asked about in my work as spiritual counsellor concerns soul mates. What are soul mates, how can people recognize their soul mates, and what kind of relationship is appropriate between two people who meet and realize that they are destined to be together? First, what is a soul mate? In general, it is a person you have known from a previous incarnation. It may or may not have been a lover or mate. It could have been a father, mother, brother, sister or best friend. One of the indications that a person was a soul mate from another life is the almost immediate psychic charge you feel between the two of you. You feel spontaneously drawn to each other, as if you intuitively know and understand so much more about each other than you could possibly know and understand from the short time you have been together. Such an intense and intimate encounter can easily be mistaken for passion.

From talking with hundreds of people about soul mates, I

am convinced that most of the soul mates we meet are not intended to become sexual partners or even life partners. Sex, as the saying goes, can complicate, even ruin, a beautiful relationship – which means, of course, that some relationships are not meant to be sexual. I believe that this is true for most relationships between soul mates. In some sense we always 'fall in love' with our soul mates. But falling in love and falling into bed are two different things. Be grateful when you meet a soul mate, but be on your guard that the relationship doesn't evolve in directions in which it is not intended to go.

HEALING

Witchcraft has always been part of the healing arts. In the earliest times healers used herbs and auras, hands and minds in addition to physical surgery and manipulation to cure diseases and heal the sick. As the practice of modern medicine evolved over the last few hundred years, the ancient methods that used herbs, auras, hands and mind/body/spirit techniques fell out of favour. Only Witches and other natural healers kept alive the art and science of healing by natural methods. Today, however, we are watching a resurgence of interest in these older and often safer methods.

One of the most satisfying and rewarding experiences for me has been to use the Craft to heal others. On an equal level with this is teaching my methods of psychic diagnosis and healing to others and watching them become healers in their own lives. By using alpha we are able to reverse physical damage to the body, restore energy and create well-being. We do this by a power that flows through our breath, our thoughts, our words and our touch.

People have come to me from all over the world for psychic diagnosis of their physical medical problems. I have successfully diagnosed tumours, blood diseases, arthritis, diabetes, heart disease, and gallstones, to name just a few. I never perform medical diagnosis, however, on someone who is not already under the care of a qualified physician, nor do I use any healing techniques as a substitute for modern medical care. Magic and medicine should and can work hand in hand as they always have.

Once a young man came to me about his girlfriend, who was in her twenties and had been hospitalized in great pain after being diagnosed by her gynaecologist as needing a hysterectomy because of serious uterine disorders. The young man sensed there was something wrong with this diagnosis and wanted my opinion. I went into alpha, visualized the young woman on my mental screen and examined her. As I looked at her body's aura I could see that there was a problem in the area of the lower abdomen because the aura's colour was absent there. But on closer analysis I saw that she didn't have uterine problems at all but a serious inflamed appendix. I told him it was almost ready to burst.

The young man rushed back to the hospital and told the doctor what I had found. The doctor objected on the grounds that he didn't need 'any of Laurie Cabot's hocus-pocus' and proceeded to schedule the hysterectomy to be done in the next two days. The young man called to tell me what had happened and I suggested that he and his girlfriend request a second medical opinion from another doctor and that I would see to it that the second doctor would find the real cause of her problems. I went into alpha and projected for the right doctor. Later that day the second doctor called into the case discovered the woman's inflamed appendix and ordered an immediate operation. The appendix burst during surgery, but the woman's life was saved.

I myself have been on the receiving end of a bad medical diagnosis. Some years ago a gynaecologist examined me and concluded without a test that I had uterine cancer and promptly ordered more extensive tests. He also scolded me for not having had a check-up two years earlier. I felt strongly that I did not have cancer, so I frantically called several Witch friends on the phone and asked them to use our method of psychic diagnosis to see what was up. They each confirmed that I did not have cancer. Later my doctor received the test results, which proved that my friends and I were correct. I did not have cancer.

You cannot diagnose yourself very well, especially when you're upset. It is human nature to be biased. Either we wish so hard to be well that we don't see what our problems are or we suffer from some degree of hypochondria and are prone to find all kinds of ailments that we don't really have. It is always best to have someone else to work on you.

Psychic Diagnosis
At the beginning of Chapter Six I told you how a typical class of mine responded to learning the art and science of psychic diagnosis. Now I will tell you the specific steps so that you, too, can use it in your own life.

First, you must have a guide or assistant to do psychic diagnosis. After much practice and after you are very good at it, you will be able to do it without someone to assist you, but it is always best to have a guide who is familiar with the case whenever possible. It keeps your diagnosis more focused and ultimately more accurate. Also, a guide with more complete knowledge of the case will help direct you because you, as the diagnostician, should begin with just a minimum of information. In general the less you know about a case beforehand, the better will be your diagnosis.

Step One: Go into the Crystal Countdown and reach your alpha state. At this point your guide will tell you verbally the name, sex, age and location of the person to be diagnosed. Place that person on your screen. At first you will see only the person'a aura, but as you proceed you will begin to recognize the specific features of the face, body and personality.

Step Two: Let the person's image fill your screen and repeat the person's name, age and location out loud. Snap your fingers quickly two or three times to help you focus. In fact, whenever the person's image starts to fade or you feel that you are getting stuck or you need to move from one area of the person's body to another, snap your fingers two or three times. The sound alerts you to the work that you are doing and pulls your attention to the area under investigation. Always begin with the person's head and face. Reach up with your hands and begin to feel the head. Outline the shape of the face with your fingertips. Describe its shape out loud. Is it oval, round, angular? Feel the hair and describe its colour and length. Let your hands run down over the forehead, cheeks, nose, mouth, chin, jaw. Describe each of these.

Your guide should be helpful and supportive, saying 'yes' and 'that's correct' whenever possible. He or she should never give hints. If your initial description is inaccurate, the guide should answer either 'look more closely' or 'I don't have that information'. Guides should never say 'no' because a sharp 'no' intimidates your psychic confidence and will make you more hesitant about verbalizing other correct information. The suggestion that you are not diagnosing correctly will also cause a rush of adrenalin to the brain which may cause you to leave alpha and return to beta.

Step Three: Let your hands scan the person's entire body. 'Touch' every part. Let your hands be drawn to any area that seems to be attracting your interest. If your hands feel naturally inclined to stop at any particular place, do so. Run your fingers down the body looking for scars, burns, rashes, diseases, warts or lumps. Then go under the skin and check the muscles. Check the organs and glands. Examine the skeletal structure. Look for broken bones or bones out of place. Feel the heart; hold it in your hands. Test the lungs and the entire cardiovascular system. You can envisage a vial of the person's blood on the screen. Shake the vial and watch the blood settle. Check the brain, the eyes, ears, throat. View the bone marrow.

As you examine the person's entire body several things may happen to you. You may 'see' clearly the part of the body that is ailing. This may happen within the first few seconds. Often you may see some discoloration in the aura at that part of the body. Or you may 'hear' (or 'see') a word naming the illness, such as 'cancer', 'diabetes' or 'slipped disc'. You may see or hear nothing but just 'know' as you probe around on a given part of the body that something is wrong there.

Do not worry if you cannot name the ailment accurately. You may be able to say only that it is 'a lung condition' or that there is 'something wrong with the digestive tract'. But, on the other hand, don't be surprised if you verbalize a medical-sounding term that you have never encountered before and which you know absolutely nothing about. This happens sometimes – you intuitively know the technical name for a disease you have never heard of. I always keep a copy of *Gray's Anatomy* on hand so that after I do psychic diagnosis I can look up the area that I was working on and learn the correct names for the parts of the body and the kinds of illnesses that can occur there.

If you feel you are not getting enough information about an area of concern, there are three additional steps you can take.

Firstly, in your mind, ask the image of the patient on your screen if he or she knows what the problem is. People usually know on a subconscious level what is wrong with them, and if their image on the screen has that information they may just need to be asked to give it to you. You may receive the

240

information through 'voices', which may sound either like your own voice or that of the patient.

Secondly, if the person on the screen will not tell you what is wrong, you can psychically 'put on his or her head' and look at the problem through the patient's own perceptions. Here's how to do it. See the person's face, life-size, looking directly at you. Place your hands on each side of the head and turn it around until you are looking at the back of the head. Then lift it up, off your screen and above your own head, and pull it down over your head like you would put on a life-size mask complete with head. Look through the person's eyes, take a few imaginary steps, hear what he or she can hear and get the feel of what it feels like to be that person. Ask yourself what is wrong and let your mind receive whatever ailment presents itself. You may 'feel' it on that part of the body or you may just intuitively know what is wrong. Then put your hands on either side of the head, lift it up and off your own head, and replace it on the screen so it faces you.

Before putting on someone else's head always check the brain for the presence of drugs, alcohol or mental illness. If you detect any of these, it would be unwise to put the head on because you will psychically experience those symptoms. Wearing the head could make you feel drunk or drugged, and this will impair your ability to diagnose accurately. The drug or alcohol condition is no threat to your own safety or well-being, but you will feel the symptoms temporarily.

Thirdly, if you still cannot find the problem, draw on to your screen light blue, gold, white or orchid light and ask the light of the Total Intelligence to give you information about the person's physical condition. This will usually provide the answers.

Step Four: When you accurately know the problem or the location of the problem, send the person healing light and

241

project for the person to be healed. See the colour totally around the aura and especially in the area of concern. Use the following colours as they correspond to the nature or seriousness of the disease:

    emerald or kelly green: minor ailments
    red–orange: critical injuries or illnesses
    bright pink: self-love and self-esteem
    violet: psychological balance
    ice blue: anaesthesia, to shut out pain
    light blue, gold, white or orchid: for Total
    Intelligence/God/Goddess/the All

Then project that the person is healed. Always visualize the end result, not the means to the end. For example, if you are working with an open wound, simply see the wound closed and healed. You do not have to visualize an operation. The reason for this is that we may not always project the best means for the end result. Lastly, send more healing light and ask that the healing be correct and for the good of all, just as you do in all your spells.

Step Five: After sending healing to the person erase the person's image from the screen and give yourself total health clearance, as you learned in Chapter Six. Relax a few moments and then count yourself back up to beta and open your eyes.

Step Six: Then discuss your diagnosis of the person with your guide. Remember that in alpha, time does not progress as we are used to it in beta. What you saw and learned about the subject may be a past, present or future condition. This is another reason for the guide never to say 'no' to you when you are commenting on the person's condition. You may be describing a condition that the person had twenty years ago and is unknown to the guide. Or you may be describing some future problem. There are even cases in which the current condition of the subject is not completely known by the guide or doctor. For example, one student told her guide that the subject, a young man, had blond hair. The guide, who was the subject's girlfriend, kept telling the student to look more closely. She did but continued to describe the man as a blond. The guide gave up and the let the matter pass. Later that day, when she saw her boyfriend, she learned he had indeed just bleached his hair!

It is important to remember that you cannot catch a disease or ailment while in alpha. You cannot get cancer from healing a cancer patient or heart disease from working with a heart patient. That is not why we give ourselves total health clearance. If you do not clear yourself before counting up, you could temporarily assume some of the symptoms of the subject's ailment. You can *feel* their problem (backache, sniffles, sore throat etc.) for a while, but you will not actually have the disease. Nevertheless, there is no reason to put up with an uncomfortable situation if you don't have to. Giving yourself total health clearance each time you count up from alpha also reinforces the healing magic in yourself as well.

Absent Healing
Absent healing is a method of sending healing energy to a person at a distance. It is the same procedure you used for psychic diagnosis and healing above, except you may not have to do the diagnosis if you already know what is wrong with the person. Count into alpha, bring the patient on to your screen, send healing light, use your hands to work the injured or painful area, ask your spirit guides to help you by sending energy to the person. When you have finished give yourself total health clearance and count back up into beta.

Laying On Of Hands
Witches take the common phrase 'magic touch' quite literally. As I studied the ways of the Craft I learned that laying on of

hands is a critical part of healing. Once again science is catching up with what Witches have known and practised for centuries. Dolores Krieger, author of *The Therapeutic Touch*, teaches nurses and other health-care personnel a method of using their hands to help and heal. Her experience shows that simple human touch can affect a patient's blood chemistry and brain waves and elicit a generalized relaxation response. Nurses who practise therapeutic touch testify that their patients recover more quickly and with fewer complications than those who do not receive this treatment.

To understand the laying on of hands try this experiment. Run your fingertips down the clothing you are wearing or across the top of a table or chair. Feel the sensations while you move your fingers. What you are actually feeling is not your clothing, table or chair but only your fingertips. We know from subatomic physics that there is molecular space between your skin and material objects. Light energy passes through this microscopic gap between hand and object. The light energy from your aura and the object's aura mingle here. The feeling in your hands or fingertips is the sensation that comes from blending the light from your aura with the light from the object's aura. Krieger's studies indicate that healers feel the energy in a variety of ways. The most common are heat, cold, tingling, pressure, electric shocks and pulsations.

Many people have witnessed the power of the aura's energy in karate demonstrations where a person strikes a stack of wood with his or her hand and shatters the boards. The secret behind this feat is that the karate expert first visualizes the aura of his or her hand slicing through the board before the hand ever touches the wood. It is the aura, as much as the hand, that shatters the boards. In the Apple Meditation from Chapter Six you drew a real apple on to the screen of your mind and felt it with your hands. The principle was the same – you had an exact replica of a real apple's aura and touched it through the aura from your finger-tips.

Here are steps for using your hands to balance energy in a sick or injured person, draw out harmful energy and remove energy blockages that prevent the free flow of health and well-being throughout the body. Laying on of hands works best in a magic circle, but the following steps can be used whether you have the opportunity to cast a circle or not.

Step One: Before seeing the patient always spend a few moments visualizing your own chakra points (see page 121) and building up your own energy. See the seven power centres in your own body and watch the energy in each one heighten and grow stronger. Reinforce your protective shield. Visualize healing light around yourself. Let your own energy concentrate in your hands, specifically in your palms, by holding your hands palms upwards for a few moments in the Egyptian prayer pose.

Step Two: When in the presence of the patient count yourself into alpha. Hold your hands so that the palms face the body of the patient. Place your hands over the head or crown chakra. Move your hands down the body, pulling and pushing away any harmful energy at that chakra. Do this as often as necessary until you see the aura glowing bright and strong. When that is completed repeat this movement at the forehead, throat, heart, solar plexus, spleen and foot chakras.

You may physically touch the person's body lightly with your hands or you may make contact only through the auras by holding your hands an inch or two away from the body. When you have drawn away the harmful energy stand back from the patient and shake your hands, releasing any of the energy that may still be in your own aura.

Step Three: Recharge your body, balance your energies and

polarize yourself by using the Egyptian Sun Meditation (see page 178) before you bring healing energy to the patient.

Step Four: Place your hands at each of the patient's chakras and channel healing energy into them.

Sympathetic Magic

Dolls have been used by Witches throughout the centuries for healing spells. It is unfortunate that many people associate their use solely with evil voodoo spells that inflict harm. In the Craft, however, we use dolls made in the image of another person to empower that person with magic or healing energy. The correct use of a doll can help treat illness, relieve pain and restore vitality. Dolls, or 'poppets', to use the archaic term, are excellent for relieving the pain of arthritis and headaches.

Step One: You can make a doll of either cloth or parchment paper or buy a small doll at a Witch shop. Give the doll the name of the person for whom you are making it and call it by that name. You could write the name on the doll or make a little name tag to attach to the doll's back. You may even use a photograph of the person pasted on to the doll's face. If you can, sew into the doll pieces of clothing taken from the person when he or she was healthy, or you can use strands of hair or fingernail clippings.

Step Two: When the doll is made locate the acupuncture points on the doll's body that correspond to the specific ailments of the patient. You can use a standard acupuncture or acupressure book for this. Then mark these spots on the doll and place straight pins into those points. Since the points on a doll will be smaller than a full-size body, you may be inserting the pins in the general area rather than the specific point. This will not interfere with the spell if you make the intention that the pin affect the true point on the patient's body regardless of whether it hits the same point on the doll. Remember that the doll is not the actual body but a representation that helps you to focus your awareness and your actions.

As you insert the pins send healing energy or coloured light to the person via the points on the doll. Leave the doll on your altar or some special place where you will see it and be reminded to send healing energy. When the person recovers remove the pins and give him or her the doll as a keepsake that will bring energy.

.8.

A WITCH'S LIFE: MILESTONES

The milestones in a Witch's life are marked by magical moments, special ceremonies and spells that contribute to the meaning and purpose of life in general and the Witch's life in particular. As we pass through the stages of life we are keenly aware that our physical life is only a part of our existence. We live on higher spiritual realms as well as on the material plane; we have a cosmic identity that transcends time and place. Whether we marry, end a relationship, give birth and raise children, prepare for death or bury our loved ones, as Witches we surround these sacred moments with symbol and ceremony to keep our awareness focused on the multiple dimensions of human existence. Here are some of the ways we mark the milestones in our lives.

Handfasting

As a minister of religion recognized by the Commonwealth of Massachusetts, I can legally marry people in the traditional Handfasting Ceremony that Witches have used to enjoin their lives and their love for each other as husband and wife. More and more American states are recognizing Wiccan priests and priestesses in this capacity, and we are seeing a revival of the Handfasting Ceremonies, even among couples who are not themselves Witches.

Before marrying, the couple should consult an astrologer to better understand their love and their compatibility and to select an astrologically auspicious date and place for the wedding.

The magic circle with a nine- to thirteen-foot diameter is formed of nosegays, flowers and ribbons. The immediate family and other Witch friends stand just inside the circle and form an inner circle around the altar, which is draped in pink, white or black cloth. Frankincense and myrrh are burning; two chalices filled with wine or spring water stand between one white and one black candle. Next to the chalices are the two wedding rings.

An assistant priestess, with two nine-foot black silk cords draped around her neck, leads the bride and groom into the circle from the north. Once they are inside, the high priestess casts the circle with her magic wand. The bride and groom greet the four archangels in the four quarters as they walk around the circle. Then the assistant sweeps the circle with a magic broom, brushing away all negative events that have transpired in the couple's lives. Then, facing each other, the bride and groom kneel on two pillows in front of the altar; the priestesses charge the rings and chalices. The kneeling couple than cast a verbal spell while looking lovingly into each other's eyes and declaring to all present and to each other their mutual love and the goals each has for their life together.

Next each picks up the other's wedding ring and drops it into the opposite chalice. While the couple's hands are crossed holding the chalices, the priestess loosely binds them in a figure-eight design with the black silk cords. They then take a sip of the water or wine from each other's chalice. The rest is poured into a bowl, the rings removed and placed on the hands of the bride and groom. The high priestess then takes the silk cord, holds it over the heads of the couple and pulls the loosely bound knot tight as she says, 'I tie the knot'. She then hands one end of the cord to the groom and one end to the bride. As they hold the cord between them the priestess places a hand on each one's head and announces to all present, 'You are both bound in infinity. So mote it be.' Then all the wedding gifts and magical presents that have been placed under the altar are charged. The circle is then opened, the ceremony is complete and the bridal couple and guests continue the celebration with gaiety and merriment.

Ending A Relationship

Ending a relationship is an important turning point in life, and too often couples today do so without a formal and sometimes personal rite of passage to ease the pain of separation and prepare them for the next stage of their lives. In spite of the pain involved, separating is often for the good of the two individuals. The ancient Celtic Handfasting Ceremony allowed the couple to pledge their love and devotion for a year and a day at a time, after which, if they were mutually agreed, they could part company and go their separate ways. Today's marriage ceremonies are often 'until death', and should the marriage not work out separation becomes a very traumatic event, filled with guilt, a sense of failure, disappointment and sometimes bitterness.

I always tell clients who come to me that if they are in a relationship that is not satisfying, or that is actually harmful, it would be best to end it. Some people think that if they can just get the right potion or spell, everything will turn out right. Magic will not change our basic personalities overnight or even over several years, and we must accept the fact that some personalities are just not meant to stay together. I do advise evaluating the situation, however, in terms of self-esteem and self-love, which are the basis for any successful magic and the basis for any successful relationship. If you love and respect yourself, you will not let others manipulate, dominate or abuse you. If you constantly project that you do not love yourself, you will continually attract partners who will take advantage of you for their own ends. You will become a victim.

Know yourself well enough, and your partner as well as you can, before deciding whether or not you are good for each other. If your magic and your own sensible efforts cannot save a relationship, then this may be a strong indication that it is time to part. At this point use magic and work spells for you and your partner's future happiness and to make the separation as painless and positive as it can be for both of you.

Here is a programme that should be begun as soon as you realize that ending the relationship is the best possible course. Taken as a whole these measures will constitute a spell to ease the pain of a broken heart.

Spell To Ease A Broken Heart

You will need the following ingredients (be sure to charge them all before you begin):

  1 bag strawberry tea
  1 small wand or stick from a willow tree
    sea salt
  2 pink candles
  1 mirror
  1 pink draw-string bag
  1 quartz crystal
  1 copper penny
  1 bowl made of china or crystal that is special to you
  1 teaspoon dried jasmine
  1 teaspoon orris-root powder
  1 teaspoon strawberry leaves

1 teaspoon yarrow
10 or more drops apple-blossom oil or peach oil
10 or more drops strawberry oil

On a Friday morning or evening (the day sacred to Venus) take a bath in sea salt in the light of a pink candle. As you dry off and dress, sip the strawberry tea. Use a dab of strawberry oil as perfume or cologne. Apply make-up or groom yourself to look your best. Cast a circle with the willow wand around a table with the other ingredients. Light the second pink candle. Mix all oils and herbs in a bowl. While you stir look at yourself in the mirror and say aloud, 'Oh, Great Mother Goddess, enclose me in your loving arms and nurture and bring forth the Goddess within me.' Gaze deeply into the mirror after you have finished mixing the ingredients and say aloud, 'I represent the Great Goddess, Mother of all things. I shine in the light of the Golden Wings of Isis. All that is good and all that is great and loving only belongs to me.' Then put half the mixture in the pink bag and add the penny and crystal. Carry it with you always. Leave the other half of the potion in the bowl, out in a room where you can smell the fragrance. Repeat this ritual every Friday if necessary.

WITCH CHILDREN

A new generation of Witches is reaching adulthood, marrying and having children of their own. With the renewed interest in the Craft over the last twenty years, we are once again entering an age when the magical practices of our ancestors will be passed down from mother to daughter, from grandmother to granddaughter. Once again we will see the family traditions of the Craft take on new strength and assume their place alongside the other traditions that have emerged over the years.

This brings us to the important milestone for many Witches – birthing and raising Witch children. When do we begin to train our daughters and sons in the ways of magic? How do we teach them to be proud of their Witch heritage? How do we instruct them in the ways to defend themselves in a hostile society?

We cannot begin too early. Children lose their magical sensibilities slowly over the first ten or eleven years of life. As Betty Edwards has shown in *Drawing on the Right Side of the Brain*, by this age children have stopped drawing magically and whimsically and become fixated with drawing exactly. They will spend hours drawing and redrawing the same figure to get it to look 'realistic'. As Edwards explains, they are beginning to think that there is only one reality – that perceived by the five senses. Their sense of imaginative realities becomes less important and may even appear to them as an impediment to entering the world of adults.

Joseph Chilton Pearce has discussed in *The Magical Child* that children have a natural rapport with their mothers and with nature in the first years of life and they lose this rapport in distinct stages, perhaps never to reclaim it. When a child expresses his or her intuitive insights into reality or a sense of oneness with nature, adults often belittle, ignore and discourage those perceptions. Witch parents, however, are different. They nurture those natural talents and help their children develop them. They create a supportive environment to keep their child's magical senses open and receptive.

Birthing A Child

In the earliest days of pregnancy a mother can begin preparing her child for birth and life in the world. It is important what the mother thinks, says and sees while she is carrying a child. Just as her food, medications and drink will have an effect on the unborn child, so too will her thoughts and emotions. Witch mothers send nurturing intra-uterine

253

affirmations to their child. While the unborn child is still part of the mother's body/mind/emotions, it is very important for her to see, think and feel the great truths of magic so that the child is introduced to them even before birth. Affirmations that a Witch repeats for herself become affirmations for the child while the child is still part of the mother. Of course the mother can also address the baby outright and repeat affirmations designed especially for it.

What should these affirmations say? You can write them yourself so that they reflect your own personality and the words you usually use in speaking, but the sentiments should reflect the basic laws of the Craft. Affirmations should begin to instil in the child a strong sense of self-esteem and self-love. The simplest affirmations could state:

'I am slowly becoming ready for a rich and fulfilling life in the world.'

'I have a mother who loves me even now and is waiting eagerly for me to be born.'

'I am a lovable child of the universe and will be nurtured and raised in a loving way.'

Instruct the child to trust that he or she is a lovable little creature and that after birth the child will be caught and held and cuddled by loving hands. Self-esteem is so important to successful magic that the foundation for it should be laid even while the child is still in the womb.

The womb is, in general, a safe and healthy place, provided the mother takes care of her own health and avoids harmful substances that could impair the baby's health. Some experts say that the child does react to the mother's fears, however, and it is possible that the intimate union between mother and unborn child at this stage may even contribute to the child thinking that he or she *is* the mother's fears. It is important to reassure the child that there is nothing to worry about and that being born need not be a dangerous or frightful experience. Affirmations about this will become part of the baby's thinking and feeling, even if only on a subconscious level.

Anointing Ceremony

After a child is born a Witch mother consults an astrological chart to determine the child's strengths and weaknesses. A good reading of the positions of the stars and planets will give a profile of the child's potential talents and possible future interests. We see what the child will be good at and what he or she may have trouble with. For example, it might appear that a young girl will be lacking in physical dexterity or a young boy may not be drawn towards doing well in school. None of these conditions indicates that the child is fated to be a failure in these areas. Rather they are signs of where a parent or teacher should direct extra attention and patience.

The next step is to plan an anointing ritual with one's coven. In the magic circle each Witch comes forward and bestows on the child gifts that are lacking in the child's chart. For example, a Witch who is athletic could project physical dexterity for the young girl. A Witch who is good at studies can project qualities that will help the young boy do well in school. In other words, each Witch should bestow his or her own personal talents as gifts upon the newborn child.

In the circle each Witch in turn touches the child, allowing their auras to mingle. In this magical moment the Witch projects the qualities that she or he wishes to give the young Witch as an anointing gift.

The Craft In The Nursery

After the baby is born jingles and lullabies become the primary means of instruction. Witch mothers are careful about what they sing to their babies. Many of the old lullabies and rhymes have developed versions that are quite violent and negative as they were passed down from generation to generation and were written up and illustrated in commercial books for children. Sometimes the original or earlier version is much more positive. Take 'Rock-a-Bye Baby' for example. The baby falling from the treetop 'cradle and all' is really not the kind of fear that you would want to instil in your child. I remember having been very frightened by this lullaby when my mother would sing it to me. Older versions say nothing about this but instead mention the tasks and rôles that other members of the family play in the baby's life.

Witch parents usually monitor books, toys and television and video programmes very carefully since they are produced by the dominant culture, which is still very hostile to the Craft and Craft values. Sometimes in the middle of the most innocent story the stereotypical evil Witch appears. Children's television programmes are powerful propaganda for mindless consumerism. They also play on the child's exaggerated sense of self-importance. In general, Witch parents want their children to grow up with a simpler, leaner lifestyle in which happiness and self-worth do not depend on material possessions. They also hope to prevent their children from becoming the demanding, often impertinent children that are presented on television advertisements.

Perhaps one of the most damaging aspects about children's tales is that they can present a false kind of evil and a false sense of security. There really is evil and danger in the world and every child should learn about this, but we don't prepare children for life by instilling in them images of evil that have very little to do with the real world. Witch parents often conduct a parallel educational programme to correct the misconceptions that the school system and media programmes instil in their children. For example, they try to instil in the child, through stories and fairy tales, a strong sense that there are solutions for every problem. They tell their children that they have the creative potential to solve life's problems and to take care of themselves.

The best climate for a raising a young Witch is one in which magic and a sense of personal power and strength are perfectly natural. As I raised my daughters I tried to provide an environment that would focus their young consciousness on nature and magic, one in which their spontaneous feelings that they were one with the universe and able to live in it magically could grow as they grew. There are powerful influences in society that threaten to tell children otherwise. As Witch parents we do not want our children to grow up thinking that they are at the world's mercy, that they have no way to control their lives or that they are not responsible for what happens to them. Children who grow up with magic know themselves and the world in deep and intimate ways. This intimacy becomes the basis for their power as Witches.

'A' Is For Alpha

Even in the first year a Witch mother can begin to teach her child how to go into alpha and meditate. The great Swiss child psychologist Jean Piaget has pointed out that the mind of a child develops over time and changes in ways that depend on the environment. He says that the way we think about everything, from how nature works to our morals, depends to a great extent on the physical features of the world in which we are immersed. He also says that not only the content of a child's thoughts but also the mode of thinking or the ways a child thinks and processes information are pre-determined by the environment.

A newborn child spends a great deal of its sleeping and waking hours in an altered state of consciousness, but gradually the child learns how to maintain the alertness we call beta. For example, the one-day-old infant can hear, smell and taste. By two or three months the child will recognize faces and will smile. By eight months the child's memory not only recognizes faces but can retrieve information from its young memory bank. As these changes occur the child is learning to hold its consciousness in beta in order to function in the physical environment. During these early months Witch parents begin to teach their child how to go into alpha.

In past years we used to think that pastel colours were best for young infants. But more recent research, such as that by Jerome Kagan, who has studied infant development for the last twenty years, indicates that babies respond best to bold primary colours, especially red, and to stark checkerboard patterns rather than plain ones. So in their earliest months they are ready for the Crystal Countdown. Witches in Salem introduce their children to the spectrum of colours from bright red to violet by using brightly coloured objects or toys. Stuffed animals, different-coloured flowers, brightly coloured sheep taped to the wall – anything will work. Many parents make a game of it to show the objects or toys in the order of the countdown and to count as they do so. They challenge the child to find or recognize the sheep or lollipops or balls in the order of the countdown. Older children can paint their walls or ceilings with these colours or make a collection of their favourite objects according to their colours.

Witch children are usually better at concentration than other children because of the time their parents spend with them teaching them how to direct their attention and observe and recognize things around them. And as a general rule, children are often more accurate than adults.

When my daughters were young I played the following game with them to teach them how to use the Third Eye in alpha. I would think of something in the room and ask them to draw it on to the screen and tell me what it was. Of course they did not always see the object clearly, but if they came close to the right colour or shape or use, I considered that a success.

One day I was playing this game with my daughter Penny and thinking of a mortar and pestle placed near the kitchen sink. Her response was 'a broken guitar', which she described as a guitar with the neck broken off and lying on its side. I was inclined to consider that a miss because we didn't have a guitar – whole or broken – in the house so I told her to look more closely. But she continued to see the broken guitar and insisted that that was what it was. Then it dawned on me that the particular mortar that I had in mind was shaped like an hour-glass, which is similar to the shape of a classical guitar. The pestle lying by its side could have been the neck of a guitar. So I told her that she had done well by seeing the correct shapes, even though she identified them wrongly. This was one of the first times I learned that psychics can get the correct information but misinterpret it. We should never decide too quickly what we think information means.

By playing the Crystal Countdown with our children and letting them see objects on their mental screens while in alpha, we teach them that thoughts are things, and that the world is not completely outside their minds. Anything around them can become part of their consciousness. In this way they will grow up to be comfortable with psychic experiences that happen to them naturally and spontaneously. Similarly, they will learn how to control their psychic experiences and be able to tune them on or off at will. When they see or hear fairies, spirits, animal helpers or guides from other dimensions, they will not be frightened nor will they dismiss them as mere fantasies. They will accept them as being real and be open and receptive to the knowledge and wisdom that they bring to us.

Dreams
Children spend a lot of time dreaming and often they hesitate

259

to talk about their dreams because parents don't take dreams seriously. Too often children wake up crying in the night from a frightening dream and parents come in, brush away their tears and tell them to forget it, that 'it was just a nightmare or just a bad dream'. No dream is bad. Even the frightening ones have meaning and purpose. A good Witch will not dismiss a child's dream but help the child to understand it and make sense of it. It is also important to ask the child about his or her 'good' dreams so that the child learns that dreams are not just the fears and anxieties that appear to them in their sleep. Witch parents make it a daily routine to ask their children what they dreamed about the night before and then, if time permits, they talk over with their children possible meanings for their dreams.

Dreams are the way our minds try to sort out information at night while we are asleep. Some of them may even be messages from other realms or experiences we have while out of the sleeping body. A powerful dream can be filled with information for us even if we never quite understand it as completely as we would like to with our waking minds. Not every dream has to be totally analysed for its power to influence us. Most of all we must let our children know that dreams are real. They are a different kind of reality from waking reality, but they are none the less real and deserve our attention.

Witches encourage their children to relate their dreams and what they think the dreams mean. In this way children learn how to talk about their dream worlds and take them seriously. The dreamer always knows on some level, even if it is unconscious, what a dream is all about. So we work with our children, asking them questions about the images in their dreams and their feelings about their dreams to help them gain insight into what is happening.

Some tribal peoples teach their children to handle frightening dreams by confronting the threatening images and making them allies. One way to do this is to tell a child who has had a disturbing dream that when the dream, or another one like it, comes back, the child has the power *while still in the dream* to confront the monster and ask it for a gift of power. In time children are able to do this and they derive strength and self-confidence from the most frightening dream.

To make a child's sense of power in a dream more real, some Witch parents fashion a special dreaming wand or dream doll to give the child to sleep with next to the pillow. We tell the child that the wand or doll will be there when the monsters come and will give the child power to confront the monster, ask for the gift, and make the monster a friend or ally.

As children get better with controlling the way they respond to disturbing dreams, they can be taught to incubate or programme dreams around topics they find pleasurable or enjoyable. I always encourage children to have dreams about flying, or dreams in which they learn things about nature, or dreams in which they will meet their spirit guides or animal helpers. Later in life they will incubate dreams to help in problem-solving and decision-making, and they will have a rich and rewarding dream life.

Protection Spells For Children

Children are vulnerable, and our society seems to be getting more violent all the time. It is important for all parents to teach children the truth about evil and danger and to teach ways that children can protect themselves against harm. One of the reasons the Witches' League is working to change the image of the Witch in children's videos and books is that it gives children a false sense of danger and security – they think that Witches are green and ugly and ride broomsticks as they go around doing evil. In reality Witches are not evil, and the real threat to children's safety lurks in many corners of our society in the guise of average-looking men and women. The outlandish cartoon characters that gnash their teeth and lick their lips and wring their hands over doing evil things are not walking the streets of our cities. Average-looking people are, some of whom are trusted family members, and we must teach children the truth about this.

In addition to educating children about safety and how to be street-smart, Witch parents also teach their children ways to deflect harm. Any of the spells and exercises in the protection section of the previous chapter can be taught to children or done for them. Witches begin to teach a child how to use magic to neutralize evil or danger as soon as the child is old enough to understand what it is all about. We put protection shields around our children, and when they are old enough to do their own, we teach them how. Protection potion can be put on a child's wrists and forehead before going to school, which will also serve as a reminder to play safe, be on guard when crossing streets and be wary of strangers.

DEATH AND BURIAL

Death is one of the most important moments in life. It is the moment we step from this physical world into that of spirit, light and energy. We step completely and finally through the *nierika*, the portal in the mind that leads into the next world. Death, like life itself, will always be a mystery. In Hindu mythology the continual rhythm of creation and destruction is expressed in the eternal dance of the God Shiva. In modern physics, Fritjof Capra tells us, 'Every sub-atomic particle not only performs an energy dance, but also *is* an energy dance, a pulsating process of creation and destruction.'

Spiritual traditions from around the world have sought to explain this mystery of life-in-death and death-in life by

262

initiation rites that centre around a hero who must undergo some form of death, often symbolically, journey into the Beyond and emerge reborn as a teacher or guide, either for other mortals or for some more cosmic enterprise. In Celtic lore we see this in the story of Arthur, who sails to the Land of the Dead to retrieve the magic cauldron from which only courageous and true heroes could eat. The cauldron nourished them with the food of immortality, thus assuring them a blessed life in the world to come. When Arthur himself was mortally wounded he was transported to Avalon, where tradition says he will wait until the world needs him once again. At that point he will return. Today when Witches use the cauldron, this ancient symbol of immortality, in their rituals, they are reminded of these sacred truths about life, death and the land where no one dies.

In modern Western society we have practically outlawed death from public and private discussion. The subject has become taboo. This attitude is unique in world history. Other cultures did not shun the topic of death as we do. In fact, teaching the 'ways of death' was part of their spiritual traditions. For example, the Orphic and Eleusinian mysteries in Greece, the Osirian and Isis mysteries in Egypt, the Mithraic mysteries in the Middle East, the Druidic mysteries in Western Europe, the Ojibwa Midewiwin society (to name merely one of many American Indian medicine societies), the Egyptian *Book of the Dead*, the Tibetan *Book of the Dead*, the Aztec *Popul Vuh*, the medieval tradition of *ars moriendi*, or the 'art of dying' – all these were attempts to give people a preview of what awaited them when consciousness left the body and embarked on its journey to the next life. Such spiritual traditions were undoubtedly powerful psychotherapy to deal with death and dying and prevent the fear and shock that seems to be part of modern man and woman's understanding of death.

Witches celebrate death in our own sacred mysteries just

as we celebrate life. Because our worldview is earth-centred and because we celebrate the changing of all the seasons, winter as well as summer, we do not see death as the end. It is merely one season on the Wheel of Life. Death is intimately woven into the fabric of the world and of all things. But then so is birth. If Persephone spends the barren season of winter in the underworld, she will surely return as the young maiden in the spring. The daughters return; the sons are reborn. The moon and sun are faithful in their cyclic journeys across the sky. By orienting our annual celebrations around the birth and death of the year, we are constantly reminded of the great rôle that death plays in the divine scheme of things.

Our rites and beliefs support the theory of the 'eternal return', and most Witches believe in some form of reincarnation. The Witches' law that what we do returns to us three-fold suggests that if we do not receive the effects of our deeds in this life, we will in the next. Witches who derive their traditions from Celtic sources are strong believers in the immortality of the soul, for it was taught by the Druids. The transmigration of souls was one of their cardinal beliefs. In Celtic society it was common for people to make loans on the assumption that if they were not repaid in this life, they would be in the next.

My own beliefs are that after death the information that has manifested in us during this life becomes part of the Akashic records. The Akasha is the metaphysical term for the ether, or cosmic energy, that pervades the universe. I believe that it is the same phenomenon that physicists call the 'quantum fields' of energy. Everything that happens, including our lives, is a manifestation of energy within these fields and is, in turn, imprinted on them. At death each of us will become part of the cosmic field as an energy packet or 'information bundle'. This is why every human being is under such tremendous responsibility to live a good life and to grow in knowledge and wisdom. Whatever we become will remain. It will be part of the universe, the Akashic records, or the Mind of the All, forever.

Witches see death as a blessed moment in the life of the one dying, even though our human response is always tinged with sorrow and sadness that a loved one is leaving us. Just as we rejoice when a baby is born, we try to be equally joyful when someone we know or love begins a new life in the next world. We wear white to send out our own energy as a sign that we would accompany the departed energy of the loved one.

Witches tend to favour cremation rather than burial. The loved one's ashes can then be used in a protection potion, kept in an urn near our altar or blown to the winds in a spot that was special or holy to the departed or to those of us who remain behind. When Witches are buried we also bury their magical tools and robes with them, placing herbs and crystals into the grave. We cast a magic circle around the grave site. Dust from the top of the grave can be used in future protection potions because some of the deceased's light energy emanates up through the earth for years after the burial. Sometimes we plant a tree or shrub for the person or invite a newborn kitten into our home in honour of the person and to perpetuate the spirit of that person. In other words, we replace life with life.

·9·

WITCHCRAFT TOMORROW

I gaze into the future and I am filled with both hope and fear. As I look at all the tomorrows that lie before us I am alternately excited by the great opportunities that await us as a species and alarmed by the many problems that lie in our immediate path. I wonder how we will reach the year 2089, a century from now. I don't think that any one path is pre-determined. We find and make our own paths. The future is in our hands and minds.

I can see into the past as well — the events of recent history, incidents lost in the mists of time, even occasional glimpses of the very earliest experiments of life on this planet earth. My heritage as a Witch is filled with life forms and animal presences and spirit helpers that abound in legendary tales from around the world. Mythical beasts, lost continents and races of people and the many ancient ways that spirit breaks through into human life — these still live in me and all those who practise the Craft. The sky gods of many cultures, the 'star people', who may have inhabited parts of the earth, the root races, angelic beings and messengers, the technicians of vanished civilizations, the elves and fairies, little people whose legendary presence is found throughout the world — these ancestors of ours are still present in the universe, imprinted on the cosmic energy fields or the

Akashic records. Their legacy is available to us in alpha. The 'time before time' still beckons us to enter and experience for ourselves our common roots and origins.

A Witch's consciousness is not time-bound in the present; it ranges to the far edges of the universe and to the extremes of human experience. As a Witch I have always had the desire to experience both the past and future, to know where we have come from and where we are heading. Many Witches feel the same way.

A surprising number of Craft people and other neo-pagans have jobs working with computers and computer programming. This is not unusual because computers are the latest in a long line of information-processing technologies that include Pythagorean systems, the Jewish mysticism found in the Kabbala, the Tarot, and the ancient runic alphabets of old Europe. Like these ancient forerunners, computer language is a kind of secret code that can access information and help shape our lives and build our futures. Witches are drawn to this kind of work. Our Craft practices prepare us for channelling knowledge through light, colour and number.

I see several scenarios or programmes for the near future and the important rôles that Witches will play in them. In this chapter I would like to share them with you.

I see Witches reclaiming the holidays of the earth and sky. The old festivals of the Witches' calendar – Samhain, Imbolc, Beltane and Lammas – will once again become important cultural holidays, vital celebrations for the wider communities in which we live. I even see people not in the Craft eagerly anticipating and recognizing the equinoxes and solstices as dramatic turning points in the Wheel of the Year.

For this to happen Witches must actively work to reclaim these days as our own. We must champion these secularized and commercialized holidays and turn them back into holy days. I propose a threefold strategy for doing this: education, public ceremonies and good works.

Education: As each holiday rolls around Witches will write to local shopkeepers and the council about the significance of the forthcoming celebration. We will point out the rich history of these festivals and explain the original intent of our ancestors who celebrated these sacred moments in time. We will offer to lecture in local schools and colleges about these days and write letters or editorials for local newspapers.

However we choose to go about it, we will see to it that accurate information is available for the public. We will use all forms of media because they are powerful vehicles for education. In our media campaign we will encourage all those who have any control over how these days are celebrated to forgo the commercialized and demeaning images that accompany modern observances and return to more ancient and accurate images. Witches will be the primary consultants in this. For those holidays that modern society has virtually forgotten or ignored, such as Imbolc, Lammas, Beltane and the equinoxes, we may have an easier time. There is less misinformation and distortion to overcome. For many people these may be totally new holidays. In time society will honour us as bringers of new joy and festivities.

Public Ceremonies: The big problem confronting the Craft in recent times has been invisibility. No one sees us. I propose that Witches go public on the major earth and sky holidays with costumes, music, dancing, singing, feasting and magic. If possible, get permits to raise Maypoles in city parks, organize parades or candlelight marches at Samhain, celebrate Yule at community centres or in Universalist Unitarian churches (which are often receptive to non-Christian liturgies). We can join with college students interested in anthropology or medieval customs and do rituals on campuses. If public places are not available, we will begin in our own back gardens. We will notify the neighbours that we are going to sponsor or recreate some 'colourful folk celebrations' and invite them to join in or just come and watch. I predict that within a few years, maybe even just one year, we will have half the neighbourhood holding hands and coiling around each other in a spiral dance! And in costume!

I think it's important that we be as open about our identities as Witches as possible. Today Salem is a safe place for Witches to wear pentacles and capes on the street and to sponsor sabbat celebrations in public places, but it was not always so. The primary reason we are accepted today is that I and other Salem Witches have stood up for our right to dress as we wish, wear what we want and celebrate our sabbats. I do not think we should hide our rites. And yet I realize that not every Witch lives in a safe town. If you cannot come out openly about the true nature of our celebrations because doing so would intimidate conservative members of your community who could cause trouble and even prevent your celebrations, find acceptable ways to explain what you are doing. Terms like 'Witchcraft', 'Wiccan', or 'pagan' may cause opposition. However, most people are not threatened by Maypoles, for example, when presented as an old English folk custom. Lammas can be explained as a simple harvest festival. Yule celebrates our need for light and warmth as the winter months approach. The equinox and solstice rituals can be described as ancient customs that focus our attention on ecology, the seasons of the year and the balance in nature. By introducing our sabbats in this way we can educate people to their true nature and purpose. In time even the most closed-minded will learn that no harm comes from our festivities but that, on the contrary, they provide joy and good times for everyone.

Some witches who produce public ceremonies actually enjoy the fact that some spectators and participants think they are engaged in mere pageantry and theatre while underneath lies powerful liturgy and sacred ritual. After all, the origins of drama, poetry and dance lay in religious ceremonies and many people came just for the spectacle, so I don't think it is wrong or misleading to emphasize that aspect if in doing so we win public acceptance of Wiccan customs. Remember that our goal is to educate first, and ritual is a most effective means of education. Make your public rituals exciting events that will awaken, inspire, thrill, delight and empower all those who are present. Let your own consciousness rise on these occasions and in so doing raise the consciousness of others.

Wearing ritual garments is important at all our holiday celebrations, not just Samhain. Children should see their parents in magical clothing around the Maypole, on Midsummer Eve, at Yuletide. Wearing sacred garments is a means of bringing power into our lives and projecting the magic and meaning of what we do. I have been disappointed at the Salem children's parade at Halloween to see how few Witches show up in costume or in their Witches' robes. I applaud those who do. It is important that we give children a sense that a Witch's life spans many worlds and moves between them. Seeing us dressed in special clothes and garbed for a different place and time is a powerful way to teach children (and adults) that we live in more than one reality.

Some Witches claim that work and careers don't give them time to prepare or hold public celebrations on these days of the year. It's true that we do not yet get time off work for our sabbats like we do for national holidays, but we can take a personal day. Some Witches make a point of asking for these days off when they apply for a job. Often employers are more than willing, especially if a Witch who takes time off for Yule, for example, is willing to work on Christmas Day. I encourage you to do this even if you don't spend the day getting ready for lavish celebrations. These days are sacred, and we should create sacred space and time in our lives by taking time off from work and spending the day consciously and productively in the ways of the Craft.

Good Works: One of the first questions asked me by a born-again minister on a television chat show was: where were my hospitals and orphanages? He insisted that to prove that I was really a 'religious' person, I should produce hospitals! Even the host pointed out to him the inconsistency in this line of logic. Not every religious group has to own and operate hospitals and orphanages. But he was adamant in quoting that 'by their fruits you will know them'. Well, on that point I can totally agree with him – we are known by our good works. And I see Witches of the future being known for their good works as we were in pre-Christian times before the slanderous campaign began to convince the world that we were capable only of 'bad works'. As part of reclaiming our traditional holidays I encourage every Witch and every coven to organize in conjunction with each holiday some form of volunteer work that will benefit the larger community.

For example, the spring holidays can include work on gardens and flower planting in civic areas. We can volunteer to help people in nursing homes plant gardens. Or we can bring bouquets to hospitals. At the summer solstice we can help the home-bound and invalids, children and senior citizens, to get outside and enjoy the warm summer days. We can provide transportation to public events, sponsor picnics, volunteer to help at local day camps.

As the year grows old we celebrate the harvests and the earth's need to recycle her energies. We can pack boxes of food for the poor. We can volunteer time with local recycling projects. We can help the elderly in our neighbourhoods prepare for the cold months ahead by installing storm windows, stacking firewood, providing insulation, putting away the gardens tools of summer.

Winter was always the traditional storytelling season when folk spent long evenings around the hearth. We can rejuvenate the custom of storytelling by volunteering at libraries and day-care centres and offering adult programmes at community centres. We can find clothing and food for the homeless or volunteer time in a local shelter. In Salem, Witches sponsor a toy-and-food drive each Yuletide for children's charities. Imbolc occurs at the coldest and bitterest time of the year, so why not sponsor a beggars' feast or a potluck for the local soup kitchen?

These are just suggestions. Gaze deeply and clearly into your own community and find what needs to be done. Then make specific plans to do it, either alone, with a couple of Witch friends or with a coven. If you live in an area that has several Wiccan or pagan communities, propose a joint effort to do good works as part of our efforts to reclaim our rightful holidays.

I see Witches becoming ever more active in ecological concerns. As the earth becomes an increasingly unhealthy place to live in and as modern civilization continues to poison the planet, Witches will speak out for the rights of the earth. Our voices will be among the loudest, calling all people to live in balance and harmony with the communities of plants, animals and minerals.

For many Witches this will mean taking stock of how they personally live on the planet. It is often perplexing to find ways to live so that our lifestyles don't contradict our values as 'keepers of the earth'. Our cars, computers, clothes, heating fuels, plastic shopping bags – so many things we find it hard to live without – may be depleting the earth's resources, contributing to toxic wastes, exploiting nature populations in other countries and fostering the mistreatment of animals. Modern life is such a complex web of relationships that it is often impossible to know what effects our actions have on others. The business and industrial network literally webs the entire world and involves everyone.

Clearly, we cannot all return to living on the land. In America alone there are too many people to do that. But I strongly believe that in small ways we can each lead a simpler life that wastes less, pollutes less, destroys less, even costs less. Witches of the future will pioneer new ways for individuals to scale down their needs and live lighter, touching the earth more gently.

If each of us would contribute just five hours a month, that's about one hour a week, to some local organization that is involved in ecological or environmental work, we would see remarkable results in our own lives and in the broader community. Clean up the parks and woods; help the Scouts collect newspapers; plant trees, flowers and shrubs. In Salem the Witches' League for Public Awareness bought and planted two hundred fir seedlings. Again I can only offer a few suggestions that occur to me. You must find your own way to become actively engaged in the health of the environment. Discover what projects are available and necessary in your community. If Witches are to have a greater impact on the future of our society, we must become more service oriented.

When it comes to environmental issues we must become more knowledgeable. We must use the media, television in particular, to learn about cultures other than our own and their attitudes towards the earth; about the science and technology that is currently polluting the environment; about the new technologies that might offer possible correctives. As informed and knowledgeable Witches we can become active in demonstrating, protesting and working for reform. We will not hesitate to work with local and national officials and legislators who have the political power to enact change.

The earth is undergoing major changes. Native Americans have predicted these for centuries, often with remarkable accuracy, and now many of them are coming true. The earth must adjust herself to the problems that human life has created for her. The great Titans of the earth are waking up to take part in this cleansing: fires, earthquakes, volcanoes, storms, droughts and floods. Humans tend to see these as 'disasters' when we view them in terms of our own petty interests. But even the end of the earth may not be a disaster when viewed from the perspective of the All. We just don't know. At best we must heed these events as messages from the earth to reform our ways and live in harmony and balance with the earth and her many communities. I see Witches performing spells for growth, cleansing and survival. I see the Craft becoming an integral part of the worldwide effort to make human life more responsive to the needs of the earth. I see Witches in league with other earth-oriented communities doing magic, sharing knowledge and working great spells of healing and cleansing.

We will look forward to future harmonic convergences and new ages, and we will work with them. The past convergence was successful in heightening awareness about the interconnectedness of spirit and earth. Harmonic convergences will not be just a fad but an ongoing call to spirit-minded people around the world to project health and well-being and balance between spirit and matter. In spite of what detractors said about the convergence being another doomsday watch for the world to end, those who took part understood its real purpose – the alignment of our intentions with the evolving future of the earth and its communities of life.

I see a future in which there is no war and no threat of war. I see the past conflict in Vietnam and remember how it was stopped by the unrelenting vision and voices of countless brave men and women protesting against its escalation and projecting for an end to it. I remember the great peace mantras of the 1960s – 'Make love not war' and 'Give peace a chance' – and the peace symbol that became an international talisman working its magic on the minds and hearts of people everywhere. Although I think that conflict is part of human existence and will always be present in some form or another, I do not think that conflict between people or nations need erupt into war, especially in the future, when more armies

274

will have nuclear weapons at their disposal. And I think that television will continue to erode widespread support for war, as it did during the Vietnam conflict, by bringing the horrors of the battlefields into our living rooms, where we cannot mistake them for glory.

Witches must make peace an important goal. We must do magic and spells to work for a war-free world. Using the spells in this book for peace may be one of our most important contributions to our children's and grandchildren's futures. We can do binding spells, using white light to neutralize soldiers, their weapons and, especially, the military leaders who send them into battle. We can put protective shields around armies and civilian populations, who, now more than in the past, are the major victims of war. We must also protect the land, its crops and its animals, which are also the innocent casualties of armed conflict. We can go into alpha and engage in dialogue with world leaders, encouraging them to negotiate with each other rather than resort to war to settle disputes. We can send pink light. We can project solutions to both internal and international problems.

We should begin educating our children about the reality of a war-free, non-violent planet. Some years ago I taught a course in the science of Witchcraft for children of some Salem Witches. One of our projects was to surround Salem in pink light, specifically to neutralize other teenagers in town who lacked civic pride and self-esteem and took out their frustrations on the environment by acts of vandalism. These young Witches did their spells faithfully for three to four months, and when the next crime report for the Commonwealth of Massachusetts came out, Salem ranked lowest for vandalism.

As the world becomes an increasingly unsafe place to live, I can see the growing need for wise and powerful healers, knowledgeable in both ancient and modern methods of healings. To find a cure for cancer, AIDS, heart disease, life-threatening allergies and the host of environmental diseases that seem to proliferate at an alarming rate will require our best minds and our most powerful magic. As the earth goes through her own adjustment and cleansing, we will see more 'natural disasters' such as drought, floods and earthquakes, and Witches will be part of the rescue missions to save and comfort the victims.

But for now the many stress-related ailments of modern civilization – heart and lung problems, backache, headache, the common cold – should become our immediate focus because they are close at hand. We know people who suffer from them. They are sometimes our own discomforts. In our traditional rôles as healers and counsellors we must offer our neighbours a healthier style of life and the science of magic to heal themselves.

Witches of the future will be part of the health-care delivery system, working or volunteering in hospitals, nursing homes and hospices, bringing people vision and hope because of our unique perspectives on life and suffering, death and rebirth, the eternal exchange of energies between the material and spiritual realms. As Wiccan clergy we should demand the same visiting privileges, which the Christian clergy now have, to counsel and heal our patients when they are hospitalized.

People are dying because of addictions, loneliness, fear and prejudice. I see Witches offering healing programmes, centred on ritual, for alcoholics and drug abusers. Our covens will offer ceremony and ritual for bereavement groups. We will bring meaning and hope to the lonely and the abandoned. As earth-centred healers we offer a new vision to people alienated from the earth and the natural rhythms that put life in perspective and create a context of meaning. We will teach meditation, offer guided spirit journeys and help individuals discover their own sources of health and happiness through ritual and magic that will bring them into contact with their deepest selves.

I see Witchcraft becoming once again a major religion, taking its rightful place alongside other spiritual disciplines. We will enrich those other religions by showing how the science of the Craft is the basis for all effective spiritual practices. But we must make the first move. I encourage every Witch who has the opportunity to become a 'certified minister' by joining the Covenant of the Goddess or the National Alliance of Pantheists, both of which have won government recognition as religious bodies with the right to 'ordain ministers'. We must realize that in the eyes of the dominant culture, labels like 'reverend' and 'minister' are necessary to give us official status. Without them our anointings, Handfastings, funerals and hospital ministrations will not be accepted as legitimate religious rites.

Whether 'certified' or not, Witches will play an ever-growing part in ecumenical activities. We will be participants in seminars and retreats at Christian, Jewish and Buddhist centres and at the growing number of inter-faith agencies and seminaries. Already Witches have been invited to such conferences because only we are truly versed in the ceremonies and rituals of the Goddess traditions that are becoming a major field in theological studies. Witches not only understand but *live* the spiritual vision of our ancestors, who recognized the divine power in the earth and in natural processes. Witches have the knowledge and the techniques for realizing our own divine powers so necessary for living in harmony with creation. What is being called 'creation theology' in some Christian circles is what we and Native Americans have been living for thousands of years. It is what the world so desperately cries out for in our own time and what may be our ultimate salvation – a spiritual vision that recognizes the sacredness of all life and the inter-connectedness of all living things.

I challenge theologians and religious scholars, and average men and women in the Christian and Jewish communities, to *study us and learn who we are.* I throw down a gauntlet to them, daring them to put aside the lies and distortions that have characterized their feelings about us and prevented them from truly understanding us. The major modern religions have studied Zen Buddhism and Native American spirituality in recent years, discovering in those old and revered traditions much inspiration and sacred wisdom. I challenge all students of religion to do the same with Witchcraft and the rich Goddess traditions from which we spring.

Not long ago Barbara, a Witch friend of mine, was a volunteer teacher in a local private school that had a distinguished reputation for providing education of a high calibre. Barbara's years of service to the school were recognized by faculty, students and parents alike. When the position of principal became vacant she was offered the post. Then word went around that Barbara was a Witch. Suddenly, a woman whose reputation in the community was beyond reproach became an 'unknown'. People reacted as if they didn't know her well. At a conference with the school officials she affirmed the fact that she was a Witch, as were her husband and children. The offer of principalship was withdrawn. Ironically, when she left the conference she walked past a classroom down the hall where a film was being shown explaining the beauties and mysteries of Native American spirituality. In the future those films will be about us. And we will not lose our jobs because of who we are.

I see the number of Witches growing by leaps and bounds, not because we recruit new members, for we do not and never have, but because the Goddess will call people to discover their original spiritual heritage. We will still require that initiates prove themselves and their intentions by studying with us for 'a year and a day' before we accept them into our covens, but more and more men and women will come forth to do so as they realize the time is ripe and perhaps that time is also short. New covens will spring up, new rituals will be developed, new ways to use our magic for the good of all will be discovered. We must be open and receptive to these newcomers. We must make ourselves available for those who are searching by living publicly as Witches, proud of our Craft and our life-giving traditions.

Today I see Western religions groping for their mystical/magical heritage, and I see them finding it in the ancient ways of the Craft. I see men and women, dissatisfied with their own religions, coming to us out of boredom and hopelessness. They will be drawn to our public rituals and to the science and art that make Witchcraft so exciting and meaningful. As the world becomes more democratized I see the spiritually-minded yearning for a sacred tradition in which both men and women can participate fully, with no hierarchy and no audience, a spiritual path on which all walk together as equals.

As people become fed up with 'revealed truths' handed down from ministers and clergy, they will ask us to show them the ways of alpha in which they can directly learn the spiritual truths of the cosmos and create their own personal relationships with the All. As other religions build walls around themselves and divide people into categories of insiders and outsiders, of 'saved' and 'damned', of 'saints' and 'sinners', people will gravitate to us where all are welcome. They will see, for example, that at our Handfasting ceremonies we do not separate the families of a wedding couple on opposite sides of an aisle but call everyone to stand together in a circle around the bride and groom, holding hands and becoming one family.

I see women of vision and power, looking for ways to express what is deepest in their feminine nature, finding us and joining our covens. Already feminist theologians (some calling themselves 'thealogians') invite us to speak, to explain the Craft, to show them our rituals. Our covens will become forums for all women's issues – social, economic, political, as well as spiritual – attracting strong, service-oriented women who want to make a change in the world and to save the earth for their children and grandchildren. I see women who will become leaders in business, government and community affairs wearing the pentacle around their necks and speaking with the wisdom of the Divine Mother.

I see a new breed of teenagers who will not find it necessary to turn to the world of Satanic rock lyrics, to films and videos that glamorize evil, or to cults that encourage violence. Unlike today's generation, which rebels against a spiritual vacuum and a growing sense of power-lessness, the teenagers of the future will know the facts about Witchcraft. If they choose to join the Craft, they will do so with the understanding that to be a Witch means to repudi-ate the notion of Satan and evil power over the earth, to reject violence and hatred as weapons of social change and to turn to the divine mysteries of the Great Mother and discover empowering rituals that inspire service and commitment to society. Witch children will grow up with the law of the Craft inscribed in their hearts, dedicated to the principle of harming no one.

I see scientists and mystics engaged in a fruitful dialogue, each contributing their own visions of the universe and discovering that they are speaking the same language and describing the same realities. This dialogue has already begun, and science and mysticism are once again becoming allies. Soon their insights will trickle down to average men and women who may for the first time realize that the universe is an interweaving of light, galaxies, stars, planets and the myriad forms of life. With fresh eyes people will see that the All is a web of energies and auras, thoughts and words, visions and voices. In time everyone will participate in the great dance of light and life that Witches have been leading for centuries.

But Witches must bring about this vision by reading and

studying science. They must become as knowledgeable about scientific realities as they are about spiritual ones. To educate, change and ultimately save society means being able to speak with facts and figures, to uncover relationships and to explain meaning. Witches must be able to speak the language of the new physics and the language of the spirit. We must stand before the world as people who can reconcile the apparent opposites in human experience, who affirm that what the world sees as 'superstition' or 'mysticism' is in reality the basis of science. We will inspire others to take to heart Einstein's words: 'Mysticism is the basis of all true science and the person who can no longer stand rapt in awe is as good as dead.' We will show the world that our 'awe' leads us back to the science of Witchcraft, which is the root of all spiritual work. By our joyful, productive lives we will convince the world that our vision of sacred reality is firmly grounded in material reality.

As we become ever more adept at using alpha to heal and teach, we will help to inaugurate the fullness of the Aquarian Age and put to rest the Piscean Age, the age of blind belief. Others will come to us to learn the ways of alpha and to discover the meaning of life for themselves rather than try to fit the personal mysteries of their lives into a standardized and worn-out paradigm that no longer reflects the new knowledge.

We need new frontiers in psychic development: instant means of transport without vehicles, sound and safe methods of bilocation, controlled techniques for operating out of the body, ways to heal instantly, perform psychic surgery, manifest our ancestors and the past as holograms so that we may study history by entering it and taking part in it.

Artists in the Craft will play a vital rôle, for symbols and images are the midwives for new ideas. They will express in their paintings, songs and poetry the interweaving of the sacred and the secular. Like Michael Pendragon, a Salem composer and musician, songwriters will use Pythagorean philosophy and astrology to write their music. Fashion designers will create clothing of fabrics and colours that are natural, comfortable and expressive of each individual whether it be to reflect the female energies of the Goddess, the male powers of the God or the androgynous blending of the two. Clothing and jewellery will become magical tools once again for all.

Strongly grounded in the Craft, artists will demonstrate that art, science and spirituality are just three sides of the same triangle. Witch artists will remind their audiences, or perhaps teach them for the first time, that all things are connected. I see a day when Wiccan songwriters, performers, sculptors, painters and weavers will influence mainstream art with our images and symbols. I long for the day when the Goddess and the God are once again the major motif of human life.

I see a future in which the current interest in science fiction among so many Witches and neo-pagans will prove to have been a wise study of things to come, not the escapist fantasy that many detractors think it is. Witches have always tended to think in terms of the galaxy as a whole, to see all time and space in the present moment, as they divine the future. Our natural interest in space and the 'times beyond time' will result in Witches being among the first to understand and accept extra-terrestrial visitors for we have already contacted them in our dreams and visions. We know that the universe is so structured that anything might be true at some time and in some place, so we are free to speculate and dream. The plans and projections that we instil in our children today may become the nucleus for life in space and in other galaxies tomorrow. Out of our dreams will come the communities and ways of life that will reach beyond the planets and lead us back to the stars.

As Plato taught, as many Native Americans knew, as

282

ancient peoples around the world surmised, and as Witches have always believed, we are sky people who have come from the stars. Birth is a kind of 'forgetting' of all the knowledge that we held while living among the galaxies, and life is a 'remembering' of who we are and for what we are destined. The root races, the ancestral beings, the original life forms that populated our planet so many aeons ago are waiting for us in the times to come. They will welcome us back.

EPILOGUE

On my altar is a sprig from an ancient oak tree in England that was struck by lightning. A modern Druid gave it to me twenty years ago, but the leaves are still green and alive. It has been charged with divine power. I like to look at it, for it always reminds me that the world itself is charged with divine power. No, the world *is* divine power. Each plant, animal, rock, river, hill, path, shadow, fire or twig has its own spirit, its own intelligence, a message. As a Lakota medicine man once said, 'Everything has a voice and wants to communicate.' Imagine how the universe would sing if humans had not lost the power to listen and hear and whisper back to the cosmos the secret desires of our hearts!

Witchcraft is very old, but in our times it is becoming the path to the future, leading us out into the furthest reaches of the universe. What will we hear out there? Nothing, if we do not first learn to listen to the voice of our Mother Earth. We cannot hear the divine voices singing in the universe if we have not learned to listen to those same divine voices singing softly within us. We do not have much time. In all parts of the world people are reporting encounters with messengers from other realms. Some of us go gladly to them; others cower in fear. Who will march bravely into the future? Who will be left behind in the debris of the twentieth century?

The Craft has always prepared men and women for the greatest challenges in growth and transformation. From Neolithic times to our own nuclear age the Witch has been able to bend, shape and change. Certainly the Craft is now preparing us for the next century and beyond, for it is truly a 'craft', a set of practices and skills. With it we can explore and search the universe for the divine wisdom with which it is charged. And we will find it, for our magic can take us anywhere – deep into the fertile secrets of the earth or high into the silent journeys of the moon.

APPENDIX OF
USEFUL ADDRESSES

AMERICAN RESOURCES

Supplies
(Laurie Cabot Products)

Crow Haven Corner
125 Essex Street
Salem
MA 01970
USA
Tel: 508–745–8764

The Magic Door (mail order)
P.O. Box 8349
Salem
MA 01971–8349
USA

Organizations

*Witches' Antidefamation
  League*
(include SAE)
Dr Leo Martello, HP
153 West 80 Street
Apt 1B
New York
NY 10024
USA

ADDITIONAL ADDRESSES

Author's Note: Please note the following listings have been kindly provided by my British editors. I cannot personally recommend these resources, as I am not familiar with them.

Supplies

Blu & Maggi
137 Central Avenue
Beeston
Nottingham
Nottinghamshire
NG9 2QT

Coranieid Crafts
The Cottage
Mt Pleasant Lane
Swanage
Dorset
BH1 2PN

Dusty Miller & Son
14 Weston Road
Strood
Kent
ME2 3EZ
Tel: 0634-718471

Martin Hinchcliffe
73 Minterne Way
Hayes
Middlesex
UB4 0PE
Tel: 081-561 5996

Rhiannon's Robes
Ael y Bryn
Lon Abram
Denbigh
Clwyd
N. Wales
LL16 3SS
Tel: 0745-715724

Seven Veils
28 Atalanta Street
London
W6 6TR
Tel: 071-381 4716

The Sorcerer's Apprentice
1 The Crescent
Hyde Park
Leeds
LS6 2NW
Tel: 0532-753835

Spellbound
Cae'r Dderwen
Troedyrhiw
Cribyn
Lampeter
Dyfed
Wales
SA48 7NR

Groups, Newsletters and Journals

Albion Arise (newsletter)
52 Black Haynes Road
Selly Oak
Birmingham
B29 4QL

Albion Magazine
43 Rowley Street
Walsall
West Midlands
W51 2AX

Ancient Ways (magazine)
The Alchemists Head Bookshop
10 East Essex Street
Dublin 2
Eire

Cambridge Pagan Fellowship
142 Pheasant Rise
Bar Hill
Cambridge
CB3 85D

The Cauldron (journal)
Caemorgan Cottage
Cardigan
Dyfed
Wales
SA43 1QU

Children of Sekhmet (magazine)
BM Box 9290
London
WCIN 3XX

Coranieid
The Cottage
Mt Pleasant Lane
Swanage
Dorset
BHI 2PN

The Crone-icle (magazine)
c/o 56 Old Oak Road
Birmingham
B38 9AJ

The Deosil Dance (journal)
Noddfa
Llithfaen
Nr Pwllheli
Gwynedd
LL53 6NN

Earth (bi-monthly publication)
20 Stonegate Road
Thorpe Edge
Bradford
West Yorkshire
BDIO 8BT

Evohe! (journal)
Box 250
Oxford
Oxfordshire
OXI IAP

Gates of Annwn (magazine)
Cartref
Conwy Road
Penmaenmawr
Gwynedd
Wales
LL34 6BD

The London Web
33 Oldridge Road
London
SWI2 8PN

Meyn Mamvro (magazine)
22 Bosorne Road
St Just
Penzance
Cornwall
TRI9 7RD

Moonstone (magazine)
BM Box Moonstone
London
WCIN 3XX

Oxford Pagan Fellowship
Box 250
Oxford
Oxfordshire
OXI IAP

Pagan Celtic Ritual Group
I Ravenstone Road
Hornsey
London
N8 0JT

The Pagan Federation
BM Box 7079
London
WC1N 3XX

Paganlink Environmental Group
43 Rowley Street
Walsall
West Midlands
WS1 2AX

Paganlink Network
Box 7
Occultique
53 Kettering Road
Northampton
Northamptonshire
NN1 4AJ

Pagan News
Box 175
52 Call Lane
Leeds
LS1 6DT

The Pagan Prattle (journal)
127b Water Street
Radcliffe
Manchester
M26 0BE

Pagan's Choice (journal)
5 Upper Brook Street
Ulverston
Cumbria
LA12 7BH

Par (newsletter)
23 Highfield South
Rock Ferry
Wirral
Merseyside
L42 4NA

Path (journal)
1 Forge Cottages
Lichfield Road
Abbots Bromley
Rugeley
Staffordshire
WS15 3AA

Pentacle (journal)
7 Mapelwood Flats
Llandaff North
Cardiff
Wales
CF4 2NA

Pipes of Pan (magazine)
Blaenberem
Mynyddcerrig
Llanelli
Dyfed
Wales
SA15 5BL

Quest (magazine)
BCM-SCL Quest
London
WC1N 3XX

Songs from the Wood (newsletter)
5 Allington Avenue
Tottenham
London
NI7 8JE

Touchwood (magazine)
P.O. Box 36
Whitley Bay
Tyne & Wear
NE26 ITN

The Wiccan (newsletter)
BM Box 7079
London
WCIN 3XX

Wiccan Gateway (magazine)
Ferns Hollow
School Road
Ruyton XI Towns
Shrewsbury
Shropshire
SY4 IJT

Wiccan Rede (magazine)
P.O. Box 473
3700 Al Zeist
Holland

Wood & Water (magazine)
4 High Tor Close
Babbacombe Road
Bromley
Kent
BRI 3LQ

THE WITCHES' CHART OF THE PLANETS, THEIR INTENTIONS AND MAGICAL CORRESPONDENCES

By Order Of Day	Symbol	Planet	Rulership	Exalted	Colour	Stone	Metal	Plant	Tone	Intentions	Tool	Element
Sunday	☉	Sun	Leo	Aries	Yellow Yellow-gold Gold	Citrine Topaz Cat's Eye Herkimer Diamond Adventurine	Gold	Camomile, Heliotrope Orange Sunflower, Marigold, Frankincense	C♯	Physical strength, success, health, winning, creativity, jewels, obtaining goals, wealth rulership, illumination	Candle	Fire
Monday	☾	Moon	Cancer	Taurus	Silver Light Silver	Pearl Moonstone Selenite	Silver	Moonwort, All night-blooming flowers, Mesquite, Willow, Bergamot, Camphor	G♯	Psychological balance, psychic ability, beauty, feminine forces, dreams, astral travel, protection, intuition	Cauldron Chalice	Ocean water
Tuesday	♂	Mars	Aries Scorpio	Capricorn	Red	Ruby Pyrite Garnet Hematite	Iron Steel	Nettle, Garlic, Passion Flower, Parsley, Cactus Pepper, Pine	D	Action, force, partnership, marriage, passion, sexual love, courage, clothing, determination, furniture	Sword	Fire
Wednesday	☿	Mercury	Gemini Virgo	Virgo	Orange Grey	Carnelian Agate Opal	Aluminium	Dill, Skullcap, Lavender, Cinquefoil, Vetivert Root, Hazel, Horehound	D	Wisdom, all knowledge, motion, communication, transportation, speed, healing, motivation, creativity	Wand	Ocean Water Earth
Thursday	♃	Jupiter	Sagittarius Pisces	Leo	Royal Blue Turquoise Purple	Lapis Lazuli Chrysocolla Sapphire Turquoise Amethyst	Pewter Tin	Cloves, Hyssop, Cinnamon Jasmine, Chestnut, Saffron, Cedar, Honeysuckle, Tonka Beans	F♯	Material logic, influence of people in high places, good fortune, wealth, success, law, business, officials, honours, expansion	Witch's Cord	Earth, Fire, Air, Water
Friday	♀	Venus	Taurus Libra	Pisces	Green Pink Copper Rose	Emerald Pink Shell Rose Quartz Malachite Watermelon Tourmaline	Copper	Adam & Eve Root, Rose, Caper, Heather, Strawberry, Tansy, Lady's Mantle, Violet, Primrose, Apple, Yarrow	A	Love, growth, health, fertility, beginning new projects, beauty, sensuality, money, jewellery, cosmetics, pleasure, friendship, prosperity	Thurible	Air Earth
Saturday	♄	Saturn	Capricorn Aquarius	Libra	Wine Magenta	Black Onyx Jet Diamond Garnet Galena	Lead	Ivy, Hemlock, Datura, Mandrake Root, Tobacco, Moss, Wolfbane, Myrrh	D	Testing, binding, to inhibit, to manifest, to crystallize things, science,concentration, maturity, to invent, pragmatism, to neutralize evil intent, discipline, longevity	Athame	Earth (Earth Salt) Water (Fresh) Air, Fire

THE WITCHES' CHART OF THE PLANETS, THEIR INTENTIONS AND MAGICAL CORRESPONDENCES

By Order Of Day	Symbol	Planet	Rulership	Exalted	Colour	Stone	Metal	Plant	Tone	Intentions	Tool	Element
	♅	Uranus	Aquarius	Scorpio	Lavender Dazzling White	Fire Opal Clear Quartz Crystal Rutilated Quartz	Uranium White Gold	Rue, Clover, Birch, Burdock Root, High Joan Root, Ebony Wood, Pomegranate	G♯	Eccentric ideas, inventions, publicity, to reform, to expand unusual ideas, to clear electrical energies, bizarre happenings, unexpected changes	Garter	Air Water Fire
	♆	Neptune	Pisces	Cancer	All iridescent colours Phosphorus Opaque colours	Sea Shell Beryl Aquamarine Bloodstone Blue Quartz Fire Opal	Platinum Pewter	Lotus, Watercress, Water Lily, Seaweed, Grapes	A	Visions, dreams, ideals, fantasies, artistic abilities, psychic awareness, healing, imagings, water, illusions, chemical change	Crystal Ball	Water
	♇	Pluto	Scorpio	Aquarius	Black	Black Coral Obsidian Black Quartz Black Aventurine Jet	Chrome Nuclear elements Plutonium	Wormseed, Hawthorn, Foxglove, Low John Root, Ginger Root, Vanilla Bean, Arrow Root, Dogwood, Bloodroot	D	To bring order out of chaos, group ideas, sudden manifestation of spells and thoughts, Witches' power, unifying or disrupting forces (use caution)	Black Cape Robe	Water
	◿	Vulcan	All Signs	All Signs	Clear, vivid spectrum of colours	All Precious Stones & Diamonds Black Tourmaline	Gold	Black Currant, Oak Bark, White Mullein Leaves, Angelica Root, Bayberry Bark, Cloves, Blue Cohosh Root, Galangal Root, Lotus, Myrrh, Frankincense, Solomon's Seal Root	All Tones	A planet yet undetected, very close to the Sun, "The Jeweller of the Gods", puts total force into your magic	Gold Pentacle	Fire
		Sparta	All Signs	All Signs	Brown	Slate Shale	Bronze	Nutmeg, Snakeroot, Potato, Barley, Betel Nuts, Shepherd's Purse, Fennel, Ginseng Root	G	A twin planet to the Earth on the opposite side of the Sun. To ground, balance, be pragmatic	Magic Mirror	Air Earth Fire Water
	◇	Earth	Taurus Virgo Capricorn	Pisces Libra Scorpio Aries	Rust Brown	Granite Marble Sandstone Smoky Quartz Clear Quartz	Brass	Mastic, Motherwort, Rue, Mushrooms, Ginseng, Orange Peel, Shepherd's Purse, Wormwood, Tarragon, Caraway Seed, Adam & Eve Root	G	Action, force, and passion, partnership building, gardening, marriage, balance, decisions, grounding, nesting, stability	Egg Animal Horn	Air Earth Fire Water

INDEX

INDEX

ARKANA – NEW-AGE BOOKS FOR MIND, BODY AND SPIRIT

A selection of titles

With over 200 titles currently in print, Arkana is the leading name in quality new-age books for mind, body and spirit. Arkana encompasses the spirituality of both East and West, ancient and new, in fiction and non-fiction. A vast range of interests is covered, including Psychology and Transformation, Health, Science and Mysticism, Women's Spirituality and Astrology.

If you would like a catalogue of Arkana books, please write to:

Arkana Marketing Department
Penguin Books Ltd
27 Wright's Lane
London W8 5TZ

ARKANA – NEW-AGE BOOKS FOR MIND, BODY AND SPIRIT

A selection of titles

A Course in Miracles: The Course, Workbook for Students and Manual for Teachers

Hailed as 'one of the most remarkable systems of spiritual truth available today', *A Course in Miracles* is a self-study course designed to shift our perceptions, heal our minds and change our behaviour, teaching us to experience miracles – 'natural expressions of love' – rather than problems generated by fear in our lives.

Sorcerers Jacob Needleman

'An extraordinarily absorbing tale' – John Cleese.

'A fascinating story that merges the pains of growing up with the intrigue of magic . . . constantly engrossing' – *San Francisco Chronicle*

Arthur and the Sovereignty of Britain: Goddess and Tradition in the Mabinogion Caitlín Matthews

Rich in legend and the primitive magic of the Celtic Otherworld, the stories of the *Mabinogion* heralded the first flowering of European literature and became the source of Arthurian legend. Caitlín Matthews illuminates these stories, shedding light on Sovereignty, the Goddess of the Land and the spiritual principle of the Feminine.

Shamanism: Archaic Techniques of Ecstasy Mircea Eliade

Throughout Siberia and Central Asia, religious life traditionally centres around the figure of the shaman: magician and medicine man, healer and miracle-doer, priest and poet.

'Has become the standard work on the subject and justifies its claim to be the first book to study the phenomenon over a wide field and in a properly religious context' – *The Times Literary Supplement*